MO FANNING

Ghosted

SPRING STREET BOOKS

promised to put things right. I should have done this before now, but we can fight about it some other time. Like when we see each other.

The thing is, Joey, I come from a different generation. I said what I said to protect you. We live in a shitty world, and I didn't mean that because you're gay it automatically meant you'd die of AIDS. How could you think that of me? Anyhow, things have changed with cures and vaccinations and stuff. I talked to a guy selling coffee in the West Village, and he told me how he's living with HIV, and it no longer means a death sentence.

Three dots.

And then they're gone.

Chapter One

Silas knows this isn't going to be his day. The Goering Brothers department store seasonal recruitment office is a windowless room with a pervading odor of unwashed bodies. A door that doesn't quite close means it's too hot to wear a jacket, but too cold to take one off. Dog-eared posters on scuffed yellow walls date back to the '90s—a time, it seems, when most everyone wore shades. A clock above the door says it's a quarter after one, so he's already been here three hours.

He arrived expecting to see familiar faces, who would welcome him back and send him right up to Santaland. Instead, some sulky kid behind a thick plexiglass divider insisted Silas complete an application form.

He asked if it was new, trying not to sound rude. "I never did one before."

The kid yawned. "Then yeah. I guess you could call it new." He surrounded the word with sarcastic air quotes.

Silas handed over his completed form. Sample question: What matters most about the Goering Brothers experience? Good Silas would admit he loved making kids believe in dreams. Bad Silas wrote: *Getting paid.*

He took a seat and waited. And waited. And then he waited some more. An hour later, a girl appeared and mispronounced his name, before telling him to follow her to a miserable third-floor storeroom, where she machine-gunned questions from a printed sheet, ticking boxes as he answered. She sent him back to the recruitment center, and this time he got a little green ticket with a number: 617.

His stomach growls for food. Silas got wasted last night, and somewhere between the fifth beer and first Scotch, mislaid his wallet, and with it his

EBT card. The benefits office on Third closes early on Fridays, and unless someone gets a hustle on, he'll need to survive the weekend on stale crackers and dry cheese.

A whiny voice calls his number, and Silas makes his way to a desk.

"Your smile came across as fake." A different kid behind a different divider holds up his creased application form, newly stamped with a red cross. "Should I validate parking?"

Silas does his level best to not leap over the divider and throttle this pointy-chinned, freckled-face, thin-lipped stick of a kid.

"I always play Santa," he says. "Children love me. You think maybe I could talk to someone higher up?"

The kid rolls empty eyes. "Whose line would you like me to try?"

"How about Bill Goering?"

As soon as he suggests the name, Silas regrets it. Bill Goering is the CEO, but takes huge pride in being seen as a regular Joe. At last year's Christmas party, Goering got everyone playing a drinking game where you asked questions, and each time your answer included the letter S, you had to down the contents of your glass. Silas had asked Bill his favorite food, and Bill said lasagna, insisting it was written with a Z. Given they were already some ways into a bottle of vodka, Silas objected more forcefully than perhaps he should have. The upshot was Bill Goering left the party with a black eye. Silas left with a security escort. It took a written apology from one man and a cursory nod from the other to let Silas keep his job.

The kid sitting opposite hasn't picked up his phone.

"What?" Silas says. "Does Mr. High-and-Mighty Goering no longer take calls?"

He yawns. "You think I have the number for the CEO?"

"Okay, so try his assistant."

With a roll of the eyes, he punches in a number, waits a beat, and hangs up. "That line is busy. You want me to try someone else?"

"I'm good to wait." Silas runs through the contents of his kitchen cupboards in his head. As well as crackers, he has pasta. That makes two meals. Enough to survive until he swings by the benefits office on Monday.

"There's a line, sir. I need you to step aside," the kid says, and then he softens. "Listen, dude, we take on older guys to hand out candy canes."

"Do I get health insurance?" Silas says.

The kid reaches for another application form and slides it under the divider. "You get every second Sunday off."

* * *

For Silas, a long walk helps stem the ongoing sense that someone up there has his name on a list of losers. Right after leaving Goering Brothers, he gets a call from his Santa buddy, Sam, to talk about the unexpected interviews.

"How about that girl ticking boxes?" he says. "Was she for real?"

Silas isn't ready to tell anyone about how he didn't get the job and so he grunts, and Sam suggests meeting up with Justin for drinks to kick off another season playing Saint Nick. He calls them the Three Amigos, adding how Marty will be there in spirit. Silas decides to lie and says he left it too late to apply for the job and, when quizzed about why, stays vague.

"I'm kinda hoping to see my kid this year."

Sam whoops. "Joey finally got in touch?"

"I guess he figured we can't go on ignoring each other forever. Life's too short."

After wishing him all the best, Sam hangs up, slamming shut the door on another friendship.

Silas enjoys playing Santa. It isn't the greatest job in the world, neither is it the worst. Some guys see it as easy money, but not him. Once a year, he gets to stop being a random grown-up, shuffling through life in the city to become someone who make kids happy. Sam, Justin, and Marty felt the same. They formed a bond. It didn't hurt that, at closing time on Christmas Eve, Goering Brothers staff got to ransack the food hall and take anything they wanted to eat, drink, and make merry.

The lie he told Sam about not submitting his Santa application on time means he can't now apply to hand out candy canes. That wasn't in the cards. Not really. He's too old to spend days on his feet in bad weather, dealing with punks out to steal money collected for charity.

* * *

Silas always finds peace within the high walls that surround the Baron Hirsch Cemetery. Rolling hills and manicured lawns help him forget how this is Staten Island. He breathes in damp November air, following a winding path, the soil giving under his feet. A route he's taken way more often than feels right.

Brown leaves rustle as he brushes them from a smooth gray stone inscribed with Nancy's name. She always wanted things simple. No embossed lettering, no inscription. Just Nancy French. Died May 19, 2005, and under that, the plot number: 406.

He places a round white pebble on the stone, before stepping back.

"The doc says I need to slow up," he whispers, since Friday morning is peak visiting time at Baron Hirsch, and ears have a way of flapping. "I told him how I'm already traveling at half speed."

Silas bites his lip. Inside his head, Nancy teases about how he attacks life like a bull at a gate and tells him to cool his temper and think twice before speaking.

"I didn't get the job." He wipes away unexpected tears. "Some wet-behind-the-ears punk reckons my smile is fake."

A woman's voice calls his name, and he turns to see Maya Shanker, middle-aged, but still striking, in a fitted dress that skims her curves. She raises a gloved hand in greeting and they talk a while, mostly about the weather. She tells him snow is on the way, and he takes her number, promising to arrange Friday night dinner. Silas won't get in touch. Nancy called her a floozy.

His cell rings, and he excuses himself, checking she's out of range before answering.

A man clears his throat at the other end of the line. "This is Mr. Silas French?"

A hollow background buzz suggests someone calling from a train station.

An intercom squawks above the hum of people, and there's the occasional burst of laughter.

"Who am I speaking to?" Silas sticks one finger in his other ear.

"My name is Zach Walker, and I'm your son's husband."

He holds his breath, and his chest constricts. The letter he finally got around to sending Joey must have reached Florida. The second he put it into the mailbox, he wanted to grab it back, sickened by what he'd put in motion. The letter would leave New York and land in Florida, setting off a chain of small explosions. Silas sits on a bench, the wood cold through his pants. His hands are shaking; his mouth is dry.

"I heard a lot about you…" Silas says, in a voice that comes out like a whisper.

"To my knowledge, you haven't spoken to Joseph in years." The guy at the other end of the line is hostile. He might be right that they aren't talking—but come on. Don't be such an asshole.

Silas tries to sound upbeat. "I saw pictures of your kids."

A long silence.

"Joseph doesn't want a relationship with you," Walker says. "He asked me to tell you to stop trying to get in touch. No more letters, no more drunken messages."

Silas steadies his breathing. "Don't I deserve a chance to make things right?"

"My husband owes you nothing."

The line goes dead, and Silas glances back, aware Maya is still hovering. Did she hear? She catches him looking and twinkles, signaling once more that he should call. He drops his cell into a pocket and hurries away.

This can't go on.

Silas balances on an ottoman, reaching up to the top shelf of his closet, sliding a hand along until he finds a square tin, and then running his index finger along deep grooves etched into the metal. The lid has grown rusty, and needs careful work with a Swiss Army knife to prize it open. Muted sunlight pouring through the window catches dust swirls.

This is all the money he has. Tips from satisfied customers who paid Silas to weed their lawns and tidy their gardens in the summer, or shovel snow from sidewalks in the winter.

Last year, his building got sold to developers, who threw a fancy drinks reception where a dead-behind-the-eyes guy promised nobody would lose their home, and yet each time a neighbor moves out or dies, in they swoop in with contractors, turning creaky apartments into places where millennials might pay millennial rents. The service fees doubled, and Silas had cause to dip into his savings. All anyone in the building saw for their money were two miserable Ficus trees placed outside the entrance. They died within two months. In his darkest moments, Silas worried about what would happen if he could no longer afford to live here. Where would he go? A chair where Nancy once sat. The drapes she sewed late at night on a busted machine after working long shifts at her father's store.

Silas lives in the older half of the building, stacked on top of strangers, brought together by narrow hallways and ladder-steep stairs. The guy in the apartment above plays conga drums throughout the night with zero sense of rhythm. Whenever his next-door neighbor showers, Silas's tub fills with grime, and he's certain asbestos lurks in the radiators. Despite the new owners, his place remains rent controlled, and although that should be a good thing, it only makes it harder to agree on repairs. Mrs. Blatter in the basement insists she saw a rat. A white rat with red eyes, and she's most likely right. The city is overrun. He read in the *New York Times* about how they're breeding faster, thanks to global warming. So much for Mayor de Blasio and his mass rodent-culling program. The lease refers to the landlord's responsibility for pest control—but says nothing about frequency. Without Nancy, he occupies nothing more than a bunch of rooms in a run-down part of the building.

This morning, when Dr. Malinowski eventually tore himself away from whoever was judged more important in the next-door consulting room, he'd explained how most of Silas's aches and pains were due to stress. Three years before, he'd suffered a small heart attack. Nothing to suggest needing to get his affairs in order, but he spent two nights at Mount Sinai Medical Center and a couple of weeks resting up. Malinowski called it a warning sign, saying next time around it would be bigger.

After putting the savings tin back in his closet, Silas pulls on a jacket, calls his sister-in-law, and invites himself over. He's sick of being on his own.

* * *

Rose runs a hand through purple hair and lights a cigarette. Silas leans back on plumped-up pillows. He should tell her not to smoke in bed, but this is her bed in her apartment.

"I ran into Maya Shanker," he says. "At Baron Hirsch."

Rose drops a battered brass Zippo into a nightstand drawer. "Is that shiksa still alive?"

"She asked me to dinner."

"You should go. It'll be one in the eye for Levi."

Silas worked for Levi Shanker for nine years, hauling heavy boxes packed with fragile glassware onto waiting trucks. It was hard work. Twelve hours a day, six days a week. Right until one January, when he slipped on ice and twisted his knee. The accident left him with a limp. Levi laid him off.

"Perhaps I will," he says, and Rose falls silent.

Even with the windows shut and a fan heater cranked up full, the rumble of traffic on the Brooklyn Bridge dominates. What would Nancy say about him sleeping with her sister? Right until the funeral, Rose and Silas kept each other at arm's length, speaking only when spoken to. Why did Rose think him not good enough for Nancy? He doesn't remember when he started coming over to visit, let alone how they first ended up in bed.

"You wouldn't be jealous if I dated Maya?" he says, with a wink.

Rose flicks ash into a pale blue saucer on the chipped melamine nightstand. "Why would I care? What we have is strictly casual."

She throws back the sheets and places her feet on the bare wooden floor, reaching with one hand to rub her lower back. She's nothing like his wife. Nancy was tall, with long auburn hair and alabaster skin. Rose is short, rotund, and pasty. And cranky.

"You should get dressed," she says. "I have a friend coming over."

Silas wonders if this friend is some other guy or one of the women she often mentions from the taxi company where she works part-time.

"I could stay and keep you both company," he says.

Rose ties her hair back. "That would be weird."

She gets dressed, first pulling on dark brown tights, before stepping into a faded denim skirt and grabbing a yellow top from a mahogany tallboy.

"I'll swing by the Widow Shanker's place," he says. "See if the offer of dinner stands."

Rose tosses bundled socks at his head.

He laughs and holds up surrender hands. "I'm not the one being kicked out into the cold, after his mistress had her wicked way."

She goes into the kitchen, and a faucet runs. They'll drink coffee, chat a little more, and then he'll head home. Or perhaps to Ziggy's Bar. Almost certainly to Ziggy's Bar.

"I realize she isn't you," he whispers to the Nancy who sits in judgment on a throne inside his head. "Right now, Rose is all I got."

* * *

Ziggy's Bar is Silas's home away from home. His sanctuary. Rickety wooden stools are covered in cracked red vinyl with burn marks on the seats. The light bulbs, yellowed with age, cast soft shadows, and there's a stench of stale beer, with a hit of lemon from citronella candles.

Silas hauls his rangy frame onto one of the high stools, and bartender Larry puts down his newspaper. "Cold enough out there for you, big guy?"

Larry insists on calling him "big guy," despite the weight loss.

"Hit me up with a beer," he says. "On my tab. I've had a shitty day."

Larry reaches for a bottle of Bud. "You meet up with the fabulous four?"

Silas takes a slug of his beer to force back a swell of sadness rising through his stomach. "I just heard. Marty died."

Larry's face falls. "For real? I saw him just this spring. He told me he could get me tickets for the Jets. What happened?"

"A stroke. They didn't reach him fast enough. He hung on for days."

Silas is repeating a secondhand story. It might be true.

"I guess that means Bill Goering needs a new Santa?" Larry says.

"Two new Santas. My smile no longer fits. Sixteen years and I'm surplus to requirement. The kid Goering put in charge knows bupkes."

"You don't have a job?" Larry hesitates before handing over a second beer. "Are you good for this?"

Silas shakes his head. "Don't screw with me, man. I ain't in the mood."

The bar is all but empty apart from a bunch of stoners feeding quarters into the jukebox, whooping and cheering as Cher breaks into "Believe."

"Happy hour hangers-on." Larry's eyes narrow. "Paid for one pitcher of beer and now they won't scoot." He picks up his newspaper and studies the sports pages. "If you didn't get the job, I guess the family reunion is off."

Silas wills his face not to burn with shame. "Joey wants to pay," he says. "Insists I fly first class." His telephone rings with a number he doesn't know, and Silas hits mute as he answers. "Joey, my boy. How's it hanging?"

A female voice on the other end sounds confused. "Hello, is there anyone there? Can you hear me?"

Larry is still watching, and although he shouldn't care about the guy who serves beer in a dive bar, he does. He needs to put on a show and so he laughs. "Sure I will, kid. I can't wait to spend time."

"This is Diana from Verizon. I'm getting in touch to ask if you're content with your calling plan, Mr. French."

"You made up my room? That's swell."

"Hello? Mr. French. Did I lose you?"

Any minute now, Diana will get bored and move onto the next name on her list, and Larry will guess the call is over. He needs to think fast. Move things along. "Great news. I turned down the Goering Brothers job. I can come right away."

Diana from Verizon hangs up, and Silas puts down his cell. Self-pity takes hold, and for one awful minute, Larry's lazy grin suggests he knows Joey didn't call. Silas looks away, swallowing hard. He forces his voice to stay even. "What do you suggest I buy for my grandkids? What are they into these days? Is Lego still a thing?"

Larry folds his newspaper in two. "Pity you have your holidays all planned out, big guy. I found you the perfect job."

He points to an advert.

Owing to illness, The Crown Atlantic Holiday Wonderland Cruise urgently needs someone to make dreams come true for all our little boys (and the occasional girl). Santa experience is essential. Apply now.

If, by some weird twist, Silas got that job, he'd have the cash to fly down to Florida and visit with Joey.

"I should tell Sam and Justin," he says. "Goering cut their hourly rate."

Larry tears out the page and folds it in two before handing it over. "You should call them right now. This was in the morning edition."

Silas studies the paper, and every part of him aches. No matter how hard he tried, the money he saved from gardening jobs wasn't nearly enough to cover flights to Florida, let alone the cost of a cheap motel, in case things didn't work out with Joey. He'd been relying on his regular Santa gig to make up the shortfall. And, yeah, Sam and Justin might be up for applying too. They both live alone. They have no ties. But Silas needs this job. He needs it badly.

Chapter Two

Ellen Gitelman gazes through Dr. Malinowski's consulting room window and out across the tops of elm trees lining Central Park. The last time she came here, spring was busy getting dressed for summer. Now, each branch is bare.

She relishes a day off waiting tables, with no need to put on sensible shoes and wipe-clean slacks. Not that she minds. Being told what to wear for half your waking hours makes for an easy life. At six-foot tall, she struggles to buy off-the-rack outfits that flatter. Fashion designers think women, especially in the larger sizes, want nothing more than to flash cleavage.

The consulting room door opens. Malinowski is thin and wiry, and wearing a tweedy jacket with elbow patches. One that reminds her of high school chemistry teachers.

"I have your results, Mrs. Gitelman," he says with a winning smile.

Ellen likes how she's Mrs. Gitelman to him. Unlike at the hospital, where the nurse who bruised Ellen's arm taking blood kept calling her Ellie. She's never been Ellie. She doesn't look like an Ellie.

Malinowski has in his hands the sheet of paper that confirms the shape of the rest of her life. He holds the power to knock her for six with one simple word. The same word he used five years before. Cancer. She's been waiting on his verdict for three long days. Now all she wants is thank him for his time and leave. She's not above sticking her fingers in her ears and singing la-la.

"Has it returned?" she says, and her tongue glues itself to the roof of her mouth.

"Your levels are near perfect for a normal, healthy woman of your age."

Even though it's good news, the phrase *"a woman of your age"* sets her on edge. A guy with mustard stains on his shirt used it just the other week at the diner, after pointing out to his buddies how the dame still had great legs, turning her into a *something* rather than a *someone*. While her heart should be all for singing, Malinowski's diagnosis fails to settle her fears. She doesn't want to argue with a man she trusts, literally with her life, but what if someone mixed up the blood samples? Labs must do hundreds each day, and sticky labels come loose, a junior technician might think he has her blood, but, in fact, it's from an Olympic athlete, who, at this very moment, is hearing the bad news that he or she is dying. What other explanation can there be for why she feels like her body is pumped full of lead? How come it's a struggle to open her eyes in the morning? Why did she miss her stop last night after falling asleep on the A Train?

"Things just don't feel right," she says, hating how vague this sounds. "When I woke today, I could barely kick the covers off my feet."

The doctor perches on the edge of his desk, and his pale blue eyes twinkle. Ellen can imagine he was quite the catch at high school.

"Did you ever hear of lupus?" he says, and she shrugs. She may have heard the word, or read it in the *New York Times*, but lupus sounds like one of those ancient diseases long since wiped out. Like smallpox or the black death.

"Should I have?" she says.

"I guess not. But you know what I mean if I talk about autoimmune diseases?"

Ellen half-watched a PBS documentary where a young, handsome medic explained how hard they are to diagnose. Every ten minutes, a ticker tape warning reminded viewers the broadcast was general in nature, and no substitute for advice from a qualified health provider.

"Everyone has a part of their body we call their immune system," Malinowski says. "It's there to help fight off disease. In some people, the immune system stops fighting and starts attacking."

"But this lupus isn't cancer?" She tries to stay hopeful. "You know how to fix me?"

He exhales. "Working out what lupus might do to a body is like chasing a poltergeist. You can't see or predict its next move. Most of the time, we doctors get called in after the fact…to clear up the mess. No two cases are alike. It's not like the flu, where I can tick off symptoms."

There's a faint roar somewhere in the back of Ellen's head. One she's heard before, and one she hoped would never again come visiting. She takes a breath.

"When you say 'clear up the mess,'" she says, "that sounds a lot like cancer."

Malinowski's eyes are kind. His brows furrow with concern. "I've heard it called the 'great imitator.' You could throw most any symptom at a person and it could be caused by lupus. I want to refer you to a rheumatologist. When the holidays are over, I'll get you in with a guy I know."

* * *

At the grand entrance to L'Elise on Park Avenue South, Ellen swaps her heavy winter coat for a lunch menu. The restaurant is warm and cozy, and a sense of peace and calm washes over her. Over by the floor-to-ceiling windows, looking out on the sidewalk, her best friend had already bagged a good table. Julia is wearing a plain, white button-down with a red blazer, and black slacks. Her golden curls bounce against her shoulders as she laughs into her cell, and as Ellen settles into the chair opposite, she holds up a finger to indicate she's almost done. Ellen often wishes she had Julia's social life, constantly juggling dinner dates, nights on the town, or cocktails with friends.

The call ends.

"Apologies," Julia says, setting down her telephone in its bejeweled case and waving Ellen back onto her feet for a hug. "I'm in high demand."

Julia spent most of her working life backstage at the Lunt-Fontanne Theatre, first in makeup, before graduating to wardrobe mistress. Her tailoring skills became legendary, and even now, most every image-conscious gay in Manhattan comes calling during Christmas Ball season.

"Tell me everything," Julia says. "Who's screwing who?"

This has been their greeting, since a friendship forged in tenth grade. A bond that lets them say most anything to each other.

"Nobody is screwing nobody." Ellen throws up her hands. "Everyone we know is too old or too dead."

They order olives to compliment a bottle of ice-cold Shiraz. Julia opts for puttanesca, and Ellen has a Caesar salad. She's wearing her one and only still-white blouse and doesn't want to risk ruining it with tomato sauce. Julia charms their waiter, telling him he ought to consider modeling, and the schmooze pays off in the shape of complimentary bread sticks. They talk Hanukkah plans, what might make an appropriate gift for Julia's butcher. Ellen shares her non-cancer news, and Julia squeals, causing nearby diners to stare, but so what? It's not every day you tell your best friend you're no longer shortlisted to die.

As Julia pushes strands of spaghetti around her plate, Ellen asks about her most recent Tinder date. The idea of someone their age risking it all by meeting strangers online has her fascinated. Julia puts down her fork, purses her lips, and runs a hand through her hair. "Henry was a total dud. Nothing like his profile picture. You know how, when you shop in Whole Foods, and you see a photo of the most delicious dinner on a box, and you get it home and heat it up, and it's not what you expected?"

Ellen nods.

"That was Henry. Add to which, he talked all night about how Mexican immigrants are taking our jobs. The guy was one spray tan short of MAGA."

Ellen refills their glasses. "I seriously don't understand why you keep bothering."

"I love a challenge," Julia says. "If there's one eligible single gentleman in this city with his own teeth and two working hips, I will track the bastard down."

They pass on dessert in favor of boozy coffees, and pretty soon, Ellen's head spins. She overslept, and breakfast would have made her late for Malinowski. Being on time matters to Ellen. She breaks into hives at the thought of letting anyone down.

"Your doctor," Julia says as she snaps shut a compact after checking her lipstick for the millionth time. "Is he procuring patients?"

Ellen narrows her eyes. Julia almost always uses words like "procure" when she means "take on." It's an affliction she tries to ignore. "Sure. I guess. But I thought you were happy with your guy."

"You say such favorable things about his bedside manner. The name sounds Slavic. I envision someone tall, dark, and brooding."

Ellen laughs. He's anything but. "I wouldn't want to spoil the surprise."

"Fine, so is he enamoring?"

"He's married with kids, but yeah, he's good-looking, and I kinda think I owe him my sanity."

Five years earlier, when Ellen found a lump, her first instinct was to pretend it wasn't there. Her second, was to call Malinowski.

"Why do you ask?" Ellen says and crosses her fingers. "You're not sick?"

She's done her best over lunch to ignore how Julia's face is pale and strained, the under-eye shadows dark, and the corners of her lips turn downward.

"I came upon a mole," she says, and the words hang between them. "It's probably a trifle, but my mother always said it's important to have these things reconnoitered."

A group of women, still in their twenties, pile jackets and scarves on the next table. They order hot chocolate with marshmallows, and Ellen tries to tune out their inane chatter.

"Did you already talk to your doctor?" she says.

"He's playing hooky until New Year, and I deduced it might be of benefit to shop around. It's likely nothing, and if you would prefer I didn't use your guy, that's fine. I'd hate for things to turn awkward between us."

Ellen scribbles Malinowski's number on the back of a napkin. "Call him right this minute." She squeezes Julia's hand. "Mention my name."

* * *

On a crisp, cold afternoon, with the sky low with heavy clouds, a frigid wind whips at awnings, swirling tiny pinpricks of rain. The sinking sun gleams off car windshields and puddles shimmer in the fading light. Julia hasn't spoken since they left the restaurant. She simply linked her arm through Ellen's and walked along, seemingly deep in thought.

"You want me to come with you?" Ellen says. "Malinowski has one of those fancy Nespresso coffee machines, so I don't mind sitting in his waiting room."

Julia's face turns distant. "This is a circumstance I must deal with on my own. And anyway, I don't need you monopolizing his time. You're sure about the long-term viability of his marital union?"

Ellen play punches her friend's arm. "Be serious."

They stop in front of a store window to admire a fake snow-covered tree, overloaded with glittering ornaments, its base wrapped in red ribbons and bows.

"Daniel called to announce they're spending the holidays in Hawaii," Julia says.

Each year, she jumps on a plane and spends December in San Francisco surrounded by her son's family. His wife, three kids, and at least a dozen cousins.

"You told him about the mole?" Ellen asks.

"Why beleaguer him? He said the kids have their hearts set on learning to surf, and asked if I wanted to go, but you know me and extended exposure to the young."

They fall into step again, the heels of their boots clicking on the sidewalk, their breath visible in the dank air. A knot of teenagers bowl around the block, laughing and shoving each other. The boys wear baseball caps, the girls hoodies. One kid brushes against Julia, who lets out a squeal.

"Asshole," Ellen yells, giving him a middle finger.

Julia turns to Ellen. "When did you become so irascible?"

Ellen makes a face. "When did anyone over sixty get invisible? Seriously, what gives them the right?"

"I love it when you act like the Terminator," Julia says, wiping one hand across her face. "Let's go watch the skaters at 30 Rock. That invariably cheers me up."

* * *

As a child, Ellen begged her parents to bring her to the Rockefeller Center. She ached for a turn on the ice, to spin like the beautiful girls in the many secondhand books she devoured. Except there was always a new winter coat to buy, or repairs that simply had to happen. As a grown-up, she comes here often with Julia. They sip mulled apple cider and eat sugared almonds, laughing as grown-ups wobble-grab for side rails and kids speed past without a care.

"I almost forgot," Julia says and dives into her bag, pulling out two sheets of creased, yellow paper. Ellen knows what they are at once.

"The bucket lists?" she says with a gasp. "I thought they went in the trash years ago."

"I was clearing out my storage unit, and they were just there. Like they wanted to be found. Tempus is fugit-ing."

Ellen takes her list and scowls at handwriting, familiar, yet distant. She used to draw circles above the letter I, something she now thinks of as affected. And the paper is familiar. Torn from a school notebook. How did they ever manage that? Their teacher made everyone number the pages in each new book. Nobody dared unpick staples and steal sheets from the middle.

"I wanted to serenade a stranger," she says, smiling at the memory of when she wrote this for the first time. "But Otto once told me my singing would make even the angels cry."

"I wrote, swimming with dolphins," Julia says.

"Doesn't everyone put that?"

Julia blinks. "Wake up in the desert. Was I under the influence?"

"If I remember rightly, we didn't have dates for the homecoming and stole a bottle of wine from my father's liquor cabinet." Ellen smooths out her list. "I had such dreams. I was going to take pictures for the *New York Times*."

After high school, she applied for, and landed, a place at college to study photography. Everyone said Ellen had talent. But money was tight, and her big chance became her biggest regret. Instead, she worked in the family general store, serving with a tight-lipped smile, while wishing for more.

"My only ambition was to land a suitable beau and march him up the aisle," Julia says, examining her fingernails. "And if I recall rightly, I auditioned my fair share of applicants."

Ellen can't ignore how seeing these forgotten wishes lights a spark inside. "We should do these things before we get old. We can still wake up in the desert, if I book a weekend in Vegas."

Julia fakes outrage, clasping one hand to her chest. "I will never get old. Not as long as there's Botox in my body." She takes a long slug of mulled cider. "What do I always say about you?"

Ellen raises a hopeful eyebrow. "That I'm your best friend and you owe most everything in your life to my wisdom and loyalty?"

"You play safe. You never take risks. Who gets to meet their maker and declare they wish they'd done less and took fewer chances?"

"Slow down," Ellen says. "I'm not ready to die yet, remember."

Julia chews her bottom lip and glances around the room. "This mole I found. What if it is cancer? I haven't seen the doctor in a while. My body could have been racking up diseases without me knowing."

"It won't be." Ellen keeps her voice steady. "Cancer doesn't run in the Hoffman family. Your grandmother lived to 105 and was in better health than I am now when she passed."

Julia sighs, and drops her head into her hands. "What if it is, though? What if this is my last New Year? My final opportunity to do any of the crazy things I always said I might?"

"I'll make you a deal," Ellen says. "First, we swim with dolphins. Unless you want me to book tickets for Celine Dion at Caesars Palace?"

Julia shudders and rubs at her eyes. "I've never been keen on Canadians."

* * *

Ellen opens her mailbox and gasps when she sees a pale yellow envelope. In

21

itself, nothing to care about, except she knows the handwriting. The ink is a rich purple, the letters run together to form a calligraphic swirl. She'd told herself that, this year, there would be no further communication. That seventeen years was enough. That maybe the sender had passed. And yet, there it is.

The doorman is at his desk and nods a greeting. "More snow, they reckon."

She hurries away, jabbing at the elevator button, the letter burning her fingers. On the third floor, she struggles to unlock her door, dropping the keys twice, before bustling inside and slamming it shut, leaning against a side table to catch her breath. With a trembling hand, Ellen sets down the envelope. She needs to sit.

It's dark outside when she rises from a high-backed dining chair to turn on a lamp.

The first Happy Hanukkah card had landed in her mailbox at the start of December 2001. Otto had been dead less than three months, and Ellen still swam deep in denial, crippled by grief. She tore open that first card without thinking. The message inside wished her well. It wasn't signed, and Ellen thought nothing of the gesture, dropping it into the trash. Jews don't send each other Hanukkah cards. One of the girls from the diner must have bought it, not understanding how insensitive their gesture might be.

The next year, another card came, postmarked Trenton, New Jersey. An embroidered silver menorah on a black felt background, and inside, the same scrawl. This time, the sender signed herself as Katharine. Ellen could think of nobody with that name and asked around, drawing blank after blank.

The cards didn't stop. Each year they'd turn up in late November and each year there was no message, just the same name, the handwriting feminine, measured, and elegant.

In 2016, everything changed. Katharine added a note.

"Thinking of Otto, and hope you are well."

It was Julia's idea to hire a PI. He scanned New Jersey voter records, and one bright December morning called to ask Ellen where Otto had been on 9/11.

"The 105th floor in the North Tower," she said, unsure why that mattered.

He'd found nine Katharines employed by an investment bank with offices spanning six North Tower floors, including 105. Only one Katharine lived in New Jersey. On Parkside Avenue. Katharine Fitzgerald. The PI gave Ellen her number, but she didn't call it. When Julia suggested they hire a car and go visit, Ellen flat out refused.

"If she was…friends with Otto. You have a right to hear whatever it is she has to say," Julia argued. "She clearly wants to talk. Why else send the crappy cards?"

"But what if I don't care how she knew my husband?"

Julia hadn't mentioned it since. The cards keep coming.

Chapter Three

The woman who answers the toll-free number at the cruise company suggests Silas come right over. She even offers to pay for a cab. Either this is a really shitty part of town or a really shitty company to work for and they're desperate. The thing is, Silas needs the job, the money, and a reason not to spend the next couple of weeks stewing on rejection.

His driver struggles to find the right place and drops Silas near the passenger terminal, where a bored security guard sends him three blocks west across a busy divided highway. Away from the traffic, each shuttered warehouse and graffiti-covered wall is the same. Silas wrapped up warm, but a winter wind chills him to the bone. He passes a piano factory, a mural of Muhammad Ali, and an empty barbecue smokehouse. On the corner of Coffey and Van Dyke, a Crown Atlantic Shipping marquee flickers above a white-painted door in a building more like someone's run-down home than the global head office of a cruise company. He should turn around and go home. But the job matters. Silas swallows nerves, tries a smile on for size, and rings a doorbell.

The guy who shakes Silas by the hand is bulky, brawny, and deeply tanned. He laughs. A lot. "Man, such a blast you agreed to come." His accent manages to sound both local and as if he blew in from far away.

Silas follows him into a bright kitchen where the air has a hint of citrus and each wall features photos of happy guests, presumably taken on board Crown Atlantic cruises.

The guy holds a white plastic beaker. "How do you take your coffee, dude?"

"Cream. Six sugars."

"Jeez. How do you stay skinny?"

"High metabolism," Silas lies. "I try to keep myself busy."

In a cramped office that reeks of paint thinners and solvent, the Crown Atlantic guy launches into his spiel, explaining how they're the tenth largest cruise company in the United States, with more than seven hundred employees and dozens of ocean liners. Silas tunes most everything out, right after hearing where the ship is bound.

"When exactly would I be in Miami?" he says.

The guy makes a face. "Nobody ever asked me that."

Silas reddens. "It's just that I have family in Florida. It might be good to meet up."

"You get there right before Christmas," the guy says, nodding as if deep in thought. "Assuming you get the job."

Silas wants to ask how many other guys have applied, and if he's the first to interview, the last, or one of many.

"You understand, this isn't a holiday," the Crown Atlantic guy says. "We'll most likely want whoever gets the job to dress up and entertain guests on that day. Not everyone goes ashore."

"Sure, whatever." His mind is elsewhere. He'll fake sickness, or find some other excuse to go ashore and find a bus to Boca Raton to see Joey.

When he tunes back in, the guy is still talking. "We're a flexible group. Looking for a jack-of-all-trades. Someone to do…whatever."

Being a *whatever guy* isn't exactly what Silas expected, but he needs the job. "The ad was to play Santa Claus," he says.

"Our Santa broke both his legs paragliding. Can you believe that? Who paraglides at 63?" Beady eyes narrow. "You're 67, right?"

"Yeah, and I leave flying to the birds."

"I'm gonna level with you, Silas." He leans forward. "We haven't been overrun with applications. This morning, I interviewed some stoner kid and a guy with meth teeth. Crown Atlantic guests expect something better."

Silas has all his own teeth. Nancy used to call them *his little pearls in a row*.

"I've never worked on a ship," he says.

The guy laughs again and slaps one hand on the table. "The minute I laid eyes on you, I said, 'This is the guy. You found your man. Crown Atlantic guests will fall in love with Steve.'"

"My name is Silas."

The guy peers at the application form, like he's sure he can't be wrong. "Is that a Jewish name?"

When Silas nods, the guy shrugs.

"My ass is on the line here," he says. "I need to fill the role, like, yesterday. You want to check if taking two weeks out is cool with your family?"

Silas flinches. "My wife passed and my son...he's kinda...doing his own thing."

The guy snorts. "Don't you hate it when they act like they're all grown up?"

Neither man expects the question to be answered.

"I'll take the job," Silas says, and the guy pretends to wipe his brow, like his life had been on the line.

* * *

For the next two hours, Silas gets the basics of a Crown Atlantic induction, filling out self-evaluation forms and reading a dog-eared copy of the company handbook. All he can think of is how he'll be less than an hour away from Joey. Close enough to reach out. Would Joey agree to talk? He shudders at the thought of a refusal, of a front door slammed in his face.

The interview guy reappears, dressed for outside.

"I need to lock up," he says. A clock on the wall reads 10:01.

"Don't you think I should finish reading the rule book?"

He flaps a hand. "You already got to the most important part, man. No mixing with the guests. Most times, we don't have to enforce that, but the gay cruises are different."

"This is a gay cruise?"

"Shit." The guy's face drops. "You didn't know that?"

Silas isn't sure how to answer. He's not anti-gay. How can he be? His son lives with another man and two adopted kids. For ten years, he worked in a warehouse where the super had a Chinese boyfriend. You'd never guess the guy was queer. He liked soccer.

"It's not a problem," Silas says, and the guy's happy expression returns.

"Good to have you on the team, man," he says with a fist pump. "I'll have Gloria call for bank details, but you get yourself to the terminal by noon on Sunday to sail at four."

Silas should celebrate. He has a new job. And with that, a new plan. He already checked, and a regular bus service leaves Miami for Boca Raton. He won't call ahead, and when Joey answers the door, he'll yell, "Surprise!" and explain how sorry he is for being such a useless excuse for a father, and how much he loves his son, that he never stopped loving him—and everything will tumble into place. Joey's barred-and-bolted heart will melt, and he'll invite his father in. Apollo and Lumen will be playing with their toys, and Joey's husband will be sitting outside, drinking a beer. Or a wine. Whatever it is the gays like these days. They'll all shake hands. Especially Apollo, who will ask who the old man is, and Joey will shrug and say, "This is your grandfather, kiddo. He's staying here a while. Won't that be fun?"

And then Silas has a thought. Joey married a guy called Walker. A miserable son of a bitch with a name that isn't Jewish, meaning they almost certainly celebrate Christmas. Like any good Santa Claus, he should arrive with presents.

* * *

The next day, Silas ventures downtown, with the collar of his jacket pulled up around his ears, and his head bowed. He takes an elevator to the seventh floor of the Goering Brothers Fifth Avenue store and follows twinkling lights and signs to Santaland. If he no longer needs to pay for airline tickets, there's money to splash on gifts for the grandkids.

"Do you need assistance?" a voice says. A salesgirl he doesn't recognize from his most recent stint playing Santa. She's young and pretty and probably only working here to subsidize her income and pay off college debts.

"What would you buy a little girl?" he says.

"What age are we talking?"

Silas has no idea how recent the online photographs might have been. Lumen looked to be about five, with long, curly locks of honey gold hair, blue eyes, and an impish grin.

"Seven next year," he says, hedging his bets, and she guides him toward the main aisle, where pink lights flicker around shelves lined with dolls of varying sizes.

"I'll need something for my grandson too," Silas says. "He's the same age."

"They're twins?" The girl claps her hands with joy. "Then you should buy him the handsome prince." When Silas hesitates, she leans in to whisper. "Unless you prefer something nonbinary?"

He isn't sure what that means, let alone how to answer.

"The prince will be fine," he says. "And I need greeting cards."

TheStaff Onlydoor opens, and one of the Santas appears. Not Bob. Not Justin. A new guy: tall and lean, and he doesn't wave or say hi to the waiting kids. Instead, he stomps past into the grotto. A wave of sadness washes over Silas. Not because he didn't land the job, but because the guy they took on doesn't understand how much of a privilege it is to play Santa Claus and see the joy on young faces.

"Sir?" The sales clerk still hovers nearby. "Are you okay? You said something, but I didn't catch it."

He rubs a hand across his eyes and finds them wet. "It's hot in here. My eyes get dry. I need to use drops."

She points to a sign for the restrooms, and he thanks her, hurrying away.

* * *

Silas flicks a switch, but the lights in his apartment don't come on. He's been telling the super for months the power on the third floor is shot but keeps getting the same excuse about how finding a good electrician takes time. Silas doesn't care if an electrician is good or bad, he wants his fucking lights to work.

He feels his way to the kitchen and finds his emergency torch, before unpacking boxes wrapped in white paper with a red bow from a Goering Brothers carrier. The girl who served him said what great stocking fillers the toys would make. Is that what he wants? Stocking fillers? Don't grandparents get into dumb fights about spoiling their grandkids? But is he a grandfather, really? What on Earth was he thinking, taking that job, and buying gifts for kids he might never be allowed to see? It's time to face facts—he has no right to intrude.

Floorboards creak as he heads for the bathroom where waits for the water to run hot before splashing his face. In the tiny bedroom, Silas takes off his shirt, undoes his belt and sits on the bed, holding his head in his hands. The glow from his battery alarm clock says it's a little after midnight. Rose might be awake.

She doesn't pick up, sending him to voicemail. He rubs his eyes. "Hey, Rose. Just checking in. I'll call you again soon. Bye."

No sooner has he ended the call than he knows he should have mentioned how they won't be spending the holidays together this year. They won't eat Chinese food and pass out on her sofa watching *It's a Wonderful Life*, and he won't buy her a gift that she'll pretend to love, and later ask if he kept proof of purchase.

Chapter Four

Penn Station throbs with a mix of sharp-suited morning commuters clutching to-go cups and people dragging overstuffed bags. The drone of conversation swells, punctuated by the squeal of an excited child. A loudspeaker announces train departures and arrivals. Julia's winter boots *click clack* on the concourse and Ellen struggles to keep up.

"Look," she says, taking a huge swallow of air. "I'm being a baby. Thousands hop on airplanes every day. Malinowski will write me a script for Valium. Let's find a travel agent."

Julia shakes her head. "We agreed. Trains not planes."

Ellen hangs back as Julia heads for the Amtrak counter and joins the shortest of three slow-moving lines. After almost twenty years, she should be over her fears, and yet the thought of being strapped into a cramped airplane seat always brings her out in a cold sweat. Even now, goose bumps prickle under her heavy jacket.

A girl of about ten, with long dark hair, dirty clothes, and empty eyes holds a handwritten sign explaining how she came here with her family and got separated, and now lives alone on the street and hasn't eaten for days. She speaks no English.

Ellen tries to mime how she only has cards, and the girl simpers politely before moving on. Otto would have insisted the girl wait while he ran to get cash. This morning, she's out of sorts. Katharine's card had thrown her. Hanukkah ended a week ago. Perhaps the card was caught in the mail. Delayed. She should have checked the postmark.

The huge clock in the middle of the departure hall shows 9:00. In under an hour, she needs to be at the diner, in the staff room, getting changed for a double shift. She can't risk being late, not if she wants to stay on her boss's good side when she asks for time off. Tony gets weird this close to the holidays, even though lunchtime trade all but vanishes as soon as all the nearby office buildings shut down.

Julia's back and the face she pulls suggests bad news.

"A rail ticket costs more than a flight," she says. "Nine hundred dollars, plus an additional consideration for something they call a 'roomette.' I told the girl we'd ponder her proposition."

Ellen bobs her head, taking in nothing.

"Are you okay, honey?" Julia says. "You're somewhat pale."

"I skipped breakfast."

"We have time to adjourn for coffee."

Putting one foot in front of the other is like trying to walk a high wire. "I'll eat at the diner. Did you ask about hotels?"

Julia links an arm through hers. "We'll use Marjorie Blackman's travel agent … and ask about prices for flights. Just in case. Doesn't hurt to have a plan B."

She wants Ellen to agree to board a plane. "Fine," she says. "I'm being dumb. It's safer than crossing a street in the city, but still …"

As they leave the station, stepping into the bitter cold morning air, the weather takes a turn for the worse, and dark clouds scuttle across a stormy sky. Ellen's sister would see this as a bad omen. Although the skies were bright blue on the day when Otto died. Too blue, perhaps. Even now, there are days when she peers up and wonders if that's the same shade of blue as on that Tuesday morning, and if something awful is waiting to happen.

* * *

The East Side Diner staff room is always too hot. Tony welded shut the windows for what he called "security reasons," and no matter how much everyone bitches, he refuses to install ventilation. An evil stench rises from a black plastic sack dumped in one corner.

Ellen gets ready for her shift, hoping today finds her boss in a pleasant mood or she can kiss goodbye to swimming with dolphins. Tony's cousin Nadine appears. Ellen likes Nadine. She acts as a buffer zone between the staff and her bad-tempered relative. She could be thirty, she could be fifty, thanks to one of those impossible-to-age faces with hair dyed silver-blond and cut into an asymmetric bob.

"Hey girlfriend." Nadine blows air kisses. "How come I haven't seen you in weeks?"

"I guess we didn't work the same shifts."

"You coming to the adoption party tomorrow?"

Ellen glances up from putting on flat shoes. "The what party?"

Nadine explains how she's being adopted by two lesbian friends, mostly on account of how her own mother refuses to have anything to do with her after a falling out ten years back. Rumor has it, Nadine tried to burn down the apartment building they lived in after her folks refused to loan her money for a new car. Ellen has always thought of her as having a short fuse.

"I don't recall getting an invitation," Ellen says, and Nadine nods thoughtfully, as if her answer makes sense.

"I guess Eloise and Sandra didn't figure it was your scene."

Ellen isn't offended but would have liked to have been asked. Of course, she'd have found some excuse and sent flowers. Adult adoption parties are more of a West Coast thing. The bullshit tolerance level in New York is usually much closer to zero.

Nadine reaches into the staff fridge and pulls out a soda. "I figure I'm gonna need this. It's a Joe day."

Joe is Tony's accountant. At the end of each month, he turns up gray-faced and grim, and after he leaves, Tony makes changes. Soap vanishes from the bathrooms, paper napkins get placed on ration, the prices inch up and customers kvetch.

Nadine flips the ring on her soda. "All the signs tell me this time it's more serious."

Ellen massages her neck. She's having a bad day and sitting on a cold bench at Penn Station didn't help. Her head aches, and her eyes are sore.

"You sick or something?" Nadine says. "You're pasty."

"Thanks for that." Ellen forces a chuckle. "And here I was trying to pass for Elizabeth Taylor in her prime."

Nadine heads through double doors. "Catch you on the front line."

The shift starts out unremarkable, with a trickle of customers, and those who venture in hunker down for free coffee refills. The tip jar won't be full. Standing around and acting pleasant becomes an exercise in endurance.

A little after three, the office door opens, and Joe leaves. His eyes are red and rheumy, and his skin a pallid shade of yellow. He doesn't say goodbye. Immediately, Tony yells for Nadine, and she's in there for ten minutes, emerging close to tears.

"He wants to see you next," she tells Ellen.

Ellen swallows her nerves and knocks on a door marked "Private." After a long pause, Tony calls her in. He's short, balding, and heavy. An oversize desk makes him look like someone melted a much larger man. He signals for her to sit. "How many years have you worked here?"

She crosses her legs and nails on a polite expression. Because Tony has no manners, that's no reason to act the same. "I've been at the diner for forty-six years," she says, keeping her tone cordial. "Close on half a century."

He chews his lip and makes a sucking sound. "You must be getting sick of the place?"

"Every day is different." Ellen hopes the words don't sound as sycophantic as they play out in her head. "The diner has become a part of my life."

"My family did you an exceptional deal."

Ellen was taken on by Tony's father, and paid minimum wage, though he threw in medical and dental. She's not rich, but neither does she scratch for pennies.

"I guess," she says.

He stops picking dead skin from stubby fingers. There's spinach on one front tooth. Tony never says what's on his mind. He's always been a beat-around-the-bush kind of guy relying on charm to make him seem more like a friend than your boss, hiding behind Nadine when there's bad news to deliver.

"You guess?" he says, in a way that suggests she has just given the wrong answer.

Family matters to Tony. She needs to play along. "Your father made sure I was looked after."

"Looked after *well*," he insists.

"Of course."

He gets up and goes over to the only window in his office with a view of the busy highway, where cars, trucks, and trailers speed by. Some days, hardly anyone stops for food.

"Joe reckons profits are in the crapper," he says, and for the first time, a tiny destructive fire lights in the back of Ellen's head. When your boss talks about profits tumbling, it's usually a way into justifying bad news. "We had the worst month in history."

Ellen doesn't dare risk words. She feels the first stirrings of nausea in her belly.

Tony turns around. "I guess you know what that means?"

She still isn't sure if he wants an answer. Seems like he doesn't.

"Restructuring."

"Oh," Ellen says, half relieved he hasn't come right out and said he plans on firing anyone or taking away benefits. Because no matter how much of a weasel Tony might be, he has something of a heart. He wouldn't fire their longest-serving member of staff a week or two before the holidays. That would be cruel.

"The rule is first in, first out," he says and Ellen startles. Did she hear him right? Surely not.

She clears her throat. "First in, last out, surely?"

Tony holds out a hairy hand. "It's been fun working with you, but you gotta let the kids have a shot. You've done well to hang on this long. I'll pay you to the end of today's first shift. You don't need to stay."

"I thought…" Ellen says, but she's not sure what she thought. That this wouldn't happen? That it would be a year or two before he worked out she was easy to fire? That he'd give her more notice? That offering to pay her for the last three hours of an eight-hour shift was typically tight.

"Sorry, Ellen," he says as if he means it. "I wish I could keep you on, but..."

"But what?" Her mouth dry.

"But we're downsizing. It's not viable."

She wants to ask if he's thought about getting rid of the agency staff, or any other less drastic measure he could take to reduce their costs, but she's too upset. She can't think straight. And while she ought to stand up to him and say how she hopes that made him feel more of a man. That his father would never have acted like such a weasel, she holds her tongue, smiles, and gets to her feet.

"I best go clear out my locker," she says.

He sits, spinning his chair so he gets a view of the busy highway. "You think you could get me a coffee?"

* * *

Ellen frowns into a single shot of malt whiskey in a heavy-bottomed tumbler. It's the color of honey and the scent is of smoke and oak. Even though the bar sits right across the street from the diner, she's never come in before. Men in flannel shirts and women in blue jeans nurse pale mugs of beer. A bulletin board dominates the one wall and huge windows look out on a patch of barren grass.

"Bad day?" The bartender is about her age, with a hoop earring in his left ear, and the kind of half-heated smile that suggests he's been there, done that.

"Possibly the worst." she says, and he pulls a towel from his belt and sets to wiping the counter.

"That has to be good, right? It means things can only get better."

Ellen is content to stay inside her bubble of sadness. Outside, a homeless woman drags a shopping cart, laden with her life and held together with a brightly colored beach towel. She mutters to herself, occasionally calling out, causing passersby to change direction. Most New Yorkers are two pay checks away from losing their home, and even though she owns her apartment, the service charge always eats into her savings, and that's before she pays out for heating, water, food. And then there's Malinowski. He'll let her off a while, but not forever. Otto's money won't cover everything.

Ellen reaches into her bag and finds a headache pill, washing it down with the whiskey, something she's sure any doctor would red light.

"Where's the bathroom?" she says, and the bartender points to a dark wooden door in the far corner.

On the way, she stops to scan the bulletin board with cards and flyers from people selling strollers, offering French lessons and piano tuning. There are jobs for cleaners and dog walkers, but everyone wants references, and given all the names she called Tony when she delivered his shitty coffee, which she hoped would choke him, that might be a problem.

And then she spots something else.

For sale: Two tickets on HOLIDAY CRUISE to Miami. Fabulous stateroom, mid-level. Food and beverages included. Make me an offer.

Chapter Five

Fine sleet falls, and Silas follows familiar streets, his hands in his pockets, still not sure that what he's about to do will end in anything but disaster—but what other choice does he have? Wait yet another year, and hope Joey comes to his senses? Malinowski didn't need to spell things out. He may not have another year to wait.

Nancy used to say, if you call the devil, he'll always hear his name, and on cue, his chest tightens. He fears he might throw up, but manages to control his gag reflex with a deep breath. Silas shelters in a doorway, glancing through steamed-up windows, and across a polished marble floor to an oak reception desk, where a pair of austere women glare back. One twitches in way that suggests she's written him off as a street bum sheltering from snow, and wants him to move on.

He reaches into his pocket for a tablet that might settle jangling nerves, and checks he still has an envelope padded with cash. His neighbor from the basement apartment started up a rumor that the super has a key to everyone's place and sneaks in and out during the day, trying to find things worth taking. Mrs. Blatter never goes out, and swears she hears apartment doors slamming long after everyone leaves for work. When Silas asked why she didn't investigate, her eyes grew wide.

"How do I know he won't have a gun? This is New York City."

She had a point, add to which the super was a weasel nobody trusted.

He catches sight of the time on a clock behind the uppity receptionist ladies. It's already ten o'clock, and he needs to get moving or the MS Viking will set sail without Santa.

Silas considers his options. A cab ride with a chatty driver and seat-back screens playing Broadway commercials would transform a nagging headache into full-on nausea. Instead, he rides the subway to Brooklyn, and jumps off two stops early to buy bodega food. At the port security gates, a burly guy bars the way, and when Silas asks where he's supposed to go, the guy points toward the passenger terminal.

Even from a distance, he can make out music.

"Sounds quite the party," Silas says.

The uniformed guard doesn't answer. He limps back into his hut, muttering something about *the fucking fags.*

"Challenge him." Silas hears Joey's voice say. "Tell him that's no way to talk about people like me. Prove to me how you've changed."

The moment is past, and the security guard has already settled by a pockmarked window and picked up his copy of the *New York Post.*

Next time, Silas thinks. *I'll get it right next time.*

Outside the terminal building, a redcap takes his bag, and when Silas explains how he's crew, motions along the sidewalk toward a green awning.

"I'll meet you on the other side," he says. "With your bags."

A grumpy official demands ID, and without bothering to examine a Crown Atlantic employment offer letter, pushes a button, sliding open doors. A wave of noise hits Silas. Guys mill around, wheeling trolleys piled high. Music blares, and he joins a line for security checks.

"Welcome aboard," says a guy with a role of stickers. "Top, bottom, or versatile?"

Silas half-smiles. "I'm sorry?"

"You look like a daddy to me. Shall we say top?" He presses a dark blue sticker onto the collar of Silas's jacket and waves him past.

He surveys the departure hall. A band plays, but he can't make out the song over laughter, shrieks of delight, and the din of loud voices.

Joey would love this.

* * *

CHAPTER FIVE

A sliver of sunlight falls across Ellen's face. She opens the taxi door, and freezing air rushes in, heavy with the smell of acrid diesel. She wrinkles her nose and her eyes water. The gray port authority building is a nondescript box dating from the 1930s, its facade dulled with a patina of grime and soot. They've dressed for a long day of sitting around and standing in line. Julia in tailored black cotton pants and a crisp, white button-down. Ellen in trouser-cut straight-leg jeans and a green Old Navy sweater.

As Ellen lugs her bag from the trunk, she spots Julia's jacket. "You still have your mink coat? Even after that girl threw red paint outside Saks?"

Julia pulls on Jackie O sunglasses. "My dry cleaner made it good as new, and anyway, this is a luxury cruise, and..."

Her voice trails away. Huge speakers blast disco music. Almost every passenger is male. Mostly young and ready to party. Yellow cabs sound their horns in unison, pink flags flap, and an inflatable rainbow bounces on a stiff breeze, threatening to escape its tether.

"The young fellow you bought these tickets from," Julia says, as two drag queens fight over stray balloons, "did he happen to mention the nature of the clientele?"

Ellen shook her head. She hadn't warmed to the morose guy in his thirties, who lived in The Village, and despite what his bulletin board notice claimed, refused to negotiate even one cent on price.

"I'm sure the cruise is more mixed than gay," Ellen says. "We're all one happy family these days, right?"

Industrial strength pain medication is helping her sound positive. At four a.m., she woke in agony. The blood in her veins was boiling, and the sheets wringing wet from sweat. It was as if her spine had twisted into a knot. Turning over caused her to scream out. Was it the same pain as yesterday? She found her cell, but her doctor wasn't on call, and his answering service suggested Tylenol. She was still lying there when sunlight finally streamed through the blinds, and Malinowski called back, offering to send through a prescription for stronger medication. She popped two little blue pills in the drug store before breakfast and floated home.

A young guy, dressed in denim shorts and a buckled leather harness, stops and wolf-whistles. "You're so authentic," he tells the two women with a whoop.

"What did he mean?" Ellen narrows curious eyes. "We're authentic?"

Julia's face darkens, and she waves down a porter. "The little punk thinks we're fucking drag queens."

Ellen tries to stifle a giggle. Two years back, they went to a costume party in the East Village, and Julia dressed as Dolly Parton with cotton candy hair, way too much makeup, and a million rhinestones. Her outfit was the talk of the evening. Most everyone assumed she was a man.

Ellen links an arm through hers. "If you want to go back home, I'll understand. We'll chalk it up to experience. Lesson learned."

"Are you kidding?" Julia says. "These are my people. After twenty-six years on Broadway, I'm on hugging terms with half the guys here."

Almost on cue, a tall Black guy with a shaved head howls her name. They hug and skip around, and Julia introduces Ellen to Levi.

"He's the best dancer in *Mamma Mia*," she says. "I was a witness at his wedding."

Still painkiller-wobbly, Ellen is keen to get onboard and find their room. The guy who sold her the tickets promised a mid-level stateroom with a tub and window.

"Levi wants to get bon voyage cocktails," Julia says. "There's a place adjacent."

A voice in Ellen's head says no, but how would that sound? She's somehow managed to book them onto a gay cruise, and the first time they get invited for drinks, she finds an excuse not to go. Over by the terminal, cannons boom and silver strands of ticker tape fill the air.

"Sure, fine, whatever," she says and fumbles in her pocket for another blue pill.

* * *

Silas follows directions to find his room. Below deck on the MS Viking, one corridor is much like the other. He turns the corner into yet another stretch of scuffed gray carpet, pale blue pockmarked walls, and dark green doors, each with silver numbers. Eventually, he finds one marked 17, and pushes it open, calling hello. The sound of running water suggests his roommate-to-be is taking a shower.

For the first time, Silas wonders if whoever lurks in the bathroom might also be gay. Not that it bothers him. Every gay man doesn't want to have sex with every guy they meet. He's acting like the jocks talking on the one occasion he made it to the pool at the Vanderbilt Y. Going on about how other guys were giving them the eye and how, if they so much as tried anything…

He shakes his head, dismissing the memory.

This is a job. On a gay cruise. In just over a week, he'll see Joey.

Silas drops his bag on the floor in front of two metal lockers. In the first, he finds a rail of sequined dresses and a row of high-heeled shoes. He's clearly in the wrong room 17. Silas tiptoes out and pulls the door shut, retracing his steps to the elevator, where a sign on the wall confirms this is the right level. Perhaps the woman in the shower in room 17 got the wrong cabin? He loiters by the elevator, giving her time to be done. And dressed.

When he gets back, the door to the room stands wide open, and a skinny guy sits on the nearest bunk, wrapped in a white toweling gown, with his back turned.

"Excuse me," Silas says.

The guy turns around. He's older, maybe seventy, and wrinkled and bony. A bad comb-over hides most of a bald scalp. His eyes are clear and bright.

"You must be Santa," he says, and Silas picks up on a British accent. "If it's okay with you, I need to sleep nearest the door. Call me superstitious. I'm Ken, by the way."

Silas sets down his bags and holds out a greeting hand. Ken's handshake is soft. Almost feminine.

"I'm also particular about which locker is mine," Ken says, with a sniff. "I trust that won't be a problem?"

Silas shakes his head and beams widely. "Right…only you were in the shower before, and I went to start unpacking, and…"

41

Ken rattles with throaty laughter. "Fuck me," he says. "I bet you thought they'd slung you in with one of the birds by mistake."

Silas isn't sure what any of those words might mean and summons a noncommittal shrug.

"My stage name is Miss Kitty Kate, I do drag, darling."

Again, Silas can't think what to say, and goes over to what must, by a process of elimination, be his bed.

"First time?" Ken says.

"As Santa, no. I worked at Goering Brothers for years."

"First time at sea?"

"Is it that obvious?"

"Which side of the stamp do you lick?"

Silas doesn't understand the question, and can't help but think it rude to ask Ken to explain.

"Are you bent?" Ken points at the dark blue sticker still stuck to his jacket. "Do you sleep with men? Not that it matters, but I prefer to know."

"I'm straight."

Ken's lips curl upward, exposing yellow teeth. "You do get how that makes you a target?"

"A target for what?" Silas's mind goes into overdrive. Will he be hated and hounded for being a minority?

"We all think we have what it takes to perform a conversion," Ken says, and laughs again. "But I'm happily married, so you're safe. Unless I have one too many G&Ts, then all bets are off."

Silas blushes, and he wants to look away or make busy unpacking. "Is there someplace to store valuables?"

Ken shrugs. "I guess you can use the crew safe, but I wouldn't trust half the fuckers on this boat. My advice is to stuff your life's savings in a sock and shove it under your mattress. Like my old Mum used to say. Keep your hand on your ha'penny."

He laughs. It's a nervous reaction, but it makes Ken laugh, too, so he keeps at it.

"It's okay," Silas says. "I'm not used to sharing a room."

Ken pulls on a shirt. One that looks expensive. White and made of silk with pearl buttons. "There's a staff meeting in an hour," he says. "You'll meet with Howdy Doody."

"Howdy what?"

Ken's chuckle is another rattle that turns into a cough, and soon his face is purple, and he's gasping for air. Silas freezes. What should he do? Get help?

Ken reaches a bony arm around and punches his own back. "Don't mind me," he wheezes. "I'm on twenty a day. Full strength. The quack keeps on at me to give up. But you've got to die of something, right?"

He staggers into the bathroom. Water runs.

As Silas hangs clothes in the empty locker, there's a knock at the door, and a short man, dressed all in black, holds out a chubby hand.

"Father Robert Casey," he says. "Bob to my friends. I'm in charge of moral fortitude on this floating sin bin. Is Miss Kitty around?"

"Miss Kitty?" Silas furrows his brow. "Oh yeah, Ken. I mean Miss Kitty. Is that right? I don't know what to call them."

"Them?" The priest raises an eyebrow. "Am I to assume you're one of those heterosexuals we read so much about in the *New Yorker*?"

From the bathroom, there's a raspy, wet sound, like someone trying to spit up trapped food.

"Am I dead-naming her by saying Ken?" Silas whispers, and Father Robert chuckles to himself.

"Ken's a drag queen, love," he says. "She'll answer to anything if the price is right. Tell her Bob needs a word about supply chain issues when she's done hacking up a lung."

* * *

Ellen could have died of shame. One minute she was enjoying the company of new friends, laughing at their outrageous jokes and trading stories of life at the East Side Diner. The next, she was lying on the floor, and staring up at concerned faces. She's now in her bed, in a room she doesn't know. The decor is bland, a mix of blues, creams, and grays, although the carpet has a dizzying swirly pattern.

"You're sure about this trip?" Julia says, plumping pillows behind Ellen's head.

"I'll be fine," Ellen says. "It's my fault for drinking on top of painkillers."

"The guest relations lady said there's still an hour before we set sail if you'd rather head for home."

Ellen sits up and rubs her eyes. "We agreed on swimming with dolphins. Nothing's going to stop me."

Almost everyone Ellen knows describes her as stubborn. She prefers strong-willed. As a woman living alone, she's run into tricksters. Guys who turn up at her door claiming to be from the power company, phone calls from the bank asking for her card and PIN number, emails from deposed heads of state, begging to hide funds in her savings account in exchange for a healthy cut of the profits.

"Do you want to go home?" Julia says. "Or we could spend the holidays at my place. I'll order in. We'll still have fun."

"That sounds like the opposite of fun. I might as well call around funeral homes and negotiate prices."

"So we're staying?" Julia raises an eyebrow. "I can inform the porters they need not collect our baggage?"

Ellen rearranges pillows, propping herself up in bed. "I want an adventure."

Julia grins. "Me too. The only risk I take these days is dropping ten bucks on lottery tickets. Shall I help unpack your things?"

"I'll do it later."

She catches how Julia rolls her eyes, but Ellen doesn't care. She's an organizer. Everything gray goes together. Everything white needs a second pile. She hates rummaging through closets and drawers to find pantyhose. Her only fights with Otto were about his habit of dropping items of clothing wherever he took them off. On the rare occasions she trusted him to put away laundry, she'd discover socks mixed in with underwear and shirts crammed into the sweater drawer.

"And get rid of that." Ellen waves a crabby hand at a foldaway wheelchair by the door. She'd suffered the indignity of being wheeled on board by a woman called Kathy Lucey, who latched onto them in the security line. A blond bubble perm with a passion for fluorescent-colored clothing. Part of a double act with Patrick, her humorless brother who teaches at community college. "The last thing I want is for everyone to call me the wheelchair lady."

"What if you need it again?"

"I won't."

"But you don't know."

"For once, can you do as I fucking ask?" Ellen immediately regrets losing her cool, and draws a ragged breath. "If I require assistance, I'm sure one of us has the power to pick up the telephone and make just such a request."

As Julia flings her clothes onto shelves and into drawers, she whistles tunelessly. A habit Ellen also detests, but has never mentioned, and given they're about to spend two weeks in close contact, now isn't the time.

"Shall we get room service tonight?" Ellen tries to sound casual. What she really wants to say is, can they hide away for the next however many days, until everyone forgets about the old lady in her wheelchair.

"About that," Julia says, turning to a mirror and checking her hair. "I promised to meet up with Kathy and Patrick. They were so kind and helpful today, and I thought it would be nice to thank them."

"Fine." Ellen tries not to sound as irritated as she feels. "Have you seen my yellow dress?"

Julia unzips Ellen's bag and pulls out two more or less identical frocks.

"The one on the right." Ellen rearranges the pillows once more, before closing her eyes, figuring if she pretends to sleep, it will help clear a filthy mood.

And Julia might stop fucking whistling.

Chapter Six

The crew office doors are already closed, and the room is packed. Silas taps on the glass, but no heads turn. He tries again, this time louder, and one woman flashes irritated eyes, before nudging the guy next to her, who pokes someone else, and then the door opens.

"Do we have a latecomer?" The guy up front talks with a midwestern twang. This must be Ken's Howdy Doody. "Let's everybody shifty on around a smooch and make sure Mr. Tardy-Pants gets to see the big screen."

With mutters and groans and what-the-fuck-mans, a way clears.

"I believe we just welcomed Santa Claus." Howdy Doody signals for Silas to come to the front and let everyone see this year's Father Christmas. "Ladies and gentlemen, this is his first time at sea, so let's give him a huge Crown Atlantic welcome."

Silas edges forward to a less-than-feeble round of applause. Howdy Doody turns out to be pasty-faced, tall and skinny, straight up and down, with no hint of a chin. The kind of guy who got picked on at high school.

"My name is Howard," he says, shaking hands with Silas. His palms are wet and the grip is loose. "My job is entertainments director."

Silas forces a smile. "Good to be part of the team."

Howdy Doody clicks his fingers, and a guy looks up from his cell phone. "Let Santa Silas have your seat, Deon. You're young. You can afford to stand."

Silas wants to argue that he in no way requires special treatment, and is fine as he is, but Howard insists. Deon looks to be in his late teens, with long dark hair, and dressed head to toe in black. Young or not, he isn't happy at being told to give up his precious seat, and glares from bloodshot eyes.

When Silas sits, someone in the row behind pats his shoulder in a "well done, old fella" way.

Howard runs through a presentation. Mostly slides of company mottoes: Smile all the while. Be the best you can be. Believe you can. Most everyone else in the room fiddles and fidgets, eager to leave. The presentation ends, and Howard signals to turn the lights back on.

"Lifeboat drill in one hour," he says as people shuffle through the door.

Silas turns to go, too, but then he's asked to stay.

"Come sit with me," Howard says. "I want to make sure you understand what it means to be a vital cog in the Crown Atlantic machine."

The ship shudders and sirens sound.

"We're off." Howard gives a contented sigh. "I always love this part of the journey. The minute where they let go of the ropes holding us down, and we float off into our magical water world."

Silas stares at the scuffed floor, wondering if he made the biggest mistake. Perhaps not of his life, but certainly the biggest this year.

"Now don't you go worrying about no initiation ceremonies," Howard says with an overly toothy grin. "Some of the crew josh around with newbies and…" He breaks off and slaps a palm to his forehead. "I'm so sorry, Silas. You must correct me each time I use an unfamiliar word. *Newbies* is what we call anyone making their first voyage."

"I sort of got that," Silas says.

"How much did the office tell you?"

"They didn't go into specifics, but I guess you want me to man the grotto, ring sleigh bells, and say *yo ho*. The usual crap."

Howard's face crumples. "Don't say you're not a true believer in the Christmas miracle, Silas? It's the most wonderful time of the year."

Silas might act tough, but he only ever does this job because he loves seeing a kid's eyes light up. The thing is, that isn't going to happen on board the MS Viking.

He curls his lips into a smile. "The most wonderful time indeed."

Howard relaxes. "I don't believe in pussy-footing around, Silas. I truly don't. And if anyone tells you different, you go tell them they don't know Howard Carpenter at all. He's not one of those men. Pussy-footing is not my thing." He takes a sip of water. "I'm going to level with you, Silas. Head office let us down. I should have two more bodies on board as part of the entertainment crew. And that means you need to help me out."

"Help you out, how?"

Howard gets up and goes over to a row of hooks. From each hangs a black cloth bag.

"This is your Santa outfit," he says. "Right here, you have a snowman. This one is The Grinch."

"You want me to wear all of them?"

Howard steps back and looks Silas up and down. "I figure they should fit."

"Do I get paid extra?"

Howard roars with laughter, dabbing his eyes. "I admire your style, Silas, really I do. Take these costumes back to your room. The lifeboat drill sirens sound at a quarter after four, and you need to be at Muster Station B6."

He scribbles the number on a scrap of paper and hands it over, still chortling to himself as he taps a computer keyboard.

Their conversation is over.

Outside the crew office, Silas spots the kid who gave up his chair and raises a hand in friendly greeting. It earns him a sneer. Ken and the priest stand arguing. There's something strange about both men.

Another blast from the horn confirms it's too late to turn back.

Silas heads for the elevator.

* * *

A digital clock on the nightstand flashes. The floor creaks and rocks. Distant engines groan. Ellen pats around for her cell phone and finds it's a little after four. She pushes buttons on an illuminated panel until lights come on. The room is much as her hazy head recalls, filled with furniture made for tiny people: a half-sized chair, a three-quarter sofa, and a side table with barely enough space for two tumblers.

Julia isn't back, which most likely means she's still having drinks with that ghastly Kathy woman and her terminally dull brother. At least the wheelchair has gone, and she spies a note on the dresser with her name scribbled large.

When she gets out of bed, Ellen's head spins, causing her to stumble, and yet this isn't the worst sensation ever. It's actually quite nice. Like floating on clouds, cushioned from the world, and she doesn't care about her clothes sitting in a mixed-up heap on the sofa. Her vision is blurred, her body tingles. She pulls a white cord to open a blind, and peers through the tiny porthole window. Gray clouds billow with snow. It's already dusk.

The bathroom door stands half open, and she nudges it with one toe, her eyes adjusting to a light that flickers into life-detecting motion. Julia has kindly unpacked her cosmetics bag, and two toothbrushes wait in a tumbler near the sink. As she cleans her teeth, her stomach rumbles, and she tries to remember when she last ate. She'd picked at stale bread first thing after cleaning out her fridge and tearing the heel of the loaf into pieces for Georgette, a rock dove who stops by most mornings. Since then, she'd eaten nothing. Unless you count the cherry in an overly potent cocktail.

Her mouth is dry, and she fills a glass with water, swallowing it in three huge gulps. It tastes weird, with a chemical aftertaste.

After jabbing at buttons near the tub, water trickles, and Ellen pulls her shirt over her head and steps under the shower. It's way too hot, but feels good against sandpaper skin, and she relaxes against the wall, her face resting against the cold tiles. Almost at once, the water is freezing, causing her to startle, and she half tumbles out, standing motionless and naked. When her stomach growls once more, she finds a room service menu to order tomato soup and a chicken sandwich.

As she's brushing her hair, a gold-embossed card slides under the door. An invitation to tonight's party: wear white and be ready to dazzle.

"What am I doing, Otto?" she croaks. "A gay cruise? Have I finally lost the plot?"

It's been seventeen years since she lost her husband, and she knows he isn't there when she talks to him. Not really. But asking questions out loud helps. And she almost always gets some kind of answer.

"I know," she whispers. "I'm on my own now. You don't get to tell me what to do."

Being in this room, with its deliberately low lighting designed to help the occupants relax, isn't helping. She needs to be out and about, mixing with people, not hiding away feeling sorry for herself. She cancels her sandwich, and picks out a blue sweater and dark gray culottes. She'll wear her hair up. Julia always says how much that suits her. She puts on the watch Otto bought for her birthday, two weeks before he died.

"I love you," she whispers.

And he whispers back.

* * *

Ellen pushes a button to call the elevator. If not for the rumble of engines, she could be in a five-star hotel. The lobby is decorated with lush green plants, immaculately groomed. A shiny brass plaque mounted on the wall, hand-engraved with the company's logo, promises the journey of a lifetime. She's excited, and a little anxious. Not airplane anxious. But still. A bunch of guys join her to wait. They're excited, planning what to do. She presses the call button again.

"Honey, we should take the stairs," one of the guys says. "This is taking for-evah."

She's about to follow, when a siren sounds, loud and shrill and piercing, and she isn't sure what to do.

"Is that a fire alarm?" someone asks.

Ellen's heart races, but still she stands, staring at the elevator doors, willing them to open. The siren is so loud, she covers her ears. Even so, she hears it. The elevator doors refuse to open.

"We need to find the lifeboats." One of the guys has a hold of her hand, dragging her toward an emergency exit. "Follow me."

Ellen tries to resist, but he tugs again, harder.

"I know you're scared," he yells over the siren, "but this is just a drill. It's safe. Come on."

She gives in and goes with him, but she's shaking. She's never been much of a swimmer, and even if this is only some kind of drill, accidents happen. Every nightmare she's had in the days since buying these tickets replays on fast-forward in her head. The guy with a hold of her hand takes her room card and points to a number printed on the back.

"This is your station. B6."

Speakers blare, and a crew member directs passengers to emergency stairs. She stumbles up them, the ship rocking beneath her feet. Her heart still pounds, but she tries to remain calm, telling herself over and over how this is a drill.

Up on deck, guys wrapped up warm wander around, some checking phones, some asking uniformed crew what gives. A woman in a yellow vest yells directions from a bullhorn, but nobody acts any way worried. The drill turns into a party, with music playing and one guy blowing a vuvuzela. Up ahead, she spots Julia wearing a sailor's hat and chatting with a tall blond guy. They laugh and point at something below. Ellen calls out, but the crowd swells, and she's hidden. Another speaker crackles, but she can't make out words.

This is ridiculous. If this wasn't a drill, and lives were actually at stake, people might die. She spots a sign for Station B6, and picks her way through, but the deck is wet and oily, and she loses her footing, falling backward, snatching for a rail, and grabbing a handful of empty air.

Faces flash by, and then she's on her back, surrounded by feet and legs and gazing into worried eyes.

Deep dark brown eyes.

One with a speckle of green.

Ellen tries to sit up, but her hip aches, and she's dizzy.

"I need assistance over here," a gruff voice calls. "A woman fell." And then his kind face turns back to her. "Can you hear me? What's your name?"

"Ellen...Gitelman. I think I bit my tongue."

"I'm Silas, Ellen. Give me your hand. Let me help you."

He pulls her to her feet, and her head spins, but the pain in her hip goes away. The eyes staring into hers convey concern and kindness.

"I'm fine," she says, brushing herself down, and feeling suddenly rather silly. "It was a tumble. Nothing to fuss over."

"Best the doc checks you."

Another face swims into view. Younger. Handsome. Chiseled. Tanned. He's saying her name. And then everything turns dark.

Chapter Seven

The MS Viking Medical Center is as much unlike a hospital as it's possible to get. The floors are a patchwork of linoleum, aged rugs, and industrial rubber. Light bulbs hang in clusters of three, lending everything and everyone a sickly glow. Windows are nonexistent, and the air tastes stale.

Ellen lies on a narrow metal-framed bed in a room so tiny, she can reach out and touch each wall. In a whispered exchange, someone discusses having her flown back to New York City.

"Hello," she calls, and a young nurse pops around, holds up a finger to signal she'll be free in one minute.

Apart from the bed, there's a chair and a small sink, over which hangs a crucifix. It's the kind of place Ellen imagines would please a very devout and very forgiving nun. The kind of place that very much doesn't suit her.

"Sorry about that." The nurse is cheerful and smiling. Young. Perhaps too young to be doing this sort of job alone. "How's the patient?"

"She's feeling a whole lot better," Ellen says, hoping the lie will stick. "Well enough to return to her room."

The child-nurse smiles once more, and Ellen senses doubt.

"We do need to carry out one or two checks," she says. "To make sure you're fit to continue your vacation."

Ellen shuffles herself up in the bed and juts out her chin. "If you have any thought of trying to send me home, please think again. I paid good money for my ticket, and I plan on swimming with dolphins."

"That sounds wild."

The young always use the wrong words, she thinks. The plan is far from wild. It's exciting and different. At the least, she could suggest swimming with dolphins sounds like fun.

"My traveling companion will wonder where I am," Ellen says, as the nurse straps on a blood pressure cuff and pumps at a rubber ball.

"We posted a note under your cabin door. You took a knock to your head, right?"

"I wouldn't call it a knock."

The nurse chews her lower lip. "We *should* ask you to stay overnight to be on the safe side. I don't like the idea of moving you. Not so soon. Not at your age."

Ellen swallows an urge to throw back the covers and run. "You can have me sign release forms and accept all responsibility. It's not like I have that long to live, anyway. At my age."

Their eyes meet.

"You heard what the doctor was saying?" the nurse says. "He wants to get you transported home."

Ellen folds determined arms. "Well, that's not going to happen."

"I figured as much." She glances at one of the machines beeping above the bed. "You'll be fine, as far as I can see. There's nothing broken."

"So you'll have a word with that ill-informed klutz?"

She laughs. "I'm dating that klutz. He'll do as I say."

The skin around Ellen's thumb and index finger is turning an angry red with a yellowish tinge. She always bruises badly. It's a family trait.

"I'm grateful for your help." She softens her voice. "This really was nothing more than a silly old woman having a tumble. If you hold up fingers, I'll tell you how many. I know who's president. I can even tell you the date, and how much they charge for pastrami on rye at the Second Avenue Deli."

The nurse puts down her clipboard. "I'll go find your things."

* * *

With his first ever lifeboat drill over, Silas goes to his room, but can't help worrying about that poor woman who fell. Mostly on account of how she reminded him of Nancy. Tall with the same long hair and pale skin. He sits on his bunk, and pulls a photo from his wallet. Nancy was so pretty. Her soft blue eyes lined by thick lashes.

"What you got there?" Ken says, and Silas glances up to find him standing in the doorway.

"Nothing." He tries to hide the photo, but Ken has already seen.

"Who's that?" he asks, sitting next to him on the bunk.

"She was my wife."

"Divorced?"

"Nancy passed. An accident. A while back."

"How long's a while?"

He never answers that question. Invariably, people give him a look that suggests that, by now, he should be over his loss, that life goes on.

"I look at her picture and work out what she might tell me about whatever it is I'm doing," he says.

Ken offers Silas a cigarette, and he takes one, not because he wants to smoke, but because he doesn't want to offend the guy. There's a knock, and without being told to come in, Father Bob pokes his head around the door, and when he spots Silas, signals to Ken that they need to speak.

"I might take a walk around," Silas says, slipping Nancy's picture back into his wallet. "Get to know my new home."

As he leaves, Bob steps to one side. "Make it a long walk, Santa."

Silas had every intention of doing just that, but something suggests hanging back and listening in to whatever the two men are plotting.

"None of your tricks this time," Ken hisses, and the priest drones an answer.

Ken speaks again. This time louder. "You flew too close to the flame, Bob. I'm not taking the rap if it goes tits up."

Tits up doesn't sound good. And Ken isn't talking like he trusts the priest. It's better to slip away and leave them to whatever fight they need to have. Except he isn't quick enough. The door opens and Bob appears.

He puts his face up close, and his breath smells of raw onion. "Were you listening in, old man?"

Silas holds one hand to his ear. "I'm half deaf. I was tying my laces."

Ken pokes his head around the door. "Is there a problem here?"

Bob stares first at Silas, then at Ken, before huffing to himself, and hurrying away.

* * *

Ellen's mouth is dry. Not need-a-drink-of-water dry. Really dry. A sticky film covers her teeth, and when she tries to swallow, her throat makes the most awful clicking sound. Julia comes into focus, dressed for dinner in a pale pink pant suit with back-combed hair. She's in their claustrophobic room. In her not-quite queen-size bed, wearing blue flannel pajamas.

"You're awake," Julia says and Ellen catches how she glances at her watch, like she needs to be someplace. "Should I call for the nurse? Do you need anything?"

"Just water."

Julia picks up a glass and vanishes into the tiny bathroom. A faucet runs, and she returns with tepid, cloudy water. There's that same chemical smell as before. It's wet, though, and that's all that matters.

Ellen throws back the covers, and immediately shivers.

"I turned on the air-co," Julia says. "You were positively decalescent."

"Now I'm frozen."

Julia aims a remote control at a gray box attached to the ceiling, and whirring fans clatter to a halt. Ellen glances at the clock. It's half after seven, judging by what little she can make out of the sky through the tiny porthole, half seven at night.

"You're dressed up," she says, propping herself up with pillows. "Hot date?"

Julia laughs. "On this trip? Hardly. I promised to meet the Luceys for dinner."

Ellen wants to point out how Julia appears to be spending more time with her new friends than with her, but holds her tongue. She's hardly been scintillating company.

"I checked with the onboard physician," Julia says. "And he agreed it's safe to leave you on your own." She steps back in to the bathroom. "Such a queer fish. His bedside manner leaves much to be desired."

"They tried to ship me home." A spark of pain ignites between Ellen's shoulders. "Any idea where my purse got to? I need one of my pills."

Julia rummages under the bed and produces a yellow plastic Walgreens bottle and takes out a single blue tablet.

"How long was I asleep?" Ellen says.

"A couple of hours. I had coffee with some of my gays from *Les Mis*."

"I'm sorry for letting you down. I promise we'll do stuff together tomorrow."

Julia squeezes her hand. "I'm perfectly fine to fly solo for a while, darling. Kathy isn't such awful company, and her brother is surprisingly conversant about musical theater for a high school teacher."

Julia fits in everywhere. She'll happily sit with a group of strangers, and leave an hour later, the closest of friends. If it wasn't for her, Ellen wouldn't have any kind of life outside the four walls of her apartment and the East Side Diner.

When Ellen coughs, Julia looks worried.

"Maybe I shouldn't go," she says. "What if your health declines?"

"I'm a stupid old woman who tripped and fell. I bumped my head, and now everyone thinks I'm about to pop my clogs. Go out. Enjoy yourself."

Julia bristles. "You make out like I'm forsaking you."

"I don't care," Ellen says, and instantly wishes she picked better words.

"The intent of this trip was to have fun." Julia's voice turns tight and precise.

"It is, and I'm sorry if I sound ungrateful. I'm sure you've done all you can to take care of me."

"All I can? What's that supposed to mean? Am I not permitted friends of my own?"

"That's not what I said."

Julia grabs her purse and swishes to the door. "I'll have my cell switched on. Hopefully, that isn't selfish of me."

What the hell? That isn't what Ellen meant, and the stupid fight shouldn't have happened. When the painkiller finally kicks in, her head eases itself away to some better place, twisting in the most delightful way. She craves more sleep, despite having been out cold for most of the afternoon.

Her body grows heavy and her eyes close.

"Otto," she mumbles under her breath. "We promised to look after each other as we got older. This is when I need you."

She pictures his face. Not as she remembers it, but as it might be now. Older. More battered by time, perhaps with a beard or a mustache, almost surely with less hair on his head. He began losing it at twenty. But the face she pictures doesn't belong to her husband. It's someone else. Someone smiling. Someone familiar.

* * *

Silas is pretending to read, fumbling as he turns the page. He left his glasses in his locker, and doesn't want to look up, in case Ken takes it as a cue to talk. And talking is the last thing Silas feels like doing. His heart is still racing, and his face feels hot.

"I don't know how much of that you heard," Ken says, uninvited. "But it isn't how it sounds."

He doesn't put down his book. "Did you say something? My hearing is shot. They got me on a list." It's a lie, but one he plans to stick to. Hear no evil and all that.

Ken gets up and goes into the bathroom. "Bob needs me to help smuggle a million bucks."

"What?" Silas says. "How did a priest get that kind of cash?"

Ken appears, his eyes narrowed. "Your hearing seems pretty damn sharp to me."

Silas blushes. "Okay, so I might have overheard you guys fighting. But that's all. I don't need to know why."

Ken goes to sit at a circular table in the middle of the room, where he's laid out stage makeup and wig stands. He leans into a mirror, and runs his hand over his head. "One little tip, Santa. Keep away from Father Bob."

"I plan on it." Silas sits up and unlaces his boots. "And whatever you two have going on, it doesn't interest me."

"That's why I'm telling you to watch your back." Ken opens a small tin of powder and dabs it across his forehead. "He might act like he's taking orders from above, but he isn't."

"Orders?"

"Don't ask." Ken pours lotion onto a ball of cotton wool. "I've let myself be talked into looking after something for him. That's where it ends."

"What sort of something?"

"It's not what you think."

Silas knows full well when someone says that, it's almost always exactly what he thinks.

And he thinks Ken means drugs.

1997

Bill Clinton was on TV, standing next to Al Gore, as supporting crowds surged to mark the start of his second term as president. Santita Jackson launched into the national anthem.

In their living room, on a wedding present sofa that had seen better days, Silas stroked his wife's hair. "You think he's sleeping?"

Nancy rested her head on his shoulder. "Can we do this? I'm not sure I'm able."

That morning, Silas had called at the hardware store, and bought two strong padlocks, three bolts, and a sheet of reinforced steel. The guy asked about the purchase, and he lied, claiming they planned on keeping chickens.

Joey rolled in after breakfast, pretending to be sober, but laughing at some joke nobody else heard. He said he needed sleep, and Silas followed him upstairs.

"What the fuck?" Joey muttered on seeing his father's handiwork. He wasn't fast enough, and Silas shoved him hard, slamming the bedroom door shut, sliding bolts into position. The padlocks weren't strictly needed. They were there for when Nancy inevitably took pity and agreed to let Joey out to use the bathroom or get fresh air.

"We're holding our son prisoner," she said. "Breaking the law."

Silas closed both his eyes. "What choice did he give us? I can't take another broken promise to get clean."

For too long, he thought of himself and Nancy as the guardian of twins. By day, they shared their home with a polite, well-spoken young man, who helped around the place, ran errands, and offered to cook dinner. After dark, things changed. Joey vanished for hours at a time, sometimes returning full of buzz, other times barely able to make it through the front door. More often than not, he didn't show until breakfast. He'd lost a lot of weight, and his skin was appalling. He lived life on a short fuse.

Once, Silas followed Joey after dark, armed with a baseball bat. The world he got to see was worse than anything he'd dare imagine. The streets were dark and dangerous, and the people his son mixed with scared him silly.

Matters had erupted two days back. Joey came home high once more, and Silas saw the state he was in and tried to keep him out on the stoop while Nancy dialed 911. The cops returned their kid a full twenty-four hours later.

Joey acted contrite, and promised to seek help.

That promise lasted half a day.

Nancy switched off the TV, and Joey's mournful voice called for his mom. "This can't continue," she said. "We need professional help."

Chapter Eight

Ellen pushes away her plate. The place they picked for a first breakfast at sea isn't busy. The only other customer is a lanky guy, with a pillow crease running the length of one cheek, sitting alone at the next table. His chair squeals on the faux wooden floor as he gets up and carries a white melamine tray to the buffet, for a third helping of eggs.

"The morning after the night before," Julia says. "If I were a bell, I'd go *ding dong ding*."

Ellen manages a lukewarm smile. More than anything, she craves one of Malinowski's magic pills, but they're in short supply, so she put them on ration. One a day. Two, if things get yesterday-kind-of bad.

"That's a song from *Guys and Dolls*." Julia says. "Sister Sarah sings it when she realizes she's in love after her beau refuses to take advantage of her drunken state. I remember the first time I heard dear little Kate Jennings Grant perform. It was like magic."

Julia is prone to starry trips down memory lane, and Ellen almost always tunes them out, but this morning she needs something to distract her troubled mind, after waking with a start and not knowing where she was. It took a full minute to walk herself back through the day before, and calm a racing heart.

"My back is sore," Julia says. "The mattress is too soft. I'll speak to guest services and see if they can't do something."

Ellen would love to be lying on a nice soft bed right now. "What's on the schedule for today?" she says, confident Julia will have scanned the activity list. "I have a bunch of catching up to do."

Julia stretches and yawns. "I promised Kathy we'd get our nails done."

"Oh." Ellen wills her face to stay smiling. "I already had a manicure. Last weekend."

Julia peers over her shades. "I forgot how much you enjoy your little visits to Queens. How is Moira?"

Moira and Julia don't get on. Nail artist Moira is tall and fierce and brassy. One time, Julia complained that her new fake nails were too short, and Moira reached across the table, grabbed her hand, and yanked them all off.

"Moira sends her love," Ellen says. "I told her you lost both your hands in an accident, and that's why you no longer need her services."

Julia makes a face. "Was that necessary?"

"It was that or have her track you down and demand an in-person explanation," Ellen says. "She has your home address. You know she'd do that."

Someone calls Julia's name, and they both turn to see a blond-haired woman dressed in magnificently ugly linen trousers and a terrible flowered top.

"Be nice to Kathy," Julia whispers. "She's my next styling project."

Kathy doesn't ask before grabbing a chair and sitting herself next to Ellen, waving for her brother to join them.

"This isn't an imposition?" he says, looking embarrassed. He's dressed in a pale pink polo shirt that drains any color from his face, and unflattering cargo pants.

"I'm Ellen," she says, before Julia can introduce them properly. "I owe you both a huge vote of thanks for helping me onboard yesterday."

"Don't mention it," Kathy says. "I try to do whatever I can to help the elderly."

Ellen senses how she's grinding her teeth down to stubs.

"So what do you do, Helen?" Kathy asks. "When you're not falling over drunk in cocktail bars?"

"I wait tables...or at least I used to." She tries to keep the bitterness out of her voice.

Julia and Kathy laugh, and Ellen wonders if an exchange of secret smiles is directed her way.

"What fun," Kathy says. "I did that job in high school."

Julia grins. "I didn't. Baruch Ha-Shem."

Ellen shifts uneasily. It's like being in high school, cornered by the mean girls.

As if sensing her discomfort, Patrick pipes up. "I wanted to ask if you two ladies might want to join me in the gingerbread house-building class today. It's being run by Mary Dawson."

Ellen has no idea who Mary Dawson might be.

"That sounds ambrosial," Julia says. "Unfortunately, we already have salon appointments."

"I'll come along," Ellen says. "I mean, if it's okay with Patrick?"

His face lights up. "I'd be honored."

* * *

Silas managed less than two hours sleep. Not because he was in a strange bed in a strange room. His mother always boasted to neighbors about how her kid could fall asleep on a clothesline. Last night, each time his eyes closed, someone else would appear at the cabin door, meaning Ken had to jump out of bed and engage in furious whispers. After they left, Ken would creep back, glancing over to see if he'd woken Silas. Silas never dared move a muscle.

Blame it on the lack of sleep, but Silas has come up with a plan. He'll offer to pay and upgrade from Santa to passenger, and get his own room. He has the money, so why not treat himself? If it leaves Howard shorthanded, he'll offer to work a handful of shifts in the grotto. The decision puts a spring into his step, and as he sits in the crew office, ready for the morning briefing, he lets himself be happy. Five nights on a luxury liner, resting up, and he'll be ready to deal with Joey.

"Good morning," Father Bob's jolly voice booms. "Ready for your first shift?"

Silas glances around the empty office. "Am I early? Where is everyone?"

Bob rolls his eyes. "The meeting was at eight today. Didn't you check your schedule?"

Silas feels his heart sink. Missing a meeting isn't going to endear him when it comes to asking for favors. "Is Howard around?"

"Probably out inspecting chlorine levels in the main pool. The man is obsessed."

Bob has settled himself behind one of the desks, meaning any chance of alone time with his boss isn't likely. Instead, Silas studies the duty board. He's rostered to ring his bell and wish everyone happy holidays in The Atrium.

The office door opens.

"Hey there, big guy," Howard says, holding up a hand to high five, and Silas curses the nickname that follows him everywhere. "We missed you at roll call."

"I'm sorry. I guess I assumed…"

Howard waves away any explanations. "It's going to be a busy day, Silas. I hope you're fit for plenty of action. This afternoon, we're trialing something new. One of Bob's brilliant ideas."

He glances over at the priest, who breaks from looking at his cell and beams. "Confessions on the dance floor. A tribute to the other Lady Madonna."

Silas wrinkles his nose. "What does that entail, specifically?"

Bob comes to perch on the edge of Howard's desk. "We play music and everyone dances, then when it stops, they have to stand totally still."

"Like statues?" Silas says. "Like the party game?"

Bob nods. "Exactly, and *you* go around, trying to make the guys move, and when they do, they have to confess if they've been naughty or nice."

"Ri-ght." Silas sounds the word out slowly. "What happens then?"

"If they've been naughty, they're out," Bob says with a shrug. "And we keep on until someone wins."

Howard chimes in. "It will be a hoot."

Should Silas ask for a quiet word with his boss or wait until Bob leaves?

"How you settling into your quarters?" Howard says. "Ken isn't snoring too loud?"

"About that." Silas goes for it. "I was wondering if I could get out of sharing a room."

Howard raises one eyebrow. "It's in your contract, dude."

"I guess I signed without reading every clause."

This earns a guffaw from both men.

"Santa Claus didn't read the clauses." Howard sounds proud of his feeble joke. And then he stops smiling, and pats Silas on the arm. "I'm afraid we got a full house, man. I could ask if anyone cares to swap."

Silas shakes his head. If he asks to switch, it might indicate he's got something against Ken. Against a drag queen. Against gay people. Word could somehow reach Joey.

"I was more thinking of upgrading," he says. "How much would it cost to travel as a passenger?"

Howard glances at Bob, and then back at Silas. "You mean like one of the gay boys?"

Silas winces. It's not the expression he would have used. "I'll take whatever room you have."

"Ken was always gonna be a hard sell," Bob says, nodding slowly. "It's the CPAP machine, right?"

"It's nothing to do with Ken." Silas needs both men to hear this. "Maybe I'm getting too old to play Santa."

Howard beams widely. "This is about the extra costumes, isn't it? Okay, so bring them back. I'll get Deon to cover."

Silas swallows, trying to stay calm. "Just tell me how much it costs to switch to a passenger ticket."

Bob and Howard exchange confused looks, and then Howard picks up the phone on his desk, punches in a number, and speaks to someone. He scribbles a number on a scrap of paper, and slides it over to Silas. The room rate is at least three times what cash Silas has.

"Can we do a deal?" he says. "I could be your part-time Santa."

Howard shakes his head. "Now we set sail, they only offer rack rate. The suits in New York won't budge. And passenger insurance won't cover you for working."

Silas is stuck with playing Santa. Stuck with middle-of-the-night visitors, stuck with the fear he might be sleepwalking into something bad.

"Forget I mentioned it," he says. "First night nerves."

Howard narrows his eyes. "There's not some other reason to swap rooms?"

Silas sees it now. A whispering campaign spreads online, and his face makes the evening news. He'll be Santa Silas French, homophobic bigot.

"Ken is a decent guy," he says, desperate to regain ground. "I struggle to make out half of what he says, but, no. I'm happy to stay where you put me."

Howard sits at his desk, and turns to his computer screen. "You'll get used to the CPAP thing. I find wax earplugs work best. They sell them in the mall."

Silas doesn't move. He's trying to get the measure of his boss. Sure, he acts like the kind of guy who might lead venture scouts, or coach a local soccer team, but there's something about the man that he isn't able to trust.

* * *

Red, green, and gold signs point the way to a gingerbread house workshop where Ellen has arranged to meet with Patrick. He says hello with a halfhearted shrug, and she follows him into a room, where the walls are covered with wrapping paper. Strings of lights flicker from the ceiling, and an over-decorated tree occupies each corner.

"Way to make a Jewish lady welcome," she says, but Patrick doesn't smile.

The woman in charge introduces herself as television's Mary Dawson. She could be anyone's favorite grandmother, with an apple-pie face that never stops smiling, and white hair, cut into a neat bob.

"Some call me Mary Christmas," she says, leaving a beat for laughter. "I'm going to teach you a skill today that will impress all your friends. And if you happen to take your new knowledge home, it'll most certainly win you big prizes."

This might be setting expectations a tad on the high side, but Ellen holds her tongue as Mary runs through a PowerPoint of previous triumphs. It's more than a little boastful, and she loses the audience fast.

"Time for you boys to have a go," she says, clapping her hands to bring the group back together. "Remember, there's no wrong way to build a Christmas gingerbread house."

They each get their own table, laid out with sheets of gingerbread, a piping bag of white frosting and a box of silver sprinkles.

"It's best you all start with a twelve-inch base," Mary says, and holds up a gold cardboard circle. "Twelve inches is all you need, any bigger, and it's too much."

Everyone snickers. Even Patrick.

Mary picks up the frosting bag, and explains how to attach side panels. "I'm going to make my house into a church. It is the holiday season, after all, and I expect most of you guys will be down on your knees worshipping."

Patrick glances at Ellen. "You cool with this? Not too churchy?"

She grins. "I think I can control any natural tendency to burst into flames."

"Hey," Mary scolds. "You two lovebirds! No whispering or passing billets-doux."

Everyone laughs, and Ellen wonders if Mary gets how this is a gay cruise. Does she not consider it strange to be teaching a room of young men in muscle tops?

Apart from her and Patrick, of course.

Mary uses red icing to pipe five pointed stars around the border of her house, adding white curlicues, and explaining how to use frosting as cement before setting the class to work.

No matter how hard she tries, Ellen's house refuses to stay standing. At first, she decides everyone must have better gingerbread and stronger frosting, but then, as her hands get covered in sticky sugar, and the gingerbread walls crack and crumble, she laughs. Soon enough, tears are pouring down her face. Patrick has built a near perfect replica of the Empire State Building. It makes her laugh all the more.

"Here now." Mary comes to her aid. "No need for tears, honey. Rome wasn't built in a day, and neither was the world's best gingerbread house. Let's see if we can't clear all this mess away and start over."

"I'm fine." Ellen wipes sticky hands. "I've already had more fun in the last half hour than in the last five years."

Mary's nose wrinkles, and she glances around. "But you don't have a house, dear. What will you give your friends?"

Ellen takes a wad of gingerbread, and stuffs it into her mouth. She immediately regrets the impulse. It's dry, and tastes more of salt than ginger.

Mary panics. "The crafting materials are not safe for human consumption."

Patrick comes to Ellen's help with a glass of water.

Much as she wants to resist, she laughs again. Her sides ache, and even though she tries, Ellen can't manage actual words. Her stomach tickles in ways she forgot possible.

By the time Mary calls events to a close, Ellen is on first-name terms with almost everybody in the room, after cooing over how great their gingerbread houses turned out. There is, however, one thing left to do: Mary wants to award the prize for outstanding achievement.

She doesn't hesitate. "Patrick," she says and everyone whoops. His Empire State Building is incredibly detailed. And incredibly perfect.

As they file out, Ellen hums along to "Let it Snow, Let it Snow, Let it Snow."

"We should get a drink," she says.

Patrick's eyes are elsewhere, staring with longing at a group of guys, maybe slightly younger, heading toward the casino.

"Scratch that," Ellen says. "I fancy chancing my luck on the slots. You up for that?"

* * *

As Silas heads back to his room, raised voices carry down the narrow hallway. The loudest belongs to Ken. The other is less familiar, mumbling and breathy, and as he reaches the door, Deon pushes past.

Their shared cabin is in darkness, with a single light is trained on Ken's face. He's sitting at the central table, holding a small circular mirror and applying lip gloss.

"Are things okay?" Silas says.

Ken picks up a mascara brush. "Why wouldn't they be?"

"The kid who was in here...he sounded kinda pissed."

"Deon is always mad about something. Trust me. You'll soon get to know him." Ken stops what he's doing. "One tip. If he asks you for money, make an excuse. You'll never see it back."

Silas goes over to his bed, and only when certain Ken is too engrossed preparing for work, slides his envelope of cash back under the mattress. With seven days to go before Miami, he needs to keep his head down and ignore whatever might be going down.

"What did Howdy Doody want this morning?" Ken says. "I saw you hang back after the meeting."

Silas shrugs. "I guess he was checking I didn't have unanswered questions."

"And do you?"

"No."

Silas reaches into his nightstand and pulls out a copy of the staff handbook. Ken goes back to applying makeup. After two minutes silence, Silas clears his throat.

"When you said you help Father Bob out," he says. "What exactly does that involve?"

Ken chuckles to himself. "Why? You thinking of offering your services?"

"No," he says, a little too quickly. "I suppose I was curious."

Ken snaps shut a powder case. "Best you don't ask, Silas. The less you know, the less you're a part of it."

Silas leaves it a beat. "What if I *want* to be involved?"

"And do you?"

Silas ought to say how whatever the priest has going on is his own business, and he's totally down with it, but he can't ignore the voice inside that nags about how something isn't right. Mud sticks, especially to Silas. When he punched the boss at the Goering Brothers staff party, he set in motion a process that, one year later, saw his smile declared fake. Even though both

CHAPTER EIGHT

men had shaken hands in the hungover light of the next morning, and Bill Goering promised there would be no hard feelings, it came back to bite him. That punch landed him on this ship.

"If you need an extra pair of hands, keep me in mind," Silas says, swallowing a mouthful of sick.

In the bathroom, he holds onto the basin and takes steadying breaths. The rest of the ship is hot and dry, but in here, it's like a tomb. A pair of black fishnet stockings drip from overhead pipes, the washbasin is dusted with brown face powder.

What the hell was that all about? Why offer to help with something that's almost certainly drug-related? He could be wrong. Ken and Bob might be trading knitting patterns or Girl Scout cookies. But who is he kidding? Silas wishes he was home, rattling around rooms, behind a locked door, ranting about noisy neighbors or turning up his radio to cover the sound of Mrs. Blatter yelling at her television set. Except he isn't, and he can't be.

"Silas," Ken calls from the other side of the bathroom door. "Can you help with this zip?"

When he steps back into the bedroom, Father Bob is sitting on a stool, filing his fingernails.

"The fucking thing keeps getting stuck," Ken says. "And Bob has thumbs for fingers."

Silas does his best and after three false starts, the zipper moves.

"Ta-dah!" Ken says and holds up his hands in some kind of diva pose. He's wearing a bright red wig, teased into a beehive, heavy stage makeup, and a tight-fitting purple dress.

"What do you think?" he says. "Kinky boots or wedges?"

Silas is tongue-tied, but the priest steps in. "Kinky boots, Ken. Every time."

Ken pads over to his locker, and Bob signals for Silas to sit.

"How are you settling in?" he says. "How's life with this reprobate treating you?"

Silas doesn't want to sound nervous. "I've dealt with worse."

"At the meeting yesterday…" Bob sounds to be picking each word with

71

care. "You remember how Howdy Doody made some kid give up his seat?"

Of course, he remembers. The same kid was here earlier, fighting with Ken.

Silas shrugs. "I guess that doesn't make him my biggest fan."

"Deon has problems, Silas. Spiritual issues, and it's my job to keep him out of trouble. Crown Atlantic has a strict three-strike policy, and that young man is on a final warning."

Silas isn't sure why he needs to know this.

"I'm a busy fellow, Silas. You wouldn't believe how many fags get married and call on my services, just because it's Christmas. I'm gonna be unavailable for a few days, and that leaves Deon without moral supervision."

Silas dreads what he's almost certain is coming next.

"I was rather hoping to subcontract the mission. To you."

Silas holds up both hands. "I have a crappy track record with kids."

Bob's head jerks back. "And yet, you play Santa Claus?"

"Little kids I can do. Teenagers not so much."

"It's easy work, buddy. Make sure Deon don't get into no trouble. Watch him. From a distance. If the slime ball goofs up, you come get me."

"Bob is an absolute softie," Ken says, as he unzips his boots. "I'd belt the skinny tyke and be done with it."

A look is exchanged between the two men. One Silas doesn't like.

"By way of showing you my gratitude," Bob says, "might you be interested in supplementing the pathetic money Crown Atlantic pays?"

Another exchange of eyes, and the hint of a shared secret sends a shiver down Silas's spine.

"I'm not doing this job for the money," he says.

Bob leans in closer. "We could all use extra cash, though? I heard how you got family. In Florida."

Silas would rather not talk about Joey. Not to this man. "My kid has his own life."

Bob takes a breath, and his eyes flick from side-to-side, the smallest of smirks on his lips. "Word is, you're not close?"

"We have a great relationship," he lies, wishing he'd kept his big fat

72

fucking mouth shut with Ken. "I see my boy all the time. They use me for free childcare, but what kind of father complains when they're such well-behaved kids?"

Bob stands and claps a hand on his shoulder. "Keep an eye on Deon, Santa. It's all I ask." At the door he stops. "If, by chance, you find yourself in need of further gainful employ, track me down. The Chapel is on level five."

* * *

Ellen fumbles one hand into her bag, finding the bottle of magic pills. Her legs and arms have turned to lead, and her joints burn. Early afternoon sunlight hits her face, and she winces halfway up the shallow casino steps.

"Are you okay?" Patrick says.

"It's my hip," she lies. "Someday soon, I plan on trading it for a new one, but not until I get full value from this showroom model."

Slot machine jingles drown out the piped holiday music. Men, young and old, happy and sad, hustle back and forth, jingling change. Handsome guys in Speedos, hold trays of mulled wine, hot apple cider, and buttered rum. Ellen risks a rum. Anything to numb the pain. Patrick sticks to cider.

"I don't drink," he says. "And yeah, before you ask, my sister happens to find that hilarious."

It's his first mention of Kathy this afternoon.

"I drink like a fish," Ellen says. "As does Julia, so they'll be having a ball."

Patrick's brow furrows, and she can't work out if he's concerned or annoyed.

"Let's try the slots." She leads the way. "Someone has to pocket the jackpot."

They buy tokens, and she drops one into the nearest machine. Lights flash and two bells land together, but that wins nothing. She tries another machine, and loses again. Her first cup of tokens is gone within minutes, and Patrick suggests they look around.

She takes his arm, and they explore the room, stopping at the roulette wheel, where a young guy in a tight black vest bets all his chips on a single number. The ball spins and bounces, and when he loses, black vest curses and slaps the table.

"If I looked like him, I wouldn't care about losing money," Patrick says. "I certainly wouldn't spend my days teaching bored stoners about oxbow lakes."

Ellen glances back. The guy is cute, sure, but only because he's young and gym-pumped, and now busy play-acting like losing all his money was no big deal.

"Tell me about your husband," she says, leading the way to a circle of comfortable chairs.

"Ex-husband."

"How long were you together?"

"Twenty-three years."

She's surprised. The law only changed a few years back. Until then, men couldn't marry men, and Ellen sort of thought that meant gays didn't give much thought to commitment. Julia told lurid tales of friends who all but lived in the New York bath houses.

"He met someone else," Patrick says. "They're getting married next year. I'm invited."

A long awkward silence leaves Ellen struggling to find the right way to either change the subject or tell Patrick that his ex-partner was clearly the stupid one. The slot machine they played earlier erupts. Lights flash, a siren sounds, and tokens tumble into a waiting bucket. Two young men high five.

"Trust my luck," she says with a groan. "Right when I thought this day couldn't get worse."

She grins at Patrick, hoping he sees the funny side, but his face has turned to stone.

"Not that I'm not having fun," she says. "This is great, right? You and me hanging out together?"

He doesn't move or speak. It's awkward.

"I need to use the bathroom." Ellen hauls herself up. "And while I'm up, I'll get more tokens. This old broad isn't beaten yet."

* * *

Silas stays rattled as he pulls on his costume. Howard has him rostered to walk The Atrium, ringing a bell, and wishing everyone a Merry Christmas. Merry is the last thing he feels. He spent the afternoon trailing Deon, ducking out of sight each time the kid turned around, and then Bob cornered him for a full report.

"The guy took photographs," Silas said with a noncommittal shrug. "In short, he did his job."

The priest scowled. "Did anything he photographed seem unusual to you?"

Silas shook his head.

"Was anyone loitering, taking an unusual interest?"

"Not that I saw."

Bob turned away after a curt nod, but for Silas, the rapid-fire interrogation flipped his mood. He'd been upset, now he was plain mad. Mad enough to punch a wall. Mad enough to punch the priest, which was about the stupidest thing he could think of.

"You go on with your job," Bob had said. "Let me know what the punk does next."

Silas stands in The Atrium, ringing his stupid little bell. Huge overhead pipes blast dry air, and young, toned men walk around dressed for the height of summer. Guys whistle and wave as he saunters past, sweating in a heavy felt jacket, forcing himself to act jolly.

He needs air.

Outside, he finds a bench, its blue paint faded. At last, he's alone, and there's space to think. He squints into murk, the sea slate gray, the mist thick enough to grab a handful. Engines drone. Waves crash. A single seagull cries. What would Nancy say? She wouldn't stand for her husband kowtowing to no Catholic priest.

"I'm trying to keep the peace." His voice is carried away on a gust of wind. "I've done nothing wrong."

He'll avoid Ken. And Bob. He'll stay out late, and only return to his room when certain it's empty. The cruise lasts one week. How hard can that be?

Newly pep-talked, Silas heads inside.

Within minutes, his undershirt clings to his skin, and droplets of sweat smear his vision. He spots Deon heading toward the casino, where a sign on the doors promises air-conditioned comfort.

There might actually be some sort of God.

* * *

Another pill washed away with another complimentary hot buttered rum hits the spot. Ellen no longer aches, her head swims in a nice way, and she's ready to gamble.

"Are you okay?" Patrick frowns like she's been acting weird. "You seem… wired."

"Follow me," she says, her voice suddenly sing-song. "I feel lucky."

At the roulette table, she bets on red, winning more with each spin as everyone watching erupts in cheers, egging her on to take *one more shot* at the jackpot. They move on to play blackjack, and Ellen hits lucky again.

"That's more like it," she says, when they stop for a breather. "What I said before about not having a good time…that was mean of me. I suppose I keep thinking of how my so-called best friend dumped me."

Patrick makes a sad face. "And left you with this loser?"

Ellen laughs. "How about tonight, I buy dinner? Just for the two of us. We'll get a table in one of the froofy places on the upper level."

"I booked an all-inclusive deal."

"It's on me. I spotted a fancy French restaurant. What do you say? Call it my way of thanking you for today, and proving I know how to be a friend."

His expression suggests someone unsure of how to answer, and Ellen knows why.

"Fine," she says. "You bring Kathy. I'll invite Julia."

Patrick shudders. "The deal is you and me. No third or fourth wheels."

"L'chaim." She raises her glass in a toast, even though he's drinking soda.

His eyes follow some young guy's tush, heading for the doors, and Ellen vows right there and then to make it her mission to find him a man.

"Hey there," someone says. A gruff male voice with a New York accent. It's Santa Claus, and his face seems familiar. Especially those eyes.

"I know you from someplace," she says.

He grins. "Lifeboat drill. You fell for me. Literally."

Ellen's face is on fire. This is who she saw right before blacking out. The guy she dreamed about.

"You lived?" he says. "Reports of your demise were exaggerated."

"So far, so good." She fist pumps the air, though has no idea why. She's never done that in her life. And then she sees how his eyes dart to one side. The poor guy needs an excuse to escape.

"We're off to try our luck at craps," she says, and when he holds out a hand, helping her to her feet, warmth rises through Ellen. A feeling she hasn't known for the longest time. She clears her throat. "I don't suppose you'd care to join us?"

He shakes his head. "I'm on duty. They'd fire my ass."

Chapter Nine

Julia holds up yet another white shirt. Identical to the last two, except this one has tiny black buttons. Her eyes grow wider, suggesting hope.

"That's my absolute favorite," Ellen says, forcing herself to sound upbeat. "You should absolutely wear it tonight."

Julia plonks herself on the bed and her shoulders sag. "What was I thinking?"

This is Ellen's cue to launch into a spiel about how Julia isn't heavy, would never be thought of as heavy, and given she barely eats, will never get heavy. Except right this minute, she's tired. Malinowski's pills seem to work their magic for an hour or two, before causing her to crash. Right now, all she wants to do is sleep.

Julia's back on her feet, gazing forlornly into a full-length mirror, and holding up outfits. "It's fine for you," she says. "You're so tall, nobody notices your enormous posterior."

Ellen bristles. Her so-called best friend almost always resorts to insults when she's in this kind of mood. She rests a hand on Julia's shoulder. "What if tomorrow we check out the mall? Shop until we drop."

"How does that resolve my immediate botheration?"

"Well..." Ellen needs to handle her next suggestion with care. "We could stay in and do our nails. I'll give you a pedicure."

"I already had one with Kathy," Julia snaps. "And what about Patrick? How are you supposed to find him a suitable companion if we order room service?"

Julia has a point. One thing was clear from this afternoon, Patrick Lucey was a slouch with flirtation. There had been one guy all but sitting on his lap at the casino bar and he didn't pick up on it.

The phone rings, Julia picks up.

"Oh," she says. "Well, that's a shame. And it's not just garlic? Because we can make a request of the kitchen…" When she hangs up, she shrugs. "That was Kathy. The Luceys won't be able to join us tonight. She has an allergy to French food."

Ellen isn't sure this isn't Patrick getting wind of her plans and crying off.

"So that's settled then," she says. "We stay in."

"Well, no…" Julia pulls the kind of face that suggests she's about to say something that will cause a fight. "Kathy managed to book a table for the four of us at an alternative venue."

* * *

Silas is alone, and the only sound is that of the ship's engines. The rolling, rough vibration of the ocean below thrums through the vessel, a giant heart beating. In quiet darkness, he's restless, and wishes for a window, so he could be sure there's still an outside world. It's a quarter to nine, and he's ready for sleep, stripped down to a too-often-laundered undershirt and Jockey shorts. He had wanted a shower, and paddled through puddles in their tiny shared bathroom only to find the water cold, no matter how long he dodged between the stop-start spurts. He tried to read, but the bulb in the lamp on his nightstand didn't work, so now, he lies on his bunk, staring at the low ceiling, thinking about how he misses his own bed. In his own apartment. And his own life.

Deon had acted like he knew Silas was watching him, slipping through doors and, when Silas followed, ducking through another. When Bob demanded updates, Silas offered nothing. Tomorrow, he plans on talking to Howard again. There has to be some give on the price of that empty room. He'll call the Crown Atlantic guy himself to see if there might be strings to pull.

The only bright spot today was getting to spend time with Ellen Gitelman.

They exchanged few words, yet he treasured each one. All he thought of as she spoke was how much how her eyes reminded him of Nancy.

"This is my friend," she said when introducing the guy she was with. "Or rather, he's the friend of a friend. Not that we're not friends. How awful does that sound? We're great friends now. We made gingerbread houses. Well, Patrick did. Sorry, I didn't introduce you, did I? This is Patrick. He hates it when anyone calls him Patty."

Like Nancy when nervous, Ellen talked a million miles a minute, jumping subjects, eager not to forget something that mattered. The voice was different, sure. Less Brooklyn, and more Upper East Side. But Ellen's energy was the same. He should have stayed to chat; instead he spotted Howard, and had to make excuses before heading away, ringing that fucking bell, and wishing strangers happy holidays.

Everyone says how time heals the heart. And Silas supposes there's some truth in that. Still, not one day passes when he doesn't think of his wife, and of the times they spent together. Things had gotten tough, especially after he lost his job and had to make do with workers' comp. He fixed shelves for neighbors, unblocked drains, and painted spare rooms. Nancy took to staying up late, watching talk shows, coming to bed without turning on lights, and then shuffling under the covers, staying as far away from him as it was possible to get without sleeping in the other room.

The morning when he left to help Solly from apartment 6 deliver a table to his brother's place, he kissed his wife goodbye and promised he wouldn't be late. She said nothing. That's when he should have known there was something wrong. She didn't remind him to buy bread or pick up milk. She didn't tell him to take care.

If only he knew then what he knows now. That Nancy would decide they'd been fighting over Joey too often, and a Friday night dinner was the answer. She'd gone to buy challah, but something must have distracted her. Why else step out in front of a laundry truck? The cops said the truck was going too fast, but breaking no speed limits, that it was one of those things. An officer pulled him aside and mumbled about how Silas shouldn't blame himself, that sometimes shit happens. At the station, an older woman with gray hair and coffee breath came to sit with him in a room usually set aside to interview criminals. It stank of nervous sweat. Back home, he found tablets in her nightstand. An unopened bottle of paroxetine. He could have told the cops, but what good would that do? It wouldn't bring Nancy back and might upset her family. Or Joey.

The ship horn sounds, and from the hallway, a voice barks into a phone. It starts far away and hangs around on the other side of the door, before moving on. He pulls a single sheet over his body, rolls over and presses his face into the mattress. It smells of the many other men who must have slept on this same bunk.

Silas doesn't mind being alone. He's gotten used to keeping his own company. He has enough friends back home. There's Rose, bartender Larry and the other Santa guys. When Nancy was alive, people showed up at their place most weekends, or they found themselves invited out à deux. There had been so many unfamiliar faces at her funeral, people he should have got to know. People she accused him of ignoring. She'd been right. Each of these strangers came to wish him well, clasp his hands in theirs, and promise a call within a week or two.

He's still waiting.

A tug in his chest reminds him to take the pills prescribed by his doctor. They'll help, Malinowski explained, but Silas would also need to monitor his blood pressure. He gets out of bed and heads to the bathroom, where he washes his face and cleans his teeth, ignoring the tired old man peering back from the mirror.

Back in bed, when he turns out the light, the darkness is instant.

Staring into nothing, Silas will find Ellen again and explain why he acted weird, why he didn't hang around, and maybe how she reminds him of Nancy, but not in a creepy stalker way.

He can't spend a week at sea with nobody to talk to.

* * *

Over dinner, in a loud, over-crowded, all-you-can-chow Mexican buffet,

Kathy dominates conversation. Each time the waiter comes to inquire if the food is to their liking, she engages him in a long discussion about how each dish was made and asks for the recipe.

"It's a hobby of mine," she says, wiping her mouth with a tomato-stained napkin. "I plan on starting up a YouTube channel, teaching people how to cook food like they serve in restaurants."

Patrick sighs and she fixes him with a glare.

"My brother thinks I'm full of hot air," she says. "But you wait until they invite me on *The View* to talk about my life's work."

Julia changes the subject. She's a brilliant dining companion. "Do either of you have bucket lists?"

Ellen holds her breath. She really doesn't want Kathy to know about their plan to swim with dolphins. Not because the idea belongs to two fifteen-year-old girls, but something suggests Kathy is the sort of woman who'd think nothing of inviting herself along for the ride. Not that Ellen's in any position to object.

"A bucket list?" Kathy double-dips a tortilla chip into sour cream. "I wouldn't even know where to start. I already have most everything I could dream of wanting."

Patrick snorts, and Kathy purses annoyed lips.

"It's why Ellen and I came on this trip," Julia says. "We uncovered examples of teenage yearnings, and now the intent is to turn such aspiration into corporeality."

Kathy's eyes shine, and the way she jiggles around suggests someone both puzzled and excited. "What kind of yearnings?"

"Swimming with dolphins," Julia says, and Ellen's heart doesn't so much sink as hit the bottom of the sea with a clunk.

"I would *love* to do that." Kathy bounces up and down in her seat. "They say dolphins are the most intelligent creatures on Earth."

Patrick mutters something about how that might be true when compared to his sister, but she lets the snark go.

"Count me in," she says. "We'll make it a girls' day out."

Ellen sits back and lets excited chatter wash over her. Her eyes sting in a way that only sleep can fix, but she's not ready for bed. Malinowski's magic pills have a way of ruling that out. She's sick of being the kind of woman who doesn't speak up when something grinds her nerves. Julia once kvetched about how Ellen would eat her salad with a piece of glass in it, if complaining might upset the server. She was right. Even though the dolphins were meant to be *their thing*, she'll agree to have Kathy tag along. They'll meet for morning mimosas, and sing show tunes on the journey, and ask their taxi driver to recommend a good place for lunch. Kathy strikes her as someone who won't be content with taking photographs, she'll insist on video, and catch Ellen at her worst, likely with her hair pasted to her head, or her bathing suit bagging around her bum. Her huge bum, if Julia's to be believed.

"I'm so sorry," Ellen says, and everyone stops talking. "Suddenly, I don't feel so great."

Kathy clicks her fingers to summon help. She stands up and calls to a waiter. "Our friend needs urgent medical assistance. Is there a doctor in the house?"

People at nearby tables stop eating.

"It's nothing like that," Ellen says, her face hot with both irritation and shame. "I have a headache and need to lie down."

"You want me to come with you?" Kathy says. "I was a registered first aider at Walmart. I got a certificate and badges. I know what to do with older people."

Ellen pushes back her chair. "I'll be fine on my own. You should enjoy the rest of your evening."

"Are you certain?" Julia's eyes narrow.

"It's nothing sleep can't fix," Ellen says. "Please. Carry on eating."

She addresses this last line to everyone in earshot and picks up her bag before heading for the door.

* * *

Silas knows he's breaking the rules by drinking in the Craic of Dublin. The alternative is the Crew Bar, where he'll almost surely run into either Father Bob or Kitty Kate Ken. He's never been much for rule breaking. When he worked for Myron Schwartz, the other drivers called him Mr. Goody-Two-Shoes, on account of how he kept his nose clean and refused to get involved with side deals.

The Craic of Dublin is much like any other flat-pack Irish bar. Guys in green shamrock t-shirts show practiced disinterest in whatever they serve. Neon signs promote Guinness and Kilkenny. A muted TV screen shows sports, and kitschy paintings of leprechauns cover every wall. The lights are dim, and the music is loud. A live band plays, a dizzying whirl of pipes and strings with a young girl singing about how she misses her home town. He supposes it's meant to be melancholy, but her voice is more playful than sad.

"Sit the fuck down," the server says. "You're making the place untidy."

After their set, the band decamps to his end of the bar, and Silas gets talking. The lead singer is called Adele and just so happens to live two blocks from him in New York. The guitar player offers Silas a drink.

"Mike," he says and goes to shake hands. "And what would you be called?"

They talk about everything they love and hate and miss about life in the Big Apple. Mike's from rural Ireland, and still misses home, but loves the thrill of a city that genuinely never sleeps.

"Are you married?" Mike says after the fourth large whiskey.

"I was, but she passed."

"Oh?" Mike's face registers surprise. "You only found out about yourself late in life?"

It's a weird question, but Silas shrugs. He still finds it close on impossible to talk about Nancy without welling up.

"And do you have a partner now?" Mike says.

Silas laughs. "I've not been looking."

Mike shifts his stool a tad closer. "They always say that's when the best things happen."

Adele interrupts. "Can I get you two lovebirds another drink before we're back on stage?"

Silas sits up straight, a rictus grin across his face. "I should probably be on my way."

"Stay a while." Mike moves a hand onto his knee. "I was enjoying your company."

Adele snorts. "Trust me, this lad won't take no for an answer."

He fucking better, Silas thinks, and then hates himself. This is a gay cruise. Mike's gay. Why would he not think the same of him?

"I'm working on the ship too," Silas says. "I play Santa Claus. This is my first time on this kind of...thing."

Mike's hand moves away, and a grin spreads across his face. "Have I got this wrong? You're not gay, are you?"

Silas wants to shake his head, but something stops him. "Not yet. I think I'm still going through my straight phase. Perhaps I'm in denial."

Mike laughs. "You should have said something before I started laying it on so thick." He turns to Adele. "Another one I got wrong. Someone needs to have a tinker with my fecking gaydar."

She finds it hilarious, and orders more drinks. What could have been an awkward moment passes quickly, and Silas pats himself on the back for handling things with grace.

"My son is gay," he tells them both. "He lives in Florida with his husband. They have two kids."

Mike takes a slug of his beer. "You visit often?"

There's a time and a place to admit you fucked up with your kid and this isn't it. How would it add to the party if Silas told the truth? He takes a breath and smiles. "We couldn't be closer."

Mike puts down his glass. "Good on you."

Silas nods. He ought to come right out with it and tell this stranger how he fucked up big time with the one remaining member of his family and never quite got around to making it right.

"All you need is love," he says instead. "That's what they say, right?"

Mike waves to the bartender and orders more beer. "Fucking A."

* * *

85

As Ellen heads for the elevators, she can't help but be drawn to the raucous sound of singing from one of the bars. A sign above proclaims this to be an Irish pub. There's a band playing, and everyone is on their feet, dancing and clapping along. She should go back to her room and sleep. At home, she would never dare venture into a place like this, but here, she can. She should get used to trying new things.

Ellen picks her way through to the bar and orders Guinness without thinking and nods when the girl serving holds up a large glass. The dark liquid is heavy and creamy, and she's not sure she'll finish a whole pint, let alone if it's wise to mix beer with powerful painkillers. The band complete their set, and the lead singer jumps around on the tiny stage. Strings cry and drums patter as they launch into yet another song.

A finger taps her shoulder. It's Silas.

"I thought it was you," he says. "Did you end up breaking the bank?"

She's not sure what he means and smiles.

"The casino. You and your friend were on a winning streak."

"Of course," she says, resting a hand on his arm. "Today has been a blur."

His expression stays warm and reassuring. "Again, I'm sorry for rushing off like that. I'd have loved to stay and talk a while."

Ellen vaguely recalls fist-pumping the air and acting weird. It's no wonder he made an excuse and hurried away. Anyone would.

"So," he says, and raises an eyebrow.

Ellen shakes her head, unsure what he means.

"How was craps? Did you make your first million?"

This time she laughs. "Nothing like such luck. I lost everything on the pass line."

Silas grins. "I've never played craps in my life. Perhaps you can show me one time?"

A spark lights in the back of Ellen's mind. Is this man flirting? She blushes. It's been so long since anyone showed this sort of interest in her, and she isn't sure what to say or do. He's handsome, in a craggy way, and smells of musky soap.

"Did you find what you were looking for?" she says, and now it's Silas whose brows furrow. "This afternoon, when you had to rush off."

He heaves a sigh. "That's a long story."

Ellen glances around. Fate has cleared two bar stools. "If you're in the mood to share it, I'm in the mood to listen."

Chapter Ten

In a dismal room that reeks of two old men sleeping, Silas ties the frayed laces of scuffed black boots. His Santa suit smells of stale cooking oil, and the faded red woolen jacket has a dubious crackle stain. When he stands, the pants flap around his ankles, exposing an inch of skin where his boots end.

It doesn't help that his head hurts. And so it should after crawling to bed at two in the morning, feeling like life at sea might not be so bad. He'd met a friendly guy called Mike and spent a lovely hour or three in the company of Ellen Gitelman. They'd agreed to meet up this afternoon for coffee.

He pulls on black gloves, and checks his beard in a little round mirror.

Ken opens one eye. "Keep your thieving mitts off my stuff, Santa."

Silas sets the mirror down. "I was just getting ready to face my public."

"Some fucker grabbed my Micky last night," Ken mumbles into a pillow. "I thought he was going to yank it off. Right in the middle of my Liza Minnelli."

Silas has no idea what any of this means, so makes do with a contrite grunt. "I best get a move on. Can't be late two days."

"Keep your hand on your ha'penny, is all I'm saying. If they'll try to touch me up, you're fair game."

"I'll stay vigilant."

Ken lifts his head. "Did Deon involve himself in any funny business yesterday?"

"Not that I saw."

"Bob's got it in for the kid, but you know as well as I do that he's like any

88

other young lad. Trying his luck. Fair play to him, I say."

Silas goes to clean his teeth and when he comes back, Ken is fast asleep, snoring loud enough to shake the walls.

* * *

Ellen closes her eyes and breathes in a heady combination of citrus and mint, stretching out and willing the tension in her body to melt away. A male voice murmurs instructions from hidden speakers.

"Imagine you're on a cloud."

She woke to yet another headache, and with Julia still sleeping, decided to check out The Spa. From a complex menu of treatments, she opted for the Rebirth Special, and was handed a white fluffy robe and told to get changed.

Tinkling piano music plays over distant running water.

"See the world below. Let your cares and worries sink into the ground. And fall away."

This ought to be relaxing, and yet she can't quite bring herself to give in.

"Now you are a ball of fire, burning to the end of a field of corn, eating up all that stands in your path, taking energy from that which surrounds you."

Ellen sits up. Is she on a cloud or inside a ball of fire? It doesn't help that the voice belongs to an actor who does insurance commercials. She often hears him talking about the benefits of annuities on the radio.

"Up ahead, you see a waterfall. Let your body soak up the cascading silver streams."

Ellen takes in the tiny room with a single white mattress on a bare metal frame. An aged bonsai tree stands on a small wooden table, the trunks wrapped in brown cloth.

The sound of water gets louder. She needs to pee.

"Hello," she calls, hoping someone might hear.

Nobody answers. Nobody comes.

"Now you're climbing a hill. It becomes a mountain. Each step you take is one step closer to where you should be."

Ellen's fingers bundle into tense fists, and she pulls on her robe before hauling open the door.

"Mrs. Gitelman." The young girl on reception hangs up her phone. "Is something wrong?"

When she asks for the bathroom, the girl signals to a bleached wooden door, and once inside, Ellen leans against a wall, breathing deep and trying to settle the start of a panic attack. Right after Otto died, they happened a lot. In the supermarket, alone at home, and once in the diner, while serving hash browns to rowdy student boys. It always started the same way. Her palms would itch, and what she thought might be a headache became so much more. Her head would slip into a vice, and her lungs would feel nowhere near big enough to keep her alive.

She splashes cold water on her face, and there's a gentle knock at the door.

"Do you require anything, Mrs. Gitelman?" a nervous voice asks.

"Everything's fine," she hears herself say. "Give me a minute."

After three deep breaths, she's able to leave the bathroom.

"Would you like a glass of water?" the girl asks.

"That'd be great."

"And would you prefer a different voice?"

"A different voice?"

"Not everybody likes the guy. You can have a woman or a child—though I should probably say, the kid did a spot for CVS. It's kinda well-known."

Ellen glances at a clock on the wall.

"Is that the time?" she says, an excuse forming. "I'm running late for a coffee date. I should get dressed."

"But you haven't been fully rebirthed." The girl's expression changes, and she scans her desk, as if searching for some pamphlet to provide munition for what she's about to say. In the end, she settles for insisting it just isn't safe to quit mid-program. "You'll need to sign an indemnity form. Releasing us from responsibility if you later suffer ill effects from not being completely reborn."

Ellen forces herself not to bite. "What if we agree to treat today's session like Braxton Hicks?"

* * *

Silas sneaks into the crew office. To his dismay, the morning meeting is in full flow and Howard is up front, pointing to a flip chart, on which he's written words intended to inspire: Confidence, Togetherness, Repeat Booking.

"Hey, man," he says, and all heads turn to catch Silas's unsuccessful attempt at once again slipping in unseen. "Just so you know, the third Crown Atlantic day starts at nine o'clock sharp."

Silas mouths the word sorry, and Howard continues.

"You guys appreciate what doesn't lead to repeat bookings?" Howard scans the room, as if expecting someone to hold up their hand and give teacher the right answer. When nobody does, he sighs to himself. "Come on, dudes. You know this one. The number one reason our lovely guests don't book a second trip is poor customer service."

The guy next to Silas yawns.

"What causes poor customer service?" Howard says.

A girl down the front holds up her hand. "Bitchy guests?"

He shakes his head. "Inconsistency."

A few people nod. Others act bored.

"It's all our jobs to keep our valuable vacationers happy, and that means making sure the service remains consistent. There's no room onboard the MS Viking for rule breaking."

He flips the sheet on his board and scribbles the number three.

"Who wants to tell me why I did that?"

Nobody makes eye contact.

"Okay, so let me go through the Crown Atlantic disciplinary process one more time. Three strikes and you're out. No discussion. No exceptions. Out is out. The next port, and you take your bags and walk away. How you make it home is your business and not mine."

Silas is the only one to react. This is what he's been looking for. If he times things well, he could punch Bob out and be offloaded in Miami. No questions asked. No need to rush and try fitting in every apology to Joey in a single day.

He has money to pay his way.

He'll find a hotel.

It stands to reason Joey will take time to come round.

Howard writes something else on his flip chart. "Three strikes," he says. "Anyone care to tell me what might score you one?"

A hand goes up. The others in the room turn to stare.

"What?" the owner of the hand says. "If we don't join in, this crap could last all fucking day."

Howard ignores a chorus of snorting laughter. "Let's hear what you've got to say."

"I guess if we download porn?"

"Precisely." Howard's smile grows huge. "Accessing pornography through the ship Wi-Fi will earn you a strike."

Another hand is up. "Stealing shit?"

And another. "Fucking a passenger."

Now everyone is talking, and Howard raises both hands, grinning, but clearly trying his best to regain control.

"So," he says, fake laughing, "I get it. You guys know the rules" He pauses for a breath. "I'm sure I don't need to mention our zero-tolerance drugs policy."

Silas glances around. Most every pair of eyes looks elsewhere.

"And by drugs, I don't mean pain meds or caffeine tablets. You are welcome to use those. Obviously. But alcohol. That's a drug."

A girl up front raises her hand. "You're telling us not to drink?"

Howard pulls a concerned face. "Have a drink, for sure, but if security or your supervisors find a crew member intoxicated, it's an instant out."

"What about when we're off duty?" says a guy two seats along. "In port?"

Howard fixes him with a bland frown. "I can't tell you what to do when we get to Nassau, but if the guest relations team reports anyone drunk on duty, it's an instant request to pack your things and leave."

A Mexican wave of muttering sets up, and Howard's face suggests he doesn't know how to regain control.

Father Bob stands and claps his hands. "My turn now, and I'm here to remind you boys to keep it zipped. Some of you may well be keen to interact with our customers, but that kind of guest relationship is strictly verboten."

Some laugh. A few of the guys down front wolf whistle.

"If you must indulge, stay safe. My church doesn't condone their use, but condoms *are* readily available."

The meeting ends, and as everyone files out, Howard calls for Silas to hang back for another quick word, signaling toward a chair by his desk, and winking like a high school teacher trying to prove he's cool and down with the kids.

"How you settling in, Silas?" he says when they're alone. "You keeping your head above water? I just figured I needed to check in, what with you being new to this environment."

"A job is a job," Silas says.

Howard opens a drawer in his desk and pulls out a manila folder.

Silas tenses. "Did I do something wrong? Because if this is about last night…"

Howard's eyes connect with his, and then dance away. "You ever heard of a secret shopper? It's sort of like a spy, only not so cloak and dagger. Kinda…sorta…"

Silas opts to stay quiet.

"A secret shopper is a way of making sure our guests enjoy the best Crown Atlantic experience. It involves going undercover and trying out the facilities."

"Okay, but what does this have to do with me?"

Howard shifts awkwardly. "I figured how, seeing as how nobody knows you. Not really. You might be perfect for the role."

"I wouldn't need to dress up as Frosty the Snowman?"

"Not for a while," Howard says. "Although we would require you to shave off that beard."

Silas lifts a defensive hand to his chin. "This is part of playing Santa."

"But don't you see?" Howard leans across his desk. "You wouldn't be doing that. And if you hate it, I'm certain we can fix you up with fake whiskers."

Each year, Silas quits shaving around April and lets his facial hair grow from stubble to a wiry mess, before white hairs dominate. Having a real beard shows dedication to the cause of Claus. Here today, gone tomorrow chancers, who wear phony beards, are considered lesser beings.

Skin Chin Santas.

Silas shuffles in his chair. "Do I have any say in this?"

Howard tries and fails to look at ease. "Your contract indicates you may be asked to perform other duties, so..."

He gets the message.

"The way I want you to think of this is like Crown Atlantic agreed to give you a free holiday," Howard says. "That's kinda what you were asking me for the other day, right? If I were in your shoes, I would be jumping for joy."

"But surely...I can be a secret shopper and keep the beard."

"The beard goes, and you change into your regular clothes and use this to fund your stay." He hands Silas a Crown Atlantic key card. "It's loaded with fifty dollars daily credit. Any extra comes direct from your pay check."

* * *

Fresh morning air shakes any last grain of sleep from Ellen's eyes. As the MS Viking heads south, the days grow warmer. It's still nowhere near sunbathing weather, but the Siberian hell of a New York winter is behind them. Ellen leans over a railing, watching the ship slice through waves, breathing in the salty air. A white feather flutters past. Her mother always said they were signs left behind by angels. If you found one, it was a message from beyond. Ellen has seen hundreds of white feathers. They couldn't all be messages from Otto.

When Julia got back last night, she was in high spirits. There had been an impromptu performance of "Hey Big Spender," followed by the sound of her whistling in the shower. She'd paddled out of a flooded bathroom, and thrown her wet body on the bed, draping an arm around Ellen, and slurring in her ears how she *loved her like a sister.*

Julia is currently having a great time with Kathy. And Ellen doesn't begrudge her that. They're not tied together, but she isn't enjoying how this trip helped point out how small her social circle has grown. Friends have moved on or died. The diner became her life, and she took on the role of mother for all the kids who passed through its doors. When she gets back home, that will be gone. She could still drop in for coffee, but how will that look? The last thing she wants is for Nadine to take pity on the lonely old lady who can't let go.

There are the *ladies who lunch*. A bunch of women who sort of know each other, who meet in whatever half-decent eatery has a blue plate special, to talk about their lives. But most every other lunching lady has a husband or a partner or a wife.

The sun breaks through clouds, and Ellen pulls out her phone to take a photograph, catching the moment just right, and once again allows herself time to play with a thought that's been gestating since the day Tony told her she no longer had a job. Lots of people her age go back to college. Gwen—a lady who lunches—took the New York bar exam at age sixty. On a whim at the end of summer, Ellen phoned a number printed on leaflets dropped at the diner, and spoke to a study counselor, who explained how her work experience might translate into college credit. She could study photography. She's told nobody else. Not even Julia.

Back inside, as she heads for the elevator station, Ellen spots Silas, sitting alone in a coffee bar, staring into nothing. She'll say hello, but as she's heading his way, a younger guy comes to sit with him, and they laugh together, before holding hands. And that's when she notices.

Right hand, fourth finger.

Silas is wearing a wedding ring.

* * *

A life size cut-out of Melania Trump poses in a swimsuit holding a *Be Best* sign, pointing to the onboard beauty salon. Silas nurses an already cold cup of coffee, watching as groups of guys pose for selfies with the First Lady, laughing and joking and having a good time.

I'm not a part of this, he thinks. I'm out of my depth.

He turns away to stare through windows at the ocean. It's a beautiful day, but he can't enjoy it. He's too distracted. The ship is huge, but it might as well be shrinking. Surrounded by two thousand guys, he's rarely been so alone. Silas picks up his cell and pages through recent calls, finding the number that will connect him to Joey's husband. The asshole who warned him not to make contact.

"Joseph doesn't want a relationship with you," Zach had said.

Since when had Joey wanted to be known as Joseph? When little, he'd railed against the name. But somewhere along the way, he must have changed his mind. It's one of those things that happen as you grow up and start becoming who you really are. Like the fact he's gay.

Silas would give everything to take back the stupid words he spoke that tore them apart. But that can't happen. The worst part is thinking Joey might never talk to him again. That they'd never have the special relationship they had before he came out. Not that it surprised either parent. Nancy had been the first to say anything out loud. One night, after switching off her bedside lamp, she asked into darkness if Silas thought their son might be different. He'd simply nodded and told her to go to sleep.

"Hey there."

Silas sees his drinking buddy from the Irish bar. "How's your head?"

Mike shuts his eyes and groans. "I'm mortal. I should never drink whiskey."

"The party went late?"

"I got talking to a guy. One thing led to another, and now I need to find Adele and ask her if I did anything shameful."

Silas signals to order two more coffees. "I'm glad I ran into you. I wanted to ask your advice."

Mike holds up the palms of his hands. "If you're planning on coming out, don't go asking me for tips. I already fucked it up big style."

Silas draws a deep breath. "I lied about my kid."

When Mike says nothing, he takes it as a signal to carry on. "We haven't spoken in years. When he came out, I told him he was going to die of AIDS."

96

Mike blinks uncomprehendingly. "That's pretty fucking toxic."

"I was dumb. I knew nothing. Joey got in the way of me lashing out."

"So…" Mike leaves it a beat. "I guess your first word to him should be… sorry?"

Silas scratches the back of his head. "I don't think that even comes close to covering it."

"My folks wouldn't have exactly welcomed me out of the closet. Dad used to say words like 'fag' or 'fairy' every time the soccer ref made a bad call. My mom gossiped with her friends about two men who lived opposite. She used to make limp wrist gestures."

He demonstrates and Silas clenches his teeth.

"I did none of that. Nancy never did either."

"I was the golden child," Mike goes on. "The classic *straight-A* student. If I'd kept my head down and toed the line, things would have been fine."

"Did you ever tell him?"

Mike shrugs. "The old bastard went and died before I had chance."

For a minute, neither man speaks.

"Were you trying to…scare your kid back into the closet?" Mike says. "Did you…want him to get sick, just to prove your point?"

Silas is horrified. "Of course not."

"So all he heard was you telling him he was going to catch AIDS, when he wanted to know how great his future would be. You made out like being gay was something to fear."

Silas avoids eye contact. Was Joey right to shut him out? If he turns up in Florida and knocks on the door, will he send the Walker guy to answer and tell him to go to hell?

"I've got friends in the closet in their thirties and forties," Mike says. "Living in fear of their bosses, or of their mates finding out. That's a shitty way to look at the world." He reaches across the table and takes Silas's hand. "People still struggle with the word gay. Just because society pretends it's evolved and because Netflix runs a Ryan Murphy show or gay films win at the Oscars. There are millions of people who still talk the way you talked back then. They refuse to change, but you're different. You want to make things right."

"More than anything." Silas takes back his hand and wipes it over wet eyes. "What do I say to him next? After sorry, I mean?"

Mike's shoulders slump. "I can't tell you that. We don't have some sort of instruction manual to explain what it means to be gay. Just like you don't have one to help you be a dad. You need to feel your way."

* * *

Ellen unlocks the door of their room and opens it a crack, before waving a paper napkin white flag.

"Come the fuck in," Julia says. "And if you happen to be in possession of Tylenol, that would be even better."

Anticipating a hungover travel companion, Ellen had stopped at the drug store and loaded her basket with headache tablets, a powder that promised instant rehydration, and a cooling eye mask. She also bought hot salted pretzels and an enormous carton of ice-cold orange juice.

"You're an angel," Julia says, twisting the lid off the juice and taking a huge slug. "Why do I always do this to myself? I'm sixty-eight years old. I should know better."

Ellen pulls the drapes, letting in sunlight, and sets to gathering discarded clothing. "I gather you and Kathy painted the ship bright red?"

"The woman is a lightweight. She turned in around the witching hour and left me all on my own. Anything could have happened."

"Where were you until four in the morning?"

Julia grabs a pretzel. "I wasn't that dilatory, surely."

"You stumbled through the door, made loud shushing noises, and ran through a selection of show tunes. Then you took a shower, and collapsed on top of me in bed."

Julia swallows two Tylenol and more juice. "I have the vaguest recollections of tequila shots in a leather bar."

Ellen bends to retrieve a red bandanna. "That would explain this."

"Where did you get to last night?"

"Nowhere, why?"

"I came to appraise your state of health after supper, but the bed was empty."

Ellen turns away, her face is on fire. "I guess I just needed fresh air."

"Believe it or not, Patrick was the one who suggested bar hopping. For a geeky guy, he's frisky with a drink inside him."

Ellen tunes her out, thinking instead about Silas, and how she'd been sure he was flirting when they met in the casino and later in the Irish bar, and then how she saw him today, holding hands with some guy.

"Honey, are you sick?" Julia puts down her pretzel. "Or am I getting the silent treatment for staying out late?"

"Of course not."

She sniffs. "I am familiar with that face. You've been with a man."

"I...maybe. Not really. I mean, yes, but..."

"You always were a crappy liar," Julia says. "What's his name? How come you found a heterosexual suitor in this gay desert? Wait. Is he crew?"

"Yes, he's crew, and no, he's not straight."

Julia jerks back her head and narrows her eyes. "You're not trying to perform a conversion job, surely? Because, darling, trust me on this, it never ever works. They'll tell you how fabulous you look in designer dresses, when all the time they're making goo-goo faces at the help."

"Fine," Ellen says, and nods for Julia to come sit. "I was coming back here when I gave the Irish bar a try. Otto always loved them, and I was having one of those days where I missed him like crazy."

"So you ended up talking to the bartender?"

"I ran into Silas."

Julia folds her arms. "He's about as gay as a badly coordinated throw pillow."

"There's something else."

"He's into kinky sex?"

Ellen fixes her with a glare. "What exactly goes on inside your brain? How is kinky sex your go-to when I say there's something I'm not sure about with a man? We had a drink. He didn't entice me back to his dungeon for a night of sin."

"Sin?" Julia pulls a face that suggests she thinks Ellen too innocent. "Try debauchery."

Ellen and Julia have only ever had one big fight. A genuine humdinger that started with Ellen suggesting a walk through Central Park, that somehow descended into Julia calling her frigid after they spotted a bunch of women sunbathing topless. Things escalated fast, and Ellen jumped in a cab and stormed away home. They didn't speak for close on four weeks.

"I have leftover treatment credit at The Spa," Ellen says. "I paid for a full rebirthing package and left early. It would sort out your hangover. You want me to call and see if they can fit you in?"

Julia buries her head in her hands. "Right now, only the blood of an infant will make me feel even halfway human."

Ellen gets through to the spa, and talks to the girl from her visit. "My friend wants to take my place for the final stage of the rebirth. Is that allowed?"

After checking with someone, the news comes that it's perfectly acceptable to send a substitute. What's more they have a free place in one hour.

"If I'm being reborn, shouldn't I wear a less somber ensemble?" Julia sniffs when handed a white sweater and black pants.

"They make you get undressed," Ellen says.

Julia starts to get dressed. "You were going to tell me something else that isn't right about Silas."

Ellen takes a deep breath. "He wears a wedding band."

Chapter Eleven

The sound of her phone dancing across the nightstand jolts Ellen from relaxing sleep and back into the here and now. At first, she blinks and looks around, unsure of where she might be, but then remembers this is the MS Viking, she's sailing to Miami with 3000 gay men, and Julia is busy elsewhere being reborn.

Her phone beeps with voicemail and she hits play.

"This is Silas," a voice crackles. "From the other night. Santa Claus. I was just wondering if you might be free tonight? I have reservations for dinner and I hate looking like a schmuck who has to eat alone."

She hits delete.

The fucking nerve of the man. He's married. Working away and aiming to turn her into one of his girls in every port. She ought to block his number, move on, and chalk this up to experience. But then she calls his bluff and returns the call.

"Sure," she says when he suggests they meet at eight in The Atrium. "And you say this place has some kind of dress code?"

Silas laughs. "They said smart casual, so who the hell knows what the means?"

After she hangs up, she clenches her fists, screws up her eyes, and screams into a pillow.

* * *

Silas sniffs at his only decent shirt. The last time he wore it was the Goering

Brothers interview, when he spilled mustard on the sleeve after treating himself to a hot dog after being told his smile was fake.

"That's all you have to wear?" Ken puts down his book. "You're taking a nice lady for dinner dressed like some street corner hobo?"

"I'll put on a jacket. She'll never see the stain."

Ken shuffles to his locker, and pulls out a still-boxed dress shirt.

"This isn't your size, and you won't be able to button up the collar, but that's how the stylish man about town wears his shirt these days. Casual is in."

Silas tries it on. It fits. Just about. Although, the box-fresh creases are a giveaway.

"It needs an iron." Ken holds out his hand.

Silas sits on his bed in a faded undershirt as Ken presses first the shirt, and then his pants.

"Shower and wash your hair with this." He's given a bottle of fancy shampoo in a pale pink bottle, with a drawing of a smiling woman on the label. "I assume you have cologne?"

Silas hurries to the bathroom, kicking off his sandals. He shakes the bottle of shampoo. The aroma of synthetic strawberries reminds him of Rose, and her lecture about him never quite getting his life together. It makes him think about what she would say about this latest mess.

"You think you can trick some up-herself broad into falling for your charms?" Rose would say. "My sister might have been taken in, but I see through you, Mr. French. Who are you seeking to fool with your borrowed clothes and lady's shampoo?"

He wipes steam from the mirror and combs his hair, forcing a side parting. Howard was right about the beard. It needs to go.

* * *

Ellen and Julia are not only different sizes, they're different shapes, and struggling to shoe-horn herself into a surprisingly slinky red gown is a move Ellen fast regrets. With her face purple and panting like she ran a marathon, she slumps against the side of the bed, the defiant dress bunched around her middle.

"You will not beat me," she mutters and gets to her feet to tug again.

The sound of fabric tearing causes her to jolt upright. Worse yet, the sound of Julia swiping her entry card against the door, sees her stumbling to the bathroom.

"I'm using the john," she calls, and Julia says something about not stopping for long. And then there's silence. "Is everything okay?" Ellen says, hoping she hasn't left evidence of her dress-up session.

"Are you recreating Cinderella out here?" Julia says. "Or did Imelda Marcos come calling?"

Ellen had been trying on shoes, comforting herself that, even if Julia's entire wardrobe proved to be a tight fit, she had decent footwear. Panic takes a hold, and she steps out of the gown before bundling it with a fluffy white bath towel and hiding it under the washstand.

"How was the spa?" She tries to sound breezy as she opens the bathroom door, clad in underwear.

"All I could think about was getting independent financial advice. The guy who does those incantations is the one from the radio commercials, right?"

Ellen laughs. "Did you get reborn?"

"The lights came back on after the music stopped. So, I guess."

"And how do you feel?"

"In desperate need of gin." She goes over to the open closet and studies the rail. "Shit."

"What's the problem?" Ellen's mouth goes dry, and her heart is in her throat.

"I thought I packed something. That new dress I got from Macy's."

She shrugs. If she says nothing, she can't later be accused of lying.

"Not to worry. It's not like I don't have enough things to wear." Julia pulls a blue floral wrap dress from the closet. "I told Kathy I'd meet her for cocktails. You in?"

"I'm kinda whacked." Ellen fakes a yawn. "Must be the ocean air."

Julia furrows her brows. "Again? You sure you're not sick?"

"I promise tomorrow I'll be the life and soul. Send Kathy my love."

"You sure about that?"

Ellen grins. "Okay, tell her I was thinking about her."

Julia spends forever in the bathroom. Ellen sits staring at her nightstand clock. It's almost seven, and she still needs to shower, wash her hair, do her makeup, and lose thirty pounds to fit into that dress. Who the hell is she fooling? After tidying away shoes, she settles on her one good pair of pants and a white blouse. She folds them carefully to enable a quick change when Julia is done.

The toilet flushes and Julia unlocks the bathroom door. She emerges holding up her red dress.

"Did you do this?" she says, her voice strained, like someone trying not to explode.

"It was an accident."

Julia throws it onto the bed. "We're nothing like the same fit. I'm a size four, you're...huge."

It's a touch on the rude side, but Ellen deserves the insult. She did, after all, ruin an expensive dress and then lie about what happened.

"There's a repair service," she says. "We'll ask them to fix the tear."

"It's ripped right across the front." Julia pokes one hand through the hole. "This is Vera fucking Wang."

"I promise to pay whatever it cost, and we'll get you something different. In Miami. Or Nassau. Do they have Vera Wang in Nassau?"

Ellen already knows there's no way she can afford a designer dress. She'll just have to cross her fingers and wait until the worst of Julia's anger passes and suggest a payment plan. Fifty bucks a month until either woman dies.

Julia gets changed into her wrap dress, without a word, sitting on the edge of the bed to do her makeup, while Ellen lurks on the sofa, her lips firmly sealed.

"I'm not sure if Kathy plans on staying out late," Julia says as she steps into low-healed silver pumps. "I'll see you when I see you."

She picks up her room card and purse and leaves.

CHAPTER ELEVEN

* * *

No sooner did Silas set to shaving off his beard, than he knew it to be a mistake. With half his chin exposed for the first time in forever, he looked older, not younger. His double chin was back, his turkey neck going the full gobble-gobble. Add to which, his left eye had developed a droop. For one short, insane moment, he toyed with spending the evening sitting side on to Ellen, and making sure she saw only his hirsute cheek.

Ken raps on the bathroom door. "Did you fall down the plughole?"

"One minute." He picks up the razor, braces himself and finishes the job.

Who is this old man? he thinks, as he rinses his naked face. *Will she even recognize me?*

Ken acts impressed. "I might have made a pass at you myself if you'd shaved that off sooner."

Silas blushes. He's just not sure what to say that won't cause offense.

"I'm kidding with you," Ken says with a guffaw. "I'm what they call a rice queen."

Silas doesn't like to dig into what that might mean and takes his newly pressed shirt. It's tight around the shoulders, and the buttons strain, fit to pop. His pants, though, are baggy, and he wishes he'd let Rose talk him into buying a new outfit right after losing all the weight. It had been the one and only time she was willing to be seen with him in public.

Ken holds out his hand as Silas ties his laces. "Wedding ring."

He never removes this remaining link with the woman who completed his life. They went together to a jewelry store in Queens, where a wiry guy measured both their fingers. Silas returned there a year ago, to have the ring made smaller after almost losing it in a washroom, but the store was gone. In its place there stood a Sephora.

"She already saw me wearing it," Silas says. "It's no big deal."

"This is a date." Ken says. "I promise to keep it safe."

When he takes off the ring, it leaves a soft dent of pink skin, and a rush of sadness fills his heart. For one whole minute, he can neither move nor speak.

"And in exchange, take this." Ken produces a padded envelope. "Deon will swing by your table. I'd look after the drop myself, but tonight's show is in an hour, and he needs the contents."

The package rustles and rattles. Silas wonders what he's agreed to do.

"It's a bunch of film for his camera," Ken says, as he sits to make up his face. "The twat is always leaving that crap lying around."

* * *

When she agreed to dinner at Bistro Pierre, Ellen didn't know it was so fancy. A uniformed maître d' greets her, failing to hide how his lip curls.

"I'm meeting a friend," she says. "Ellen Gitelman."

He pulls a pad from his pocket and studies it. "I don't have you."

"Try my friend's name, Silas."

The waiter raises an eyebrow. "Would Silas have a last name?"

"I'm afraid I couldn't say."

The snooty head waiter peers down his nose. "Our policy is not to seat guests without reservations. If you give me a few minutes, I'll find a place for you to wait. In the meantime, I would request that you refrain from speaking to other diners."

He gestures toward a circular bar off to the side, and Ellen knows that this is where Julia would politely, but firmly, insist on speaking to someone in charge, and if he claimed to be the one in charge, she'd ask who he reports to, and then demand that they be found.

An awful man has judged her and decided she doesn't fit in. And then, she catches sight of herself in a full-length mirror and sees mismatched shoes. Please come back, she thinks. I need to explain how this is my first date in forever, and I didn't even notice the shoes. I had a fight with my best friend over a ruined Vera Wang dress, and now all I want to do is hide in my room. The cleaning crew will find my corpse, one hand reaching for the door.

The waiter clicks his fingers to get her attention. "Madame. Suivez moi."

She picks her way between tables and follows, even if he acts like he's leading her to the kitchens, where he'll likely eject her through some secret

CHAPTER ELEVEN

exit. He bobs his head over at a high stool, set away from other guests, and clicks his fingers once more.

Ellen sits alone, wishing the bartender would hurry. She needs a drink. A huge drink. Fast. Perhaps she should have got a message to Silas and explained how she couldn't come after all. As it is, she's going to spend the whole evening staring at his wedding ring. She ought to find Julia and make up.

Even though she's a fish out of water, she can't deny how this restaurant is beautiful, with smoked-glass windows and fake candles flickering on each table. The linens are white and the chairs plush red with backs carved to mimic signs from the Paris Metro. Still, the air smells like every other part of the ship. A weird mix of furniture polish, floral disinfectant, and swimming pools.

She can hardly chug beer at such a fancy joint, so Ellen orders a martini, but it's too dry. Her eyes go back to the where the snitty head waiter stands guard over anyone trying to sneak in and sit at one of his precious tables. She still has time. She can escape.

There's a tap on her shoulder, and Silas shares the widest grin.

* * *

He spots her before she sees him. She's beautiful. Dressed like one of the women he sees outside The Met, smoking or barking orders into phones. Very European with her hair up in a loose knot. A white blouse and stylish gray pants.

The guy at the door sends him over to the bar, adding that his dining companion is waiting, making it sound as if he's done something wrong.

"I should go talk to her?" Silas says, earning himself a withering look.

"Unless you have some place else you need to be, monsieur."

After one deep breath, that leaves him wishing his shirt was one size larger, he makes his way over.

"You look great," Silas says. "I'm late. Time got away from me."

"I was early."

GHOSTED

She sounds nervous. Is that a good thing?

The bartender signals a greeting, and Silas goes to order drinks. But then he sees that Ellen already has one. Should he ask for another round of whatever she's drinking or is that like calling her a lush? Or will she think he's trying to get her drunk? What if he says he'll have what Ellen is having? He'll struggle to finish the drink if it's something weird. Was dating always this difficult?

"A beer," he manages, and Ellen's face lights up as she pushes away an expensive cocktail.

"Same here," she says.

* * *

A far nicer young man leads Ellen and Silas to a table at the far side of the room, hidden behind a screen, and way too close to the bathroom.

"Do you have anything less intimate?" Silas says.

The server is confused. "You don't want privacy? The maître d' suggested I put you here."

Ellen glances over to the door where her nemesis has turned around, keen to see their faces, and chalk up some kind of victory. The bastard can go to hell.

"It feels like we'd be eating dinner in a restroom," she says. "I can't sit here."

The waiter balks. "I should check with Henri…"

Ellen points to an empty table in the middle of the room. "What about that one? I see no reserved sign. Would Henri be pissed if you were to seat us there?"

"But that's a table for four."

"I'm greedy," she says, walking away before he can come up with another excuse. "I always eat for two."

The young guy's hands shake as he pulls out the chair, and Ellen takes deep breaths. She's never been so rude to anyone in her life. Ever. She conjured up her inner Julia Hoffman. And it worked.

108

"Wine," she says, without bothering to look at a nervously proffered card. "Something French and red and full-bodied. Please don't insult me with the house selection."

The waiter unfolds cloth napkins, handing one to Silas and one to Ellen before backing away, promising to give them time to read the menu.

"You scared the poor kid," Silas says.

Ellen blushes. "Was I too horrible? It's just the head waiter guy acted so mean."

"You mean the dude at the door acting like he smelled rotten fish?"

Ellen dares herself to glance over to where their waiter is talking to the rosy-cheeked maître d, with his piggy round eyes, short and stubby nose. He's furious and scowling in her direction. She turns his attention to the menu and shrugs. "Henri has some kind of chip on his shoulder."

Silas glances up and grins. "I figure I might order the lamb."

He folds away his menu and rests it on the table.

He's not wearing his wedding ring.

* * *

Dinner is wonderful. Silas savors every bite, and their server can't do enough, even if Henri continues to flash icy glares. The dessert menus arrive, and Silas raises an eyebrow at Ellen, who grins, and they ask for ice cream.

Over coffee, talk turns to life back home.

"I used to wait tables," she says. "So I get why that poor guy fears his asshole boss."

"Where did you work? Maybe you served me."

"The East Side Diner."

He screws up his eyes, trying to recall all the places he ever ate in New York City, and draws a blank.

"I don't think we ever made Zagat," she says with the smallest of smiles. "What do you do when you're not dressing up as Santa?"

One time Maya Shanker asked him the same question. He'd been at some

109

sort of community gathering, feeling out of his depth, missing Nancy. He told Maya he was a garden design specialist, servicing the Upper East Side. She acted impressed and requested a business card. He said they were still in the print shop because of a redesign.

"I dig gardens and pull weeds," he says now. Why lie?

Ellen laughs. "I thought for sure you were going to tell me you worked in a bank."

He glances at the table. "Are they the hands of a guy who pushes a pen around?"

And when he looks down, all he sees is that soft pink bump where his ring ought to be. It's faded a little since earlier, but still...

She tells him how she's at her happiest walking through Central Park, and they trade stories of buskers and magicians.

"You ever see the clown with the trained mice?" he says, and Ellen shakes her head. "He was there the one time we..." Silas stops. How could he be so dumb? He's thinking of that one time he was with Nancy, and how she screamed when a mouse peeped from the clown's breast pocket, and then she hid behind him when three more scattered from a yellow box.

Ellen's eyes meet his. "You're remembering better times?"

A ball of tears rises. He won't cry. Not in front of the first woman he's got up the nerve to ask out for actual dinner in forever. Takeout with Rose doesn't count.

"I come with a history," he says.

She smiles. "Everyone our age does."

He takes a breath, and holds up his hand.

"You see this mark?" he says, and when she nods, takes a deep breath. "That's where my wedding ring should be. My roommate said I shouldn't wear it. Reckoned it would send out the wrong message."

She ducks her eyes. "And what sort of message do you want to send out?"

His face is hot. How could he be so dumb? "It's not like that. Really it isn't. I didn't *want* to take it off. Truth is, without it, I feel naked. But I got told not to wear a wedding band for a date."

The corners of her mouth twitch. "That's what this is, then? A date?"

"Sure. I mean, no. I mean..." He stares at the table, at the sauce stains from his entrée, at the rings left behind by a coffee cup.

Such a bum, Nancy used to say. *I can never take you anyplace nice.*

Ellen reaches out and soft fingers stroke the back of his hand. "Don't worry about it."

"I'm not usually like this. I guess I..." He shakes his head and looks away, swallowing more tears.

"This was dinner between two new friends," Ellen says. "Not the start of some grand love affair."

"I didn't want to take it off," he says, again. "Nancy would never..."

"Your wife's name was Nancy?"

"She passed," he says, like that might not be obvious. "Some years ago."

Ellen's face softens. "The first time I took off my wedding ring, I cried for two whole days. I got asked to leave a bodega, on account of how I was upsetting the other customers. How long were you married?"

"Twenty-six years. She was hit by a truck. Never recovered. It was quick."

"Otto died on 9/11. He was a contractor, and got called off a job in Midtown, and sent to the 105th floor of the North Tower. Some investment bank needed work done fast."

She makes like there's something in her eye.

"I'm sorry," Silas says, and wonders why people say that. He's not sorry. Not as such. It's not as if he can do anything about what happened.

"It made no sense." She looks down at the table. "The company he worked for dealt with family businesses, not Manhattan corporations. Everyone told me it must have been a new client. A big name bank, or something."

"I still talk to Nancy," he says.

Ellen's eyes are wide. "I still chat with Otto. Right before I came here tonight, I had a long conversation about whether he was fine with me meeting you."

Silas leans back in his chair. She's a handsome woman. It was her smile that first held his interest, but now he's struck by slate gray eyes, and her features, which are just as pleasing. "Nancy didn't raise any immediate objection."

She laughs. "Otto warned me he'd track you down if you tried anything."

"Such as what?"

He doesn't get an answer.

An awkward minute passes when the check comes and Silas insists on using his Crown Atlantic card. He's barely touched the $50 allowance. When they're alone again, Ellen asks if he has kids, and he tells her about Joey. "He lives out of town."

"But you see him often?"

He neither nods nor shakes his head. "Joey would get a hoot out of seeing me right now. In the middle of a gay cruise, talking to you."

She's confused. "He doesn't think his father should be dating? Or is he massively homophobic?"

"My son is gay. He lives with his husband in Florida. They adopted two kids."

"That's great." Ellen's happy expression returns. "You have grandchildren."

Silas looks up, and spots Deon. He's hard to miss, dressed for the pool in shorts and t-shirt and shades, and headed for their table. He wants to intercept the kid. Stop him from playing any role in such a fine evening, but isn't quick enough.

"Dude," Deon says without bothering to acknowledge Ellen. He's chewing gum and scratches at his crotch. "You got something for me?"

Silas reaches into his jacket pocket for Ken's envelope. Deon grabs it and without another word, walks away.

"What was that about?" Ellen says.

"Ship stuff."

Their evening is spoiled, and there's every chance Silas has turned into a drug runner.

1998 - Part I

Nancy glanced over at Silas as their borrowed car crawled up a gravel path past a neatly clipped hedge, leading to the doors of what their family doctor called a sobriety facility. From the outside, it could be any public building. A library. A community hall. A school. Except the windows had bars, prompting Nancy to think of it as a jail. A jail with a hospital attached.

"You think this is too soon?" she whispered, as they sat together, neither ready to open the car doors. "What if he relapses? Do we bundle him in someone's truck and drive him back?"

"He won't," Silas said, and rested his hand on hers.

"How come you're so certain?"

"I know my boy," he said. "Joey is a good kid at heart. He found his way into a bad group of people, but they're gone now. They have no power. The hardest part was getting sober, and he already did that."

Nancy wants to agree, and tell herself her husband is right, and that she's overthinking things. She simply can't.

"The doctor told me he might benefit from more time," she said.

Silas snorted. "And *he* might benefit from more of our money."

So, it is about that, Nancy thought. Trust doesn't come into it. When his hand strokes the side of her face, she flinches. "Not here."

"We have to be strong," Silas said. "Show him we understand."

But she didn't understand. Not now. Not then. Not ever. The boy she loved had vanished. She didn't recognize the Joey they'd checked in three weeks earlier. The way he was talking, and the way he was acting. He'd become a shell of her son. Once through the facility doors, they exchanged sorry looks. The lush green gardens masked a building that could only ever be described as institutional. Recent rain left the place smelling like a damp basement. A woman who forgot to treat anyone like fellow human beings barked their name.

"Through the red door," she said. "Wait for it to close and lock behind you. You'll hear the next one open."

Time slowed right down as the first door shut, and for one awful second, Nancy feared the next might never open. That they'd been lured into a trap. That the lunatics had literally taken over the asylum, and this was where they would die. But then, the lock clicked, and Silas led the way.

Here, there was a different smell. One she couldn't pin down. Disinfectant for sure. And something else. The musty scent of people sleeping in cramped rooms with no windows. She followed Silas down a dark hallway, pausing outside the only half-open door.

"You ready?" He looked at her.

"No," she replied.

"Me neither," he said.

The room was tiny, with three wooden chairs and a table with a vase of plastic daisies. Yet another door opened, and Joey appeared. Nobody moved. The moment froze in time. And then, Nancy ran to her boy, gathering him in her arms, sobbing and laughing, stroking his head, burying her face in his hair, breathing him in. Silas reached out to shake his son's hand, but Joey let it hang.

"We're here to take you home," Nancy said. "It's all going to be fine."

Chapter Twelve

Silas opens his eyes, certain he detects the faintest scent of roses. A memory of Nancy's perfume. The scent swamps him. Of all the things that smell like her, nothing remains as precious to Silas. He buries his head under a thin pillow, and wishes he could hide from everything, finding no comfort in the thought.

Behind the bathroom door, Ken showers and coughs, hacking up more phlegm. The hot water pipes groan in protest.

"Give me some warning before you die of pleurisy," Silas calls.

Ken pads back to his bed, still clearing his throat as he wipes his mouth on the sleeve of a grubby nightshirt.

"I smoked forty ciggies last night," he says. "My mouth is like the bottom of a fucking birdcage."

Silas shuts his eyes, pulls the cover up over his head, and tries to sleep. For an hour or so, he drifts away, and then Ken turns on his tinny radio, blaring sixties pop tunes and sings along.

"Rise and shine," he calls from the other side of the room. "Just because you've landed a cushy number, doesn't mean you get to rest your lazy behind in that flea pit all day."

Silas gazes at the blank ceiling, his frustrations bubbling. He tossed and turned all night, trying to get comfortable. A knot in his back formed from lying crooked, and his skin was hot and itchy. Last night with Ellen was great, so why does he feel so much like someone who cheated on the woman he loves?

"Look lively, mate," Ken says. "The last thing you need is Howdy Doody on your case."

Silas grabs a towel, rubbing sleep from his eyes, and swings his legs out of bed before heading for the bathroom. The putrid stench hits like a punch to the gut, and he comes to a stop short of the doorway.

"For the love of God," he says. "Can you just once remember to flush the john?"

Ken laughs. "I wanted you to admire my latest efforts."

* * *

Kathy cackles, spraying breakfast cereal onto the table. Her tongue is coated in the remnants of frosted flakes, like she licked the bottom of the box.

"Julia blew their socks off," she says, when she consumes enough to manage a breath. "You missed a great night, Helen."

They're sitting in the only breakfast bar that doesn't pipe Christmas music. It was Ellen's idea, after declaring she couldn't promise not to flip if she heard "Little Drummer Boy" one more time.

Things remain tense with Julia. After their fight, she stayed out late. Ellen didn't sleep, worrying where she might be. Julia slammed through their cabin door just after two in the morning, and bumped into furniture, cursing her way to the bathroom. She took a shower and stumbled to bed. Within minutes, Ellen heard snoring. This morning, when Ellen woke, Julia was already out and about. She has no idea where. It's only now that they've come face to face for the first time since falling out, and Julia is in no mood to talk, hiding behind shades and picking at pastry with a look that could curdle milk.

"I'm not much of a singer," Ellen says. "That's always been Julia's bag."

Kathy lunges across the table reaching for a jug of juice. "It's the sing-off tonight. Straights against gays. We're defending our title."

Patrick sighs. "When did it become a competition?"

Julia coughs and clears her throat, then motions to Ellen. "She has an excellent voice. A natural mezzo-soprano."

"The diner had a choir." Ellen ducks her eyes, furious at her friend for telling Kathy anything. "That was years ago. I can't remember the last time I sang. Not even in the shower."

"In which case, join our team," Kathy says in a way that suggests she'll accept no excuses. "We're doing 'Girls Just Wanna Have Fun.'"

Ellen tunes her out. She'd had a lovely evening with Silas. Even though she'd been self-conscious, they got on just great. There had been that awkward moment when he talked about his wedding ring, and they both lapsed into the dating red card discussions about their dead spouses, but otherwise, the evening was textbook perfect. Afterward, as they walked arm-in-arm down the sweeping Atrium stairs, she suggested a nightcap. Silas asked for a rain check, saying he was tired. They didn't kiss. At the elevator doors, he bowed his head and wished her goodnight, then turned and walked away.

Kathy clicks her fingers. "Earth to Ellen. Are you receiving us? Let's hear about the big date."

"It wasn't a date."

"I heard you wore Spanx. In my book, that makes it a date."

Ellen groans. "I had a lovely meal with a pleasant man. That's all there is to say."

"What about afterward, Helen? Did you offer him dessert?"

Ellen fingers a strand of tinsel, wound around a banister, and ponders if it might be strong enough to garrote someone?

"Silas went his way," she says, "and I went mine. Now what's on the agenda for today?"

"We're getting pedicures," Julia says. "I'd ask you to join us, but we already made the reservation."

Ellen forces a smile. "That's okay. I thought I might send postcards."

"They do a treatment where you put your feet in a box of warm water, and little bitty fish chow down on all the dead skin," Kathy says. "I can't wait."

"I might go for a swim," Patrick says, pulling a disgusted face. "Before I hurl."

Ellen needs to be quick. "Can I join you?"

"You don't swim," Julia raises an accusing eyebrow. "And what about your postcards?"

"I'm more of a doggy-paddler than a swimmer," Ellen admits. "But I packed my bathing suit, and it's such a lovely morning. The postcards can wait."

* * *

The pool shimmers in soft, citrus sun. Gone are the heavy, gray clouds that dominated Ellen's first two days at sea. Crystalline water beckons and teases. Half-naked men lounge around. Speedos are this winter's *must-have*, and body hair is back with a bang. Ellen was nervous about wearing a five-year-old swimsuit, but finds she's wonderfully invisible.

Patrick is more toned than a wardrobe of formless t-shirts and cargo pants suggest. In a pair of tight blue shorts, his lily-white chest bulges, showing off a spider tattoo and pierced nipples.

"Did that hurt?" she says, as she spreads a towel on a nearby lounger. "I worked with a woman who swore she never got over breastfeeding."

He grins, and Ellen can't help but think how much it suits his face.

"It stung like hell," he says. "I wasn't tempted to pierce anything else."

She shuts her eyes, enjoying the warm sun on her face, and taking a lungful of salty air. As pleasant as this is, she knows to coat herself with SPF. One of Malinowski's leaflets warned about how lupus doesn't play nice with UV rays.

"I'm a bit of a sun-wuss," she says as Patrick rubs a greasy cream into her shoulders. "I burn the second I dare venture out. Never used to be the case. I guess you learn to be more careful when you get older."

Patrick isn't listening. He's watching some guy in red trunks swim laps. His motion is fluid, and his body sinuous.

"You know him?" Ellen takes off her shades to get a better look. "I'm no expert, but he's quite good. He looks to be on his own."

"I came here with you."

"Spare me the perfect gentleman shtick. You like him, go talk."

He grunts to himself. "Who mentioned anything about liking him?"

For a while, neither of them speak, and Ellen fears she may have said the wrong thing. Patrick lies on his back staring up into the sky, both eyes open.

"Tell me about yourself," she says. "I know plenty about your sister, but almost nothing about you."

"There's not much to tell. I teach geography. My husband left me."

"Ran off with a younger model?"

"Wheeled himself through the front door." Patrick sits up. "Alex used a wheelchair."

Ellen hates herself for being so flippant. How the hell do you claw your way back after that kind of thoughtless mistake?

"I'm sorry," she says. "I was being insensitive."

"The younger model part, or the fact my husband was disabled?"

"Both," she admits. "I'm still getting used to making sure I use the right pronouns talking about people."

Patrick grins in a way that suggests he gets it.

"At least here, you're free to be yourself," she says. "There's no nasty homophobic gay bashers."

He clicks his tongue. "Gay men are the worst. We worship the body beautiful. Anyone whose face doesn't fit gets pushed to one side. I mean, look around. Where are all the heavy guys, the older guys, the ones who don't walk so well?"

He's right. Aside from a few prematurely gray heads, most men onboard the MS Viking are young, muscled, and impeccably tanned.

"Perhaps the misfits are the smart ones," she says. "Holed up someplace else, sipping gin slings and taking life easy."

Patrick sighs to himself. "Maybe."

He asks if she minds if he listens to music, and she waves to signal that he should go right ahead. Ellen fishes a book from her bag, one she's been meaning to read for a while. About the wife of a sporting hero who catches him in bed with their fertility specialist, and has to rebuild the life she thought was hers forever.

Why has Ellen never tried to rebuild *her* life? She lost Otto, but was young enough for a second bite at love. Somehow, the idea of having to get to know anyone new, and deal with seeing each other naked for the first time, or worse, trying to get through an agonizing night not daring to pass wind. And then…hanging over every part of her life was Katharine Fitzgerald. Until Ellen knew for sure that the shiksa who sent Hanukkah cards meant nothing to Otto, she couldn't truly move on.

She puts down her book. Her eyes refuse to focus on the words. A guy with drinks wanders past, and she orders a beer. He nods at Patrick.

"Your cute friend want one?"

Ellen shrugs winningly. "You should ask him."

* * *

Silas has searched high and low, with no sign of Ellen. After dinner, he wanted to spend more time talking, but couldn't stop thinking of how he was doing the wrong thing. That Nancy wouldn't approve. He made a range of dumb excuses, none of which sounded remotely plausible, and hurried back to his room, only to lie on his bed, staring into darkness, straining for Nancy's voice, and trying to summon up her face. She refused to come.

This morning, he woke with a single mission in mind. Find Ellen Gitelman. Ask if she wants to get a coffee, and then suggest another dinner. One where he won't run away the minute the check comes. He already tried calling her room, but nobody picked up, so she must be out and about. He started his search up high on the observation deck. Next stop, the pool.

He scans the loungers, figuring a middle-aged woman would surely stand out a mile. There she is. Over the far side, with some younger guy rubbing sun cream into her shoulders. Suddenly, he's shy. The young guy hunches his face toward Ellen, laughing, and Silas doesn't want to interrupt, but then again, he doesn't want to lose his chance. He finds a bar stool at the Rikki Wikki Bar, where a guy in tight white shorts flirts hard for tips.

"You know we accept cash?" the bartender says. "And any gratuities are happily received."

"I don't doubt it."

Ellen is reading a book, and the guy with her spreads out on a lounger. She glances up, as if looking for something, and he ducks behind a post.

The bartender is back. "You need another beer?"

"I only just got this one."

"The seats are for people ordering drinks. You can't just come here and take a load off." He waves toward the pool. "Use the loungers and chairs."

Silas regards him with a thin smile. "You sure about that?"

"I'm not interested, old man. I don't do daddies."

He toys with freaking the guy out, like Ellen did with last night's snitty waiter, then thinks better of it. The stool is uncomfortable anyhow, and the blazing sun too hot. Once more, he replays how, when Ellen suggested an after-dinner drink, he made a dumb excuse, and her expression changed. She wasn't so much hurt as confused.

Nancy would like her. He's sure.

The thought of his wife causes his chest to tighten. He's barely managed three steps before the pain surges, so much so that Silas fears he might pass out.

Is this it? The big second heart attack Malinowski promised? It's hardly fair. It shouldn't happen here. On a gay cruise. Before he even gets to talk to Joey. A guy on a nearby lounger stares with round, worried eyes, and Silas tries to signal everything is cool, but the pain is unbearable, and he struggles for one breath, then the next. He can get air out, but can't get more in. Silas falls to his knees, gasping, tasting blood in his mouth.

"Jesus," someone says. "Call a doctor. Fast!"

Silas manages to grab a barstool and haul himself up, as a sea of frightened faces stare in horror.

"What's happening, dude?" someone is saying.

He wants to speak, but the words stay trapped.

"Help is coming."

He shuts his eyes, and the only sound is his breathing. In and out. Slow and deliberate. His chest rising and falling. The air is humid. Sweat flows in little streams. He concentrates on the pattern of air. Coming in. Going out. His pulse slows, to match the rhythm. His heart slows. In his chest.

He is calm.

He knows one thing.

One thing only.

Nancy isn't here.

Of all the times he would expect her to appear, surely *this* is the big one. She'll be waiting to talk him through whatever comes next.

Olam Ha-Ba.

Chapter Thirteen

The ship doctor removes blue plastic gloves, and checks the screen beeping next to where Silas lies. She stares in silence, and then nods to herself. "I'm going to suggest you had a panic attack. All your vitals are good."

Silas sits up, gulping in the humid air of the medical center. "So it wasn't my heart?" He wipes a sleeve across his forehead, and a wave of dizziness washes over him.

"All looks steady to me," she says. "You have history?"

Silas explains about his earlier incident, and the latest advice from Malinowski.

"To be fair, we doctors say shit like that to everyone your age." She grins for the first time. "No offense."

He forces himself to return the smile. "None taken."

She tells him to rest for another half hour, drink plenty of water, and when up to walking, return to his room for an early night. There is to be no more secret shopping. Not for today, anyhow. A familiar face appears around the curtains. The last person he expected to see.

"Santa Silas." It's Father Bob. His shabby coat hangs open, revealing a grimy blue shirt. "Word is you almost died."

The doctor clicks her tongue. "Way to make my patient feel good about himself."

When she leaves, Bob comes to sit on the end of the bed, and at first, he doesn't speak, looking at the covers, smoothing them with his hand, before his eyes lock onto Silas.

"What happened?" he says.

Silas shifts uneasily, feeling under investigation. "The doc thought it might have been a panic attack."

"You're a huge guy, for Christ's sake. Strong as an ox."

"Must be the heat."

Bob draws a rattling breath. "And these *attacks*? You ever get them before?"

Silas shakes his head. "I figure I'd have known better how to handle shit. Don't they say to breathe into a brown paper bag? Count backward from a hundred?"

Bob taps at his cell. "Just letting Ken know you're in safe hands," he says before dropping it back into his inside pocket, and fixing Silas with another full-on stare. "Young Deon got into trouble. Fighting."

Silas isn't sure how to take the news. First up, he couldn't care less what Deon has or hasn't done. Second, he doesn't like the way he's being told about the incident. Like he was involved. Or worse, like he might be a part of whatever happens next.

"Howdy Doody put the kid on limited duties," Bob says, examining manicured fingernails. "And I get that. I really do. The guy had to do his job, but Deon performs an important function for me."

Silas holds his breath, and his raw stomach heaves. He wants to ask what was in the padded envelope Ken insisted he hand over the other night.

Bob leans forward. "I guess you could say, I'm here today for a favor."

Silas shuffles further up the bed, trying to put more space between them.

"We need someone to take over where Deon left off," Bob says. "A person who has regular contact with the passengers, who gets to mingle, who won't get spotted. And who better than the MS Viking secret shopper?"

Silas doesn't care for where this sounds like it's going. One of the machines connected by wires to pads suctioned on his chest beeps a warning, and an alarm blares. The doctor from before comes running.

"What happened?" She aims a filthy glare at the priest.

"We were just shooting the breeze," he says. "Me and Santa Silas here. Then World War Three broke out. You need someone to check out these machines. They maybe got faulty—"

She pushes a button to cancel the alarm, and the numbers flashing red turn green.

"I need you to leave," she says. "I need you to stop bothering my patient."

Bob gets up, and brushes down his pants, curling his upper lip and turning to Silas. "Think on what we talked about, Santa. As soon as this pretty lady gets you back on your feet, come find me."

After he's gone, the doctor shines a pin torch into Silas's eye. "Your pupils are fine, but it might be better if you stay a while longer."

He signals understanding, unable to speak, stunned by how sudden a new chest pain took hold. And this time, Nancy had deigned to appear. He saw her standing at the foot of the bed, glaring at the priest like she wanted him gone.

"You need to rest," the doctor says. "I'll write you up for a sedative."

She turns out lights, and rearranges the plastic curtain.

In the darkness, Silas squints at the screen next to his bed, watching as the numbers go ever so slightly up, ever so slightly down.

* * *

Ellen is certain the party of four seated to her right in the all-you-can-eat seafood buffet will ask to be reseated. Kathy is midway through a shaggy dog tale that involves a rabbi, a priest, and a prostitute. It doesn't help that she keeps forgetting parts of the story, and repeating herself, or pointing out the point of her joke is how Jews are purportedly good with money, priests supposedly like boys, and prostitutes like both.

"You do get how we're Jewish?" Ellen eventually says.

Kathy waves a prawn on the end of a wooden fork. "Then you'll know how true the story is. I once read somewhere, the best jokes come from real life."

Ellen doubts Kathy ever stopped talking long enough to take in anything more involved than a limerick, and much as she should point out how anti-Semitic her supposed joke is, she holds her tongue. She's seen firsthand how defensive Kathy could get when pulled up on something. Just yesterday, as they passed a group of well-dressed guys, she sighed and said how *the gays* always know how to dress. When Patrick fumed and called it a generalization, she sat down on the floor, and folded her arms, refusing to go one more step until he issued a full retraction, in front of witnesses.

"Some of my best friends are Jewish, Helen," Kathy says, as if this extra layer of defense makes anything anti-Semitic perfectly fine. "So you can't accuse me of being a racialist."

If blame is appropriate, it should be laid at Julia's door. When Ellen finally got her alone and asked how they could get past their fight, she'd insisted on dinner with the Luceys.

"You think they have hammers for the crab?" Kathy says. "I heard they boil the little critters while they're still alive. Or am I thinking of lobsters? Or chickens?"

Patrick groans to himself. He's spent ten minutes poking at bland white rice with a fork.

The idea of eating any creature boiled alive makes Ellen want to hurl.

"I might have salmon," she says.

Kathy is having none of it. "You should totally get the crab."

"We're Jewish," Julia says. "We're not allowed to eat shellfish."

Kathy is scandalized. "What? How do you have a Christmas Eve dinner and not eat calamari?"

Patrick's eyes are rolling. "Let's order."

It's a good idea. The menu occupies Kathy for a full five minutes.

"What is everyone planning for tomorrow?" she says, as a waiter does his best to ignore their table. "Personally, I can't wait to get my feet back on solid ground. Don't they say it takes a while to find your land legs?"

The MS Viking is due in Nassau at ten o'clock. Ellen and Julia have already agreed on a light breakfast, followed by a pre-booked taxi to something called The Dolphin Experience.

"I was going to look into how long I might serve in jail for sororicide," Patrick says.

Kathy chuckles. "You don't want to go killing yourself, Patty. Not while your credit card is paying for my onboard expenses."

Julia reveals their plans to swim with dolphins, and Ellen regrets not asking her to keep quiet. Kathy's eyes grow super wide.

"That sounds like such a hoot," she says. "Did you know dolphins try to have sex with you?"

When Patrick suggests they might draw some kind of line for his sister, Ellen is the only one to laugh.

Kathy glares. "I get that it's been a while since anyone showed interest in your bits and pieces, Patty, but I would thank you for keeping a civil tongue. Helen and Julia don't care for toilet talk."

Patrick bunches a paper napkin and tosses it onto the table.

"Seriously, sis," he says as he shuffles from the bench. "I've listened to you dominate conversation, telling knuckle-dragging jokes that make us sound like we come from some town where cousins fuck, and you tell *me* to keep a civil tongue?"

Kathy's lower lip wobbles, and she puts down her fork, before bursting into tears.

"There now," Julia whispers, rubbing her hand. "Patrick didn't mean it. It's been a long day. Everyone is tired."

"I did mean it," Patrick says. "She needs to hear this sort of thing."

Kathy glances up, her face a mess of mascara. "You're being horrible because of Ironside."

Ellen glances first at Julia, then at Patrick.

His eyes narrow. "What did you say?"

"This is all down to Alex. Ironside. The ordeal on wheels," Kathy says, and Ellen assumes it to be some kind of dig at Patrick's ex. She knows that she ought to step in before what's already started ugly turns truly grotesque.

"You're a total cunt," he says, and the guys at the next table cheer.

Patrick pushes back his chair, nods grimly, first at Ellen, and then at Julia, before ripping off his plastic bib and heading for the door.

After he's gone, Kathy sniffs mournfully, and dabs at her eyes.

"I must apologize for my brother's language," she says, partly to Ellen and Julia, partly to their way-too-eager audience. "My brother was recently abandoned by a very cruel man, and he somehow finds a way to blame me."

Ellen wants to ask why he thinks she had anything to do with the guy leaving, but now isn't the right moment. Instead, she hands Kathy a stack of branded Seafood Buffet napkins.

"I've had a great idea," Julia says. "You and Patrick need a time out…"

If Ellen's hip wasn't aching, she'd dive across the table and lace her fingers around Julia's throat. Anything to stop what must surely be coming next. The polar opposite of a great idea.

"Why doesn't Kathy come with us to the dolphins tomorrow?" Julia says. "We'll swing by the guest relations desk after dinner, and buy you a ticket. We already have a ride booked."

* * *

Out on the observation deck, Ellen finds Patrick smoking. Or rather, doing his best to act like a man who smokes. He leans on a rail and stares at the sea, his cheeks sucked in, his hands still shaking with rage.

"Are you okay?" she says.

He shrugs, but doesn't speak.

"I get why you want to have your sister fitted for concrete Louboutins, but she probably didn't mean to upset you."

"She never does," he says with a hefty sigh. "And whenever I point out how what she says could offend other people, she turns on the fucking waterworks, and I end up feeling like I'm the one being unreasonable."

"At least you haven't had your best friend invite her to spend the whole day with you tomorrow."

His face falls. "Oh, Ellen, I'm sorry. Let me have a word and explain how this is a special thing for your guys. She'll be fine. We'll go shoe shopping, and I'll act like the perfect gay brother."

"It's okay." Ellen holds up her hands. "I'll live."

"Kathy's not a bad person," he says. "It's just, sometimes, I wish she had some kind of off-switch."

Ellen comes to lean on the rails. "You don't happen to have a spare cigarette?"

He pulls out a pack and a battered brass Zippo.

"I gave up twenty years ago," she says. "And even when I did smoke, I never really liked it. Back then, it was the only way to get a break at the diner. I hid near the overflow freezers, and enjoyed ten whole minutes to myself."

"Alex was always on at me to quit," Patrick says. "I gave up three times last year. Once we paid over two hundred bucks for some shrink, who claimed he had a ninety-nine percent success rate. Turns out there was small print. I was the one percent."

For the longest time, they don't speak, and when Ellen stifles a shiver, Patrick offers his jacket.

"How about we go inside?" she says. "Find some place where Kathy isn't."

"About the dolphins," he says. "You think I might come too?"

She exhales. "Sure you can, and between us, we'll take turns at trying to drown your sister."

Chapter Fourteen

Silas sits on the edge of his bed, examining his hands. Still shaking, but not as bad as when he got back to his room. The clock reads four a.m., and the only sounds come from Ken's CPAP machine and the engines that groan below. Silas's mind races, replaying events in rapid succession. Images spin like a movie, as he tries to make sense of what happened. He stands up, and goes to the bathroom. From the mirror, an old man greets him. Dark circles outline bloodshot eyes. He turns on the faucet, holding both palms under a stream of cold water. For the longest time, he lets it swirl away, before reaching for a towel, and running a comb through his hair. He pulls on a fresh shirt.

Back in his bed, he sits on the covers, picks up his phone, and dials.

"What the fuck," Rose croaks. "You don't know some other schmuck you can wake in the middle of the night?"

"You were right."

There's a rustle, the sound of a drawer opening, and the click of a lighter. She exhales. "Right about what, exactly?"

"About letting Joey get on with his life."

Another short pause. "Hallelujah."

No sooner has he pledged to leave his son in peace, than he regrets saying it out loud. What he wanted more than anything was for Rose to argue. To order him to take a chance. Or say that she'd be happy to switch places. Or something other than halle-fucking-lujah. He wanted to admit his fear, and have her say it was foolish.

"Rose?"

"Yeah, I'm here."

"I called because I couldn't sleep. Wanted to hear your voice."

She laughs. A throaty chuckle. "Should I be flattered or insulted?"

"Something happened today."

Static crackles the line. "You got hit on? Silas, it was bound to happen one day. You always had that girlish gait. I don't know why nobody ever thought to mention it."

"I had a panic attack."

Her voice softens. "Talk to me."

"One minute I was fine, the next…"

"You have to come home," Rose says. "Isn't this some kind of sign? Nancy wouldn't want you half killing yourself to make things right with some kid who needs a kick up the butt."

Until now, Silas had only ever known Rose lavish praise on her nephew.

"I'm sorry," he says. "I shouldn't have called."

Rose sighs. "If you need the cash for an airplane ticket, I have savings. My rates are reasonable."

"Don't be so damn nice to me."

The line goes quiet. Then she says, "I'm invariably nice to you."

He knows she's right.

"Thing is, I'm glad you called," she says. "You need to understand what you mean to me."

Silas has no idea how Rose sees him. A friend with benefits? Something more? He wishes he could tell her how she's kept him going in recent years. That she's the only reason he hasn't given up completely and moved to live on some street corner near a branch of CVS.

"I met someone," he says.

"On a gay cruise?" There's that rattling laugh again. "So you *did* call to tell me something important."

"A woman."

There's a long crackling silence. He knows she's still there.

"I'm sorry," he says. "I didn't mean to…"

"I'm glad you're happy, Silas. That's all I want."

"I'm sorry."

"Stop saying you're sorry." A pause. "This woman. She feels the same way?"

"We didn't really talk much yet."

"Then you'd better." Rose is firm. "Many people pass through your life. Not many leave their mark."

After hanging up, he lies back on his pillow, staring into the darkness. Nancy's face floats before his eyes. She's smiling, just like she did all those years ago, the first time he saw her.

* * *

As Ellen runs a blue washcloth across her face, she flinches. Her skin is on fire, and the pain causes her teeth to grit. Too exhausted to scream, she slumps on the side of the tub. Why didn't she listen to Malinowski? Avoid the sun, he said. SPF won't protect you anything like enough. She'd read in a booklet about some woman with lupus who got sunburn under her chin from standing next to a car for ten minutes on a hot day. Another woman wrote about having to wear a wide-brimmed hat to hospital appointments. Even indoor lighting was tricky.

"Hurry," Julia calls from the other side of the door. "Some of us need to pee."

Ellen hates acting the flake, but she's almost certain she won't make it off the ship today. And if she does, the odds of swimming with dolphins hover close to zero. She grabs onto the washstand and hauls herself toward the door. Each movement is a struggle.

"About time." Julia barges past. "When you reach our age, bladder control isn't an optional extra."

What Ellen would like to do is curl up in bed. Possibly forever. She reaches for the sofa to steady her passage, but doesn't make it, instead slipping to the floor, pain lancing through joints. Julia's scream shakes her from a brief but delicious sleep, where colors had danced and gentle voices whispered her name.

"I thought you were dead." Julia licks her thumb and rubs it along Ellen's cheek. "You're overheated. I'll call for a doctor."

"One of my pills will fix everything." Ellen looks around, taking in the room as if seeing it for the first time. The maid hasn't vacuumed under the bed. "Perhaps I caught a chill. My head is kinda stuffy, and my joints are killing me."

Julia finds the tablets. "I'll get water."

Ellen shuffles until she's propped up by the sofa, where she swallows one tablet, followed by a huge gulp of tepid water. It catches in her throat, and she chokes, spitting the pellet back into her palm before trying again.

"Better?" Julia says after what felt like hours, but might have been three seconds.

"I don't think I can go to the dolphins," she says. "I'm sorry if I've ruined everything."

When she regains her strength, Ellen drags herself up to the edge of the bed, as Julia fishes her cell from a drawer and jabs at the screen.

"I'm calling Kathy and Patrick," she says. "They can go alone. I'll stay here with you."

"Please," Ellen croaks. "I want you to have fun."

"And leave you like this?"

"This is some twenty-four-hour bug. You can't miss out on the chance of a lifetime."

Julia acts unconvinced, but still her thumb hovers over the "call" button.

"You'll take loads of pictures, won't you?" Ellen says.

"Of course I will."

* * *

Silas knows Howard is talking to him, but the words take forever to connect in his head, like tuning in a distant radio station. He squishes his eyes shut, and when he looks again, Howard's lips are still moving, his face is open, happy, and excited as he holds out a sheet of paper.

"I have the addresses here," he tells Silas. "It's simple enough. You grade each aspect of service in four local establishments. Crown Atlantic has partnership agreements, and if we're recommending a place to our guests, we want to be assured they stay on message."

Silas takes the paper and smooths it out, scanning the four names.

Howard is still talking. "More than anything, you're looking for a warm welcome, quality food, and no added extras when the check lands."

"Great...sure...yeah. Whatever."

Straight after breakfast, Silas had marched into the crew office and closed the door behind him. Howard glanced up from rearranging rosters, and Silas explained how he needed to talk. He was determined to get to the bottom of whatever Father Bob was up to, but somehow the words wouldn't come. At the back of his mind, Silas couldn't help but wonder if Howard might be involved.

"Is everything cool with you?" Howard says now. "Did the doc say to take a time out?"

"I was given the all clear."

"But there's something eating at you?" He bobs his head for Silas to sit. "Talk to me."

Before he can hold his tongue, Silas blurts out about how Ken gave him a package to deliver, how Deon acted weird, and how he'd gotten veiled threats from Father Bob. Howard listens without interruption, eyes narrowed and head tipped.

"You know, people hear and see what they want to hear and see," he says eventually.

Silas shifts in his seat, heat crawling up his neck. "You think I'm making this up? Imaging things?"

"Sometimes it's best not to get involved."

"But I'm being involved. Against my will. And if this is drugs..."

At first, Howard narrows his eyes, and then his face clears, and he grins.

"Oh, Silas, no!" he says. "I promise you it's not drugs. Not on the MS Viking."

"How can you be so sure?"

"Trust me, I know the ship."

Silas searches Howard's face, desperate for the truth.

"Tell you what," Howard says. "What if we have a get together? You, me, Bob, and Ken. Shoot the breeze. Chew the fat. Break through any misunderstandings."

Silas's stomach tightens. That's the last thing he wants.

* * *

Ellen loves having the pool to herself. She takes her book and a towel and picks a lounger, shaded from harmful UV by a huge umbrella. The pills changed everything. After waking in pain, she now felt relaxed, content, insulated from the world. She didn't want to think about anything. Maybe this was the secret all along. One pill wasn't enough. Two helped. But three hit the sweet spot.

She dozes, waking to the sound of footsteps. It's Patrick.

"Shouldn't you be swimming with dolphins?" she says, shading her eyes.

He sits next to her, his face serious. "Kathy and I had words. She's gone alone."

"Oh, no." Ellen is concerned. "What happened?"

"She accused me of not taking her seriously. One thing led to another, and we both said some pretty cruel things." He signals to the next lounger. "You okay if I join you?"

"Of course." Ellen lays down her book and prepares to listen, but Patrick leans against the back of the lounger and gazes up into the sky. His eyes close. She picks up her book and continues reading.

"I think…" he says suddenly, "I should tell you about Kathy."

Ellen looks up.

"The reason we came on this trip together is that she went through something bad."

Ellen waits for him to go on.

"A year back, she lost a baby. Her first pregnancy."

She doesn't know what to say. For one thing, Ellen sort of assumed Kathy was single.

"She was in a relationship with a drifter guy," he says, "and the fucker didn't want kids. After the miscarriage, he sort of vanished."

"Oh, no. That's awful. I'm so sorry."

"It wasn't good. Kathy kinda…died inside, and I suppose I figured if we came away on this trip, it might help."

"And it hasn't?"

"I'm in a pretty bad place too. I suppose I got it into my head that, together, we might be each other's bright light and pull our way out of the dark."

Ellen nods slowly. "It sounds like what you both need is some kind of therapist."

Patrick turns to her. "I didn't mean to lay this on you. I'll get out of your hair. I guess I'd better make a call to Kathy and apologize. Will you excuse me?"

* * *

Silas was one of the last ashore, and his stomach growls, reminding him how he skipped breakfast and pretended to sleep, even after Ken turned on his radio.

"Dude!"

He turns around and sees Mike.

"You wanna hang with us?" He's with the other band members, dressed for the beach. Each of them raises a hand in casual greeting.

"I have something to do," Silas says. "But later?"

He pulls Howard's list from his pocket. Four cafés, and in each, he's meant to order the same. A coffee and a sandwich. He's allowed to ask for food to go, but must taste everything served. There are boxes to tick for speed of service, cleanliness, value for money, and overall impression. Howard wants a fifty-word summary, and provided a map to help find each place.

"We're heading for Junkanoo," Mike says. "Follow the signs."

The first port of call for Silas is in Shirley Street, a part of Nassau known as Over the Hill. He needs to find a joint called Rick's, where he should ask for the owner—confusingly named Johnny. Silas has dressed casually, hoping to blend in, wearing a threadbare sweater and baggy jogging pants.

"You sure about Shirley Street?" a cab driver says after he gives directions. "It's sketchy."

As they leave the docks, the busy streets empty and the shopfronts grow less welcoming. People don't so much walk as loiter, and the buildings are set to crumble. Not that Silas fears the worst parts of any town. He used to drive a delivery truck through no-go zones in Queens, and gets how safety comes down to how you act. Keep your head up, your eyes straight ahead. Do what you came to do and disappear.

The car stops.

"That's the place?" He stares through the taxi window at a boarded-up warehouse. "There's not some other joint called Rick's? A bar, perhaps?"

"Go around the back," the driver says, and Silas pays with Crown Atlantic money.

The young guy moves his hand from the steering wheel to the stick shift. Wheels skid, kicking up a cloud of dust.

Rick's Bar reminds him of Staten Island dives. A single, small, fly-specked window is the only source of daylight, and the air is dense with a blue haze of cigarette smoke. Faded, torn posters cover the walls, and bare light bulbs flicker. Heat leaches through cinder blocks, turning the place into a furnace. Guys in tattered jeans and work shoes shift to see the stranger who walked in.

"I'm looking for the owner," Silas says, determined to keep his visiting time to an absolute minimum.

"That'll be me." A stout man with hands like ham hocks rests his elbows on the counter. "The name is Johnny. What can I do for you?"

"I'm from Crown Atlantic." Silas hears how his voice wobbles.

"What happened to Deon?"

"I need a coffee and whatever sandwich you recommend."

Silas lets his eyes scan a dusty shelf. The chances of this place serving coffee are slim. The idea of food, even more distant.

Johnny folds his arms across a filthy grease-spattered shirt. "Show me what you got there."

"This?" Silas protects his checklist. "It's nothing."

"You strike me as the kind of dude who prefers a dark spirit."

Sensing this to be a nonnegotiable signal to sit, Silas climbs onto a rickety stool. He's poured a hefty measure and gulps, cringing as paint stripper brandy cuts a fiery road to his gut.

Johnny holds up a dirty burlap sack. Its contents rattle. "Remind your boss he still owes me."

* * *

Ellen's raw stomach growls a demand for food. She skipped breakfast, and lunch is long overdue. A quick scan confirms most every place onboard is closed, and her best option is a row of vending machines stocked with candy and chips. It's not what she had in mind, so she walks out on deck, scanning the horizon. Across the bay, alongside an inviting beach, sits a row of brightly colored wooden shacks, with mismatched tables and chairs. She takes the elevator to level six, where a boardwalk leads to the shore.

In a quiet café, seashells cover the driftwood counter, and blown-glass fish adorn the walls. Plastic flowers droop from a vase. When Ellen hobbles in, the guy in charge doesn't look up from his newspaper.

"Make yourself at home," he says in a deep, gravelly voice. "I'll be right over."

She drops her bag on a table, and plops down on one of the stools, its seat warm from the sun. Her body still hums from the magic pills, and she takes in the golden sand that tips gently away from the land, and a sky the most incredible shade of blue. Out at sea, a tiny boat cuts across the horizon, trailing a plume of spray.

"What can I get you?" the guy in charge calls over.

"A coffee. The strongest one you do. And maybe some lunch?"

For the first time, Ellen suspects she might have been happier traveling solo. Free of needing to say the right thing, and having to hold her tongue whenever Kathy cracks another offensive joke.

"You'd have loved it here, Otto," she whispers. "It's your kind of place."

"Lady, did you say something?"

Ellen breaks from a dream. The owner stands over her, holding a jug of stale-smelling coffee.

"Food will take a while," he says, and without waiting for an answer overfills a cup so it flows onto the table, before heading outside to settle into a beach chair, pulling a cap over his eyes.

* * *

The late afternoon air turns heavy, suggesting an approaching storm. Thick clouds skim the sun and Silas wipes sweat from his brow. This time, he's sure he's carrying drugs. The bag he was given is filled with plastic containers. The kind you get in Walgreens. Each contains little pink pills.

He's trying to find signs for Junkanoo beach, but the streets have gotten quieter. The bars around look to be closing for a late afternoon siesta. Silas slows and stops at a corner to rub the back of his neck. An uneasiness forms in his gut. How the hell did he let himself become a hypocrite? He drove his son to a rehab facility after lecturing him about how drugs destroy lives. Now he's a part of that same evil machine. A tiny cog turning against another cog, and then another, moving poison around.

Gulls squawk overhead, and the air smells of salt and oil. A beach shack is still open. A beer might help settle fried nerves.

The girl inside can't be old enough to work, let alone serve alcohol. Her hair is caught back in a messy bun, and her makeup is limited to a swipe of eyeliner and blush. Her hands are red from hot water and a sudsy bar rag, used to wipe tables. Silas orders a Bud and glances at the time. The beer is flat and warm.

* * *

Ellen steps from her shoes, enjoying the warm sand between her toes. Fine and smooth, and almost like flour. She licks dry lips, and tilts back her head to breathe in the scent of salt. Something about the threatening sky suggests rain, but right now, she can take on the world. Everything is going to work out. She has no clue how or why, but it will.

Otto loved the sea. They often took the Sandy Hook Ferry, and spent weekends camping on a beach, paddling in the ocean. He never swam in the breakers, always wading in a little way. Otto loved the water.

She sits and leans against a rock. It would be so easy to not go back to the boat, and instead, find a job waiting tables in the sun, making new friends, and blending into the background. Julia would take care of the apartment until she sold up. And who would miss Ellen Gitelman, anyway?

There's a rumble. Like thunder. And the sun ducks behind dark clouds.

"Here comes the rain again," she sighs, as a man wanders into the waves. He's about Otto's height, with the same stick-thin build and straw-colored hair. As she watches, he turns around, sees her and beckons.

"Come for a swim," he calls, as he wades out.

She laughs. "I can't. I don't know how."

"I'll teach you. Come on."

The water reaches her thighs, and still she follows. Her skin prickles and the sand shifts beneath her feet.

"I'm not going any further," she calls out.

The water rises. He says something before diving beneath the surface.

"I can't hear you..." She trails off and looks behind her. The shore is gone. Everything is dull and gray. A vast expanse of sea.

"What am I doing here?"

The water is too deep to find a footing, and she struggles in fading light.

"My heart," she splutters. "Where are you?"

Salt catches in her throat. Tides swirl, pulling her deeper. Aching arms and legs flail. She reaches out again and again, but the waves close over her head.

A girl with a red dress walks along a shoreline of pink sand. The glittery, crystalline sea laps at her bare toes. She has long dark hair, a pert nose, and denim shorts, cut off at the knee.

"Coming for a swim?" a man's voice calls.

"Yes." The girl holds out her arms.

"Be careful, Ellen," the man says. "It's deep from here on out."

She wades into the ocean and soon the water reaches her middle.

"It's beautiful," she calls.

The water swirls pink, the sand runs away.

And then, she's gone.

Chapter Fifteen

Silas hates being told to relax, and if the fucking nurse says it one more time, he'll be forced to excuse himself and head back to his room. He takes a deep breath, holds it, and then exhales slowly. His lungs still burn, and the bright lights of the medical center cause his skull to pound. The air is crisp with antiseptic, and the sheet he's lying on scratches like hell.

"Your blood pressure is on the high side," the doctor says. "And your color isn't good."

He wants to remind her how, given he recently saved someone from drowning, it's only to be expected. But he glances at the monitor next to his bed, pulsing in time with the *thud-thud-thud* between his ears. Whenever he closes his eyes, he's back in the water, clawing for the surface, two lives slipping away. Nancy in his ear, calling him *a dumb fuck.*

A putz.

A nar.

Anyone else would be signing autographs and playing the homecoming hero. Exchanging stories about how it was touch and go and, for one minute, he was sure he'd gotten himself in too deep. Literally. How he found Ellen in the nick of time, and dragged her to the surface, where she gasped for air. And then, he carried her lifeless body to the shore, and laid it down, as the sun ducked behind more clouds. A cold wind had caused her hair to muss around her beautiful face, as he bent and blew into her mouth, tasting her lips.

"What were you thinking of, Silas?" the doctor says. "You only just got out of this fucking bed."

CHAPTER FIFTEEN

He turns his head toward the wall. She's right.

"You go ahead and sulk," she says, reaching over to adjust a monitor. "You know I'm right. You're way too old to be playing Superman."

Silas saved a woman's life. Surely that deserves more than this patronizing slap on the wrist. And he wouldn't be here if the emergency team who came to help hadn't insisted he get checked over.

"Did you swallow a lot of water?" she says.

Silas shrugs.

"Is that a, yes, I swallowed lots, or no, you're too fucking stupid to remember?"

He shrugs once more.

She hands him a scuffed plastic beaker. "I need you to piss in this."

* * *

In their room, Ellen waits until Kathy ducks out before turning her irritation on Julia.

"Why is she here?" she says through clenched teeth. "And why did she insist on bringing me back in that wheelchair again? Everyone was staring."

"Kathy has convinced herself you'd have been fine if we hadn't gone to see the dolphins." Julia holds up a bottle of tablets. "How many of these did you take?"

Ellen turns away. "Malinowski said to have one when required."

"The label says a maximum two pills a day. How many did you take while we were away?"

"I don't recall."

"Two, three?"

Ellen wants to snatch the bottle and swallow the lot. Anything to stop her feeling so damn stupid. When a hand hauled her from the ocean, all she could do was ask where they put Otto, and if the little girl was safe. They said she swallowed contaminated water, and fed a tube into her throat. It hurt. A lot.

Kathy is back.

"It might be better if you let one of us have your tablets," she says. "That way you won't end up taking too many by accident."

Ellen closes her eyes and counts very slowly, and very deliberately, to ten.

"She means well," Julia whispers. "And I *will* keep these for now. When you need one, you have only to ask."

Ellen groans. "I don't need a grown-up monitoring my medicine. Why can't everyone go away and quit treating me like a meshuggener?"

"How's the patient?" Kathy says for the billionth time, and leans in close. "Do you want anything, Helen?"

"I'd prefer for you to stop talking like I mislaid a fucking chromosome," Ellen snaps.

Julia leads Kathy away. "It might be best to let her sleep. What if we get coffee and cake?"

Kathy's eyes light up. "That would be wonderful." And then the brightness fades. "But what about Helen? What if she has a relapse?"

"A relapse of what?" Ellen croaks. "I almost drowned. It's not likely to happen again unless the tub overflows."

"I'll have my telephone switched on." Julia ushers Kathy toward the door. "If Ellen needs anything she can call."

Kathy hesitates, but the lure of cake is too strong.

"It's a deal," she says. "And while I think of it, you're both coming to our room tonight for dinner."

"Oh, no." Ellen tries to sit up, alarm rising through her at the thought of deathless small talk. "We couldn't. Absolutely not."

"I won't hear another word," Kathy says. "We have a suite with a huge dining table going to waste. You're too sick to sit in a restaurant. People will stare, and you might put them off their food. Let me look after you. I've always been good with old people."

"Don't you need to check first with your brother?" If Ellen is quick enough, she can call Patrick and tell him he needs to find a reason dinner can't happen. She's prepared to offer money.

"Patty can't join us," Kathy says with a roll of her eyes. "There's a talk on Bahamian culture."

Julia hurries her out. "Maybe we'll see how Ellen feels later?"

* * *

Bob's face turns a worrying shade of purple, and Silas gathers he's in for a roasting.

"You left the bag behind?" he says, speaking very slowly, sounding each word out. "What if the cops find it?"

"There's no way to connect it with me."

"Did anyone see?"

"It's possible. But again. I don't think they'd know I'm from the ship."

Bob straightens up and runs a hand through thinning hair. He was waiting when Silas got back from the medical center. There was no sign of Ken, and Bob told him to close the door. He started off calmly, asking how Silas felt after his heroic act, and if there might be any long-term damage, before inquiring after the bag. Silas explained what had happened, and the priest went quiet.

And then he exploded.

"You spoke to the fucking cops!" he all but screams. "They have your name on record. They know you work onboard."

"Nobody asked me about the bag."

Bob buries his head in his hands. "I knew I couldn't trust a fucking newbie. Why the hell did Howard suggest using you?"

Silas swallows. "Howard is involved?"

"You didn't get that from the way he sent you on a mission to collect the gear?"

"What gear?"

Bob's eyes narrow, and then he laughs in disbelief. "Oh, this is too fucking precious. You seriously don't have a fucking clue what was in that bag, do you?"

Silas does, but he senses it's better to feign ignorance.

"I was told to review cafés," he says. "And then the guy who owns the first bar told me to take the bag."

There's a gentle tap at the door. It's Howard, and like Bob, he goes through the motions of pretending to care before asking if anyone gave him a bag.

Bob interrupts. "He lost the fucking pills."

People speak about color draining, but never has Silas seen it happen until now. Howard turns a shade of what can only be described as gray. His mouth opens, and sounds emerge, none of which could reasonably be called words.

Bob slams an angry hand on Ken's makeup table. "Fucking Jiminy Cricket here claims he didn't know what was in the bag."

"I dropped it when I went to rescue Ellen," Silas says. "The medics brought me to the ship."

If anything, Howard's face grows paler, and his expression suggests someone ready to burst into tears.

"We have alternative product," Bob says. "Enough to keep the boys happy. We'll arrange a new drop in Miami. And this time, we trust Deon, not some useless old man."

Although he's relieved to be let off, something tells Silas this is far from the end of matters.

"Tonight," Bob says. "You need to put on your Santa suit and do the fucking work you're being paid for."

Silas sets his jaw. "The doctor told me to rest up."

The priest throws up his hands, howling in frustration. "Why the fuck did head office send us this loser? Did they really have nobody else? If I say you play Santa, you play Santa. Am I making myself understood?"

He clicks his fingers, and Howard holds out a yellow metal tin.

Silas inhales. "What's in there?"

"Why?" Bob pushes his face close. "You plan on leaving it some place?"

Howard opens the tin to reveal glass vials of brown liquid. "Meth if you want it. Heroin if you can afford it."

Silas presses his eyes shut. Bile rises in his throat.

* * *

Kathy's home video show is in full swing. She aims a remote control at the screen and turns up the volume. "This is you, Helen. What is it you're saying?"

Ellen sighs to herself. Surely even a baboon with limited eyesight can lip-read how she's telling Kathy to fuck off.

"I can hardly keep my eyes open," she says, stretching and fake yawning. "I might get an early night."

"But you didn't touch dinner. I can order up a sandwich."

Kathy means well, and reminds Ellen of her own mother, who would let no guest leave their house unfed or unburdened by something they happened to mention liking. She once had her father unhook a painting after one of the neighbors admired it in passing. Her mother was a decent person. Kathy is too.

"I'll stay," Ellen says. "But if I fall asleep, don't take it personally. I'm on heavy duty narcotics."

"You shouldn't be alone." Kathy brushes her arm. "What if you have some kind of flashback, remembering how you almost lost your life?"

"If that happens, maybe you'll be around to make sure I don't skip any vital details."

Kathy's eyes widen, and her brow furrows, and Ellen thinks there's every chance she might burst into tears.

"I've had a shitty day," Ellen says quickly. "This isn't because of you. It's me being a bitch, and you happen to be in range."

"It's okay." Kathy's features soften. "I guess you want to find Silas and thank him for saving your life."

Ellen's face burns. "I don't wish to bother him."

"But he did something real special, and I overheard the doctor saying he needs to get tests. The water caused some kind of rash."

A shudder of alarm rises through Ellen. "I didn't know that."

Julia cuts in. "Apparently, you elected to swim right where the ships dump raw sewage. I'm surprised your epidermis isn't peeling."

Ellen runs an involuntary hand over her arms. "It's better I keep out of his way. Perhaps I'll send a get well gift basket."

Kathy jumps up, and dances from one foot to the other, looking over at Julia. "She can't remember, can she?" she says.

Ellen half closes her eyes. "Would one of you care to enlighten me?"

"You said Silas was your hero." Kathy's voice is a flutter. "That you thought he didn't like you, but now you know better."

"I'd been deprived of oxygen. And now according to Julia, I probably swallowed raw sewage. I must have been hallucinating."

"You told everyone how you wanted to marry him." Kathy skips around the room. "Can you imagine a Christmas wedding? It's so romantic."

Ellen tries to signal to Julia, but she doesn't pick up. Could she knock Kathy out cold with the glass fruit bowl, roll her in a rug, and dump the body at sea?

"You held his hand," she says. "They couldn't get you to let go. You claimed he was your soulmate."

Julia interjects. "To be fair, Ellen also mistook me for her mother."

Kathy's features soften. "You know whose advice I follow in these sort of things, Helen? Carrie Fisher's."

Ellen glances over at Julia, who's busy helping herself to more red wine.

"Carrie says to stay afraid, but do things anyway," Kathy says. "Don't wait to get confident. Do the thing you're scared about, and confidence will come. If you think Silas is your soulmate, you need to let him know."

For one moment, Ellen is back in the dark water, with a hand reaching for hers, lifting her to safety just as she's sure the end is near.

The door bursts open, and Patrick staggers in.

"Water," he gasps, before falling to his knees and then flat on his face. His body convulses like someone suffering an electric shock. Kathy wails, and Julia takes charge, telling Ellen to call for help.

She picks up the telephone and dials zero.

"They say to lie him flat," Ellen says, parroting the calming voice at the other end of the line. "Loosen his shirt and make sure he gets air."

"We don't have windows," Kathy whines. "We're below the waterline. Patty was too mean to pay extra."

"Any air." Ellen scans the room. "That fan. Point it at his face."

Julia trips over Patrick's arm, causing him to yowl.

By the time the emergency crew arrives, Kathy is inconsolable, and it takes both women to coax her into the bedroom, while the medics do their work. Ellen and Julia sit with her, each holding one hand, neither woman talking, fragile with fear, and straining to make sense of each muffled sound.

"He can't die," Kathy says, her voice little more than a whisper. "My Patty isn't allowed to die. He's my very best friend."

There's a knock, and Julia takes charge, while Ellen squeezes Kathy's hand. "I'm sorry I was such a bitch to you. I guess we both had a scare."

Kathy is sobbing too much to manage words.

Julia returns and her face is pale. "They need to take him to the medical center. He's breathing, but his temperature is way up. Could he have ingested anything?"

Kathy's mouth drops open. "Patty? No way. He even drinks decaffeinated coffee."

Ellen glances over at the nightstand. One drawer is pulled out, and she spies a small plastic bottle. "What's this?"

Kathy squints and studies it. "Something the doctor prescribed? He never tells me anything."

"I should show the medics," Julia says and hurries to the other room.

Chapter Sixteen

Patrick lies in bed, his eyes closed, and his face pale in the harsh fluorescent light. Machines, tubes, and wires fill the cramped space, and a mask placed over his nose and mouth amplifies each wheezing breath. Kathy sits and waits, her eyes rubbed red and saying nothing. Around three a.m., Ellen suggested sleep, but she shook her head.

"What if he dies, and I'm not here to hold his hand?" she says. "Patty can't leave on his own."

Other faces drift in and out of the tiny room. A doctor, three different nurses. Everyone offers to find them coffee, but Kathy waves away the kindness.

"I'm fine," she keeps saying. "But thank you."

The agreement is to share *Kathy Watch* with Julia, six hours each, but Ellen craves sleep, feeling an ache in her back and heaviness in her shoulders. She toys with a call to Julia, but it's unfair to intrude on her downtime. Instead, she pulls her chair closer to the bed, and listens to Patrick's breathing.

"Helen?" Kathy is looking at her. "I know I haven't said it before, but you're a good friend."

"It's the least I can do." She tries for a reassuring smile, remembering Kathy's kindness when they first met. How she wheeled Ellen to her room, refusing any help.

"I don't know what I'd do without you and Julia."

Around seven, Kathy tiptoes away to wash her face in the bathroom. Through the walls, Ellen hears sobbing, but by the time she emerges, Kathy has rearranged her features into hope.

"I might get that coffee, now," she says, forcing a smile. "You think you could ask someone?"

Ellen's knees click as she stands. "What about breakfast?"

"I'm not hungry. You go right ahead."

All at once, the faux bravado is gone. Kathy has gotten smaller. Like a let-down party balloon. Telltale strands of hair stick to her cheeks with dried tears. Her face is creased and the lines around her eyes deep. She looks a hundred years old.

Ellen kisses her on the cheek. She already knows how Kathy takes her coffee, having watched in horror as she spooned sugar into something already laden with calories.

"A double cappuccino coming right up with extra marshmallows," she says. "I'll be as quick as I can."

* * *

Silas is alone in the coffee bar, holding a half-empty Styrofoam cup. An hour back, drunks stumbled by, arms slung over shoulders, laughing and singing. How could they be so happy when a man might be dying?

Ken had been the bearer of bad news, bursting into their room as Silas turned off the lights to try for sleep.

"We're in deep shit," he said, hauling open his locker. "A kid died. Everything needs to go."

Silas jumped out of bed and rubbed his eyes. Bob appeared minutes later. And Howard and Deon. Together, they gathered different size boxes, bags, and tins and took the fire stairs to level five, where the surveillance cameras are shot.

Once there, they tossed contraband into darkness.

Someone had died. Or almost died. They couldn't be sure. Ken's face was white with fear, and Bob no longer strutted about like he owned the place. The only person acting as if he didn't care was Deon.

Afterward, Bob insisted they go to the chapel.

"We need to agree our stories," he said. "The cops will ask questions."

"What stories?" Ken had all but shrieked. "I had fuck all to do with this. I was helping. Letting you store your shitty drugs in my room."

It would have done no good for Silas to point out how Ken's room is also his room. That he might be in trouble too. He stayed silent as three grown men argued over who would say what. A man had collapsed and was hooked up to machines. He might die. Silas pictured Joey. In a filthy motel room. Alone. Needing help. "One day away from the end," the detective in charge had told Nancy, wondering out loud what kind of parents let that happen to their kids.

And now, as he nurses cold coffee, all the lights are turned down low and "White Christmas" is on pause. The only noise comes from the engines below, growling on like some great beast trapped in the ship's belly. A low throaty sound that quakes the floorboards and rattles tables.

He thought of calling Rose, but she'd only cuss and hang up.

The sun will soon rise, and piped music will play once more. Bells will jingle. Herald angels will sing. Guys will emerge, blinking into another day at sea, not knowing that someone is fighting for his life.

Because of what Silas let happen.

* * *

"He's awake."

Ellen rolls over in bed. For a minute, she's back at home, and listening for the sound of familiar traffic or the coo of a rock dove demanding scraps of bread, and then she remembers where she is. And what happened.

"Patrick," Julia says. "He woke up."

She rubs her eyes. "Is he okay?"

"They think so."

Ellen forces her legs to move, and limps into the en suite. Her hair is a mess, her clothes wrinkled and rumpled. She didn't undress before climbing into bed, exhausted.

As she runs water, Julia waits in the doorway.

"He's confused," she says.

152

"About what happened?"

"About everything."

Ellen's heart hammers a little faster. "But he's out of danger?"

"The nurse said it's perfectly normal when you've been out cold. The body has this way of taking you some place safe, where you come to no harm, and when you jump back into the here and now, it can be a shock."

"How's Kathy?"

Julia turns away, as if making sure Ellen can't see how hard she's trying to keep it together.

"On cloud nine," she says in a voice that wavers on the edge of tears. "She's refusing to let him do a thing for himself. They're about ready to come to blows."

Her breath catches between a sob and laughter. Ellen is happy.

"So he's not *that* confused," she says, dabbing at her own eyes. "He remembers what she's like."

* * *

The medical center vending machine whirs into life, and Julia leans against the wall, arms crossed. Patrick's collapse took it out of her. For the first time, she isn't her usual happy-go-lucky self.

"I want to shake him," she says. "He's fifty-one and acting like a rutting teenager. Whatever happened to dignity?"

Ellen rarely risks speaking when Julia picks a position. Stubborn doesn't come close. They can't afford another fight.

"You think he took drugs?" she says.

Julia sighs and takes a sip of coffee. "He told the nurse it must be some kind of allergy."

"And she believed him? Shouldn't someone report this?"

"If he won't talk, technically there's no crime."

"This isn't a parking ticket," Ellen says. "Someone's selling poison."

Julia runs a hand through her hair. "Right now, I need a hot shower and breakfast, then a strong mimosa by the pool."

More than anything, Ellen wants to ask for one of her pills, but given they just talked about someone almost dying of a drugs overdose, now isn't the moment. Julia's phone buzzes with a text.

She glances at it, narrows her eyes, and drops it into her purse. "Some schmuck trying to sell me a funeral plot," she says.

Ellen leaves it a beat. "I used to get those. Right after my diagnosis."

She all but hears the shutters slam.

"What's that supposed to mean?" Julia says.

"Nothing. Those people know how to pick their moment."

Julia heaves a sigh and turns around. Her eyes search Ellen's face. "Forgive me for losing my cool. It's not every day a man collapses and almost dies in front of me."

This is pointless, Ellen thinks. When Julia gets defensive, there's no way back. She needs to change the subject. Fast.

"There's a cake decorating master class," she says. "I thought we could go."

Julia shakes her head. "Kathy needs me. By now, the poor woman has probably decided whatever crap Patrick took is all her fault."

The ship doctor appears at the waiting room door. "Would you two ladies mind taking this someplace else? I have a sick man to take care of, and you're adding to his distress."

Julia rallies to fight back, but Ellen grabs her elbow.

"I can't drink this vending machine sludge," she says. "Let's go find you that hot shower."

*　*　*

Howard calls a meeting. Everyone attends. He starts by standing very still and very quiet, staring at the floor. He lifts his head slowly and scans the crew office.

"A guest almost died," he says. "And New York has been on the phone. They want information."

He scratches at his chin. The room stays silent. He paces.

"This isn't a joke, people. Our guests pay good money to be kept safe." He faces the group before taking a deep breath. "Who knows how drugs got onto this ship?"

No one speaks. No one so much as twitches.

"Somebody has to know." Howard manages a slight shrug. "One of you has information that can help us understand what happened. I've had to inform the authorities."

Bob has been standing behind him, arms folded, doing his best the-almighty-wouldn't-like-this expression, and nodding at each sage word. Now, he steps forward.

"I'll be taking confession as usual this morning, between ten and eleven. If anyone does wish to contribute anonymous information, that might be an opportune moment."

Silas can barely believe their polished double act. A few hours ago, they were frantic and fighting like cats in a sack. There had been a set-to. He'd yelled at Bob. Punches were thrown.

"Meeting over," Howard says. "Let's get back to work."

Silas leaves, feeling he's the only one who's done anything wrong. He should have raised his hand and told everyone what happened. By saying nothing, he became a part of the problem. How many of Joey's friends knew what was going on back then? How many of them came to the apartment, and sat in their living room, chatting with Nancy as if butter wouldn't melt? If only they'd have spoken up. He's been stupid. How could he let himself get involved when there was so much to lose? The guy didn't die, but the cops got involved, and the incident will almost surely make local news channels. If word reaches Joey, when Silas turns up at his door, what exactly can he say? That he knew nothing? That he wasn't involved?

He'll go to hell for adding one lie onto another.

* * *

Ellen watches as Julia mashes a Danish into pieces, using the tip of a butter knife spread with jelly. Her teeth, stained by black coffee, are clenched.

"We should arrange to have our things moved to that medical center,"

Julia says, with a heavy sigh. Her eyes are dull, her voice flat. "I've spent more time there than sitting by the pool."

"Is this what our lives have become?" Ellen tries to make light. "A succession of hospital beds?"

Julia squeezes a caramel into her coffee. She's hitting the sugar big time.

"Tell me to mind my own business," Ellen says. "But is everything okay with you?"

Julia turns to face her. "I didn't sleep so well."

"I'm always tired," Ellen says. "Welcome to the club."

Julia runs the tip of her finger around the edge of her coffee cup. "Was I a good mother?"

The question lands out of the blue.

"You need to ask?" Ellen says. "You fought to get Daniel into a great school. Literally. The head teacher got a black eye."

"But was I a *good* mother?" she persists. "I mean, could you tell, as he grew up, that I loved him?"

Ellen thought for a moment.

"Yes," she says, sure of her answer. "You took him places and listened to what he had to say."

"Did I love Daniel, though? Was I doing that because it's what a mother is supposed to do?"

"I always thought you were a great mother," Ellen says, and Julia seems satisfied.

"I loved him all the time he was growing up. I still love him. When he was little, he got upset if he couldn't get stuff to work. And I would hold him, and he calmed right down."

Ellen swallows. "Are you sure everything is okay?"

Julia shakes her head, and rubs the back of her hand across her eyes. "If anything happens to me, promise you'll keep an eye out for Daniel. He acts like he's all grown up, but he isn't."

* * *

156

Silas is in the bathroom. An overhead light casts long shadows, bouncing off the soap-spattered mirror. Exhaustion clings to the inside of his eyelids like wet tissue paper, and his skin reeks like he spent the night in a dirty dive bar. A cool breeze plays across his skin, causing him to shiver.

Ken appears in the doorway.

"Hey, pal. You look like shit," he says.

"Thanks." Silas rubs his face and studies his reflection. A large bruise, the shape of a fist, blooms along one cheek.

"You're not planning on saying anything to anyone?" Ken says and Silas turns away.

"I figured it might be better not to associate myself."

"Good move." Ken pauses. "But you know, if you did happen to consider helping Howard's investigation, you could suggest someone look into whatever Deon is up to."

A spark of fear jumps through Silas. "What are you suggesting?"

"The kid has form," Ken says. "And Bob reckons he's becoming a liability."

Silas chokes back a laugh. "What do you mean, *Bob reckons?*"

Ken sighs. "All right. Father Bob is a little concerned."

"Concerned?" Silas repeats. "Is that why the fucker punched me?"

Ken steps a little closer, his voice still friendly. "It's a mess, but we can fix it."

"And this fix…I guess it involves me?"

"Chances are they'll send DEA guys to meet the ship in Miami, and we'll all get interviewed."

Silas startles. He's allowed just six hours to get the Boca Raton bus to where Joey is staying with in-laws. He can't waste one minute talking to cops.

"I see how this looks, Silas," Ken continues. "I only agreed to look after the stuff if nobody else got involved, and Bob swore he only sold pills."

Silas swallows. "So you knew he was selling some kind of drugs?"

Ken shrugs his shoulders. "It's not like any of us are perfect."

"And the other night, when you told me to take that package for Deon. Was that drugs?"

He nods.

"So you turned me into your mule."

Ken raises his palms, and takes a step back. "That's a harsh way of putting it. But yeah, I guess you could say I put you in a difficult situation."

Silas glares. "Get the fuck out of my face."

* * *

Julia and Ellen persuade Kathy to take a break from nursing her increasingly grumpy brother for an afternoon by the pool. The sky is a deep, vibrant blue, and the sun shines brightly.

"How is he?" Julia says.

Kathy's shoulders slump. "Better, but he wants to sleep all the time."

Ellen pats her knee. "That'll change. You'll see. He'll be back to grouching at you for most everything soon enough."

"Did you manage to get through to your folks?" Julia says, and Kathy's face colors.

"It's a bad time to call. They go grocery shopping around now. I'll try later."

"You could send them a text message. Or an email. They have a right to know, surely."

"I'll call tonight." Kathy voice turns nasal and screechy. "It's not like Patty is in any immediate danger. Why worry them?"

Ellen interrupts. "Did the doctor say when he might be getting out?"

"Later this afternoon. Perhaps. Maybe tomorrow morning." Kathy looks at the ground. "For now, he's fine where he is."

A server passes, and Julia orders iced tea.

"Patty won't tell me where he got the drugs," Kathy says. "Perhaps if one of you speaks to him?"

Ellen shakes her head. "What makes you think he'll tell one of us?"

She presses her fingers to her lips. "I just want to find out who did this. They're probably selling the same crap to all these beautiful young men, and someone could die."

Ellen scans rows of lounge chairs, each tied to its neighbor with a rope that loops back and forth, each with its own colorful umbrella. Kathy sniffs and hastily wipes away a tear, before taking a huge breath and puffing out her cheeks.

"The man who sold Patty that crap might be sitting right over there, watching us and laughing. It could even be one of the crew."

Ellen bites her lip. She has a way-in to the crew and could ask Silas if he's heard anything.

"Let the cruise company take care of things," she says, as Julia snuffles and grunts.

"Is she asleep?" Kathy looks around. "In the middle of all this?"

Ellen watches her best friend sleeping. Sooner or later she needs to ask what Malinowski found when he carried out tests. And then there had been all that talk about Daniel? She fears more bad news.

The iced tea arrives and Julia sleeps on.

At last, Kathy relaxes and lies back to enjoy the sunshine, while Ellen tries yet again to get into her book. She barely manages a page before her eyes grow heavy and she drifts away to dreams.

* * *

Julia has spoken little since they got back from the pool. She spent forever in the bathroom, taking a shower, and now she's sitting on the edge of the bed, staring into nothing. Like something weighs heavy on her mind.

"Did you get through to Daniel?" Ellen tries to sound chipper. "How are they enjoying Hawaii?"

"What? Oh, yes…sure. They're having a whale of a time."

"If it's Patrick you're worried about. Don't be. The doctors say there's no lasting damage."

Julia shakes her head, still deep in thought. "I know."

Ellen comes to sit next to her friend. "Is there something else? Something you haven't told me?"

Julia jumps up to gather and fold clothes. "I'm frazzled, Ellen. It's been a long day. You think perhaps, tonight, we could simply luxuriate in our quarters?"

"Whatever you want." She leaves it a beat. "If something is bothering you, though, I'm here when you need to talk."

"Confabulation is the last thing on my mind."

"Okay," Ellen says. "If you say so."

Julia stops and straightens up, but doesn't turn around. "You know why I wanted to come on this sojourn with you?" she says. "Why I wanted to swim with dolphins?"

Ellen says nothing.

"I miss my old friend. The Ellen who didn't worry about what might have been every day. So you lost your husband? People lose their loved ones all the time."

This takes Ellen by surprise, and she swallows something that could be fury, or simply the ongoing pull of grief.

"That was cruel," she eventually manages to say, and hears how small she sounds. "Why would you say that?"

Julia comes to sit and reaches out a hand, and at first, Ellen resists, but she knows her friend isn't the sort to give up.

"I loved Otto too," Julia says. "How could anyone not? He was a benevolent man. When he left my life, I railed against the world too. I thought about how hard it hit you."

When the cops had delivered word that Otto was almost surely in the North Tower around the time the first plane hit, Ellen had been at home, calling around to most everyone, trying to track him down. Short of taking the subway to Midtown, there was nothing to do. And word was the trains had stopped running. The intercom sounded, and someone barked her name. She let them in, and as she listened for footsteps on the stairs, the world around her slowed. The air grew colder. She sensed bad news.

There had been two of them. A man and a woman. He flashed a prerecorded smile, like this was the hundredth home visited. She spoke quickly, asking too many questions, and not listening to the answers. Filling dead air.

Ellen stayed upbeat and offered them a drink. The woman refused. The man said water would be fine. Ellen brought three glasses anyway.

Otto was gone.

The man delivered the news, and when he stopped, the woman folded her arms and talked about how Ellen's husband likely died a hero, helping people get to safety. Saving lives.

Ellen nodded. It was a nice story. "You're certain that's what happened?"

"Things are sketchy," the man said. "But yeah. Sure. That's what happened."

After they offered their condolences and left, Ellen stood near the window. A bird flew past. She sat and cried, and then got ready for work.

"The day he passed, my friend died too," Julia says now.

Ellen regards her with scorn. "That's low. Even for you."

She sees how Julia's eyes narrow, like she wants to bite back.

"Eventually, you'll find a way to call the only person who can tell you what Otto was really doing in the tower on that day," Julia says. "Why spend all that cash finding out where she lives if you don't plan on doing something about it?"

In the New York Public Library, Ellen had logged onto one of the reading room computers and searched for Katharine Fitzgerald's home, zooming in on overhead photographs of the street where she lived, and printing out a map, a list of nearby stores, and restaurants. A direct train would take one hour. She'd imagined Katharine Fitzgerald walking a dog, going to work, and coming home, sitting in the nearby park with a book, or on the stoop with friends.

Her life went on. She didn't die.

Perhaps Katharine Fitzgerald had been one of these people her hero husband saved.

"I'm not going to do anything," Ellen says, but can't keep from glancing at her purse, where she keeps an address book "Maybe I'm waiting for something. Like a sign. Something to say it's okay to move on."

Julia leans forward. "That's not going to happen."

Ellen's hands fall to her lap. "I used to be ashamed of doubting my husband.

I'd get upset if anyone ever found out. That's the past. I don't feel ashamed at all. I don't feel anything." She looks to Julia. "What do you think of when you think of your husband?"

Julia sits back, her eyes grow distant. "I suppose I remember something he once said. Sometimes, I picture his face, or try to remember the words to a song he may have sung for me. He had such a lovely voice. I never want to forget him."

Ellen can hold back no longer. "We shouldn't have secrets."

"Agreed." Julia squeezes her hand. "You know my every deepest, darkest moments of shame."

"So why don't you want me to know what Malinowski found?"

Julia freezes.

Chapter Seventeen

Silas sits on the floor, and polishes his one good pair of shoes with a rag and cotton cloth, working swiftly, moving smoothly but methodically, not stopping or slowing. Ken has been reading a book for almost half an hour. Its gaudy cover shows a man with a long red coat and flowing blond hair, one arm outstretched as if trying to capture the reader. Now he closes it with a satisfied sigh and sets it on the nightstand, his gaze stealing over Silas.

"Very well," he says. "I'll bite. What's her name? I assume it's a her?"

The last thing Silas wants to do is talk about Ellen. He doesn't want to talk at all, because that would make Ken into a friend, and he's not in the market for friends who lie to people and sell drugs.

"Can't a guy take some care over his appearance?" Silas says, gathering his shoe brush and polish and carrying them over to his locker.

Ken purses his lips. "If you don't want to talk, that's fine with me. I was just making conversation. If I've said or done something wrong…"

Silas's hand tightens on the handle of his locker, willing his voice to stay even. "You haven't upset me. I'm fine."

"Right you are." Ken tries for a smile. "We oldies need to stick together."

It's an innocent enough remark, and yet it causes bile to sour in Silas's stomach. That he has anything in common with this sorry excuse for a man. Back on his bed, Silas laces up one shoe, and then the other, and as he goes to stand, the floor tilts.

"Storm," Ken says, as the room rights itself. "Happens at this time of year."

Silas takes a long breath, and slowly lets it out.

"Only lasts a few hours, unless it's got a temper. My advice is to stay put." Ken winks, and the dark circles around his eyes crinkle. "You'll have to keep your lady love waiting a while longer."

A voice sputters from a speaker overhead.

"Attention please. This is your captain with an important announcement. We are approaching rough seas. There is no immediate danger to our passengers or the ship, and no reason to be alarmed."

The room tilts again. This time violently, and Ken's book flies from his hand. Silas closes his eyes and tries to think past the pounding dread.

"If it gets bad, they'll reroute us," Ken says. "Bimini is supposed to be nice this time of year."

Silas rolls onto his side, but can't seem to find a comfortable position. "Where's that?"

"The Bahamas. We get to spend Christmas Day on the beach."

They can't do that, Silas thinks. *Surely*. This ship is built to weather storms.

"Looks like your family reunion will have to wait awhile," Ken says, retrieving his book and going back to reading.

* * *

When Ellen learned she had cancer, one person stayed by her side throughout. Julia was there until the last subway of the night, and they whiled away sticky summer afternoons playing canasta. When the pain became too much, Julia slept on the couch to be on hand no matter when. She ran towels under a cold tap, and wiped Ellen's brow. She sat by her side, recalling stories long forgotten, helping her through the darkest nights and days. Julia was there for every medical procedure—ultrasound exams, CT scans, PET scans, enzyme and hormone assays, biopsies to probe suspicious tissue. She was there when Ellen had her first session of chemotherapy, holding her hand as the needle was inserted into Ellen's arm, and the drugs flowed into her body. She was there when, six sessions in, Ellen's hair dropped out, leaving a pale, newly shorn scalp.

Ten minutes earlier, on the ship, Julia's cell had rung. She picked it up, glanced at the screen, and something in her eyes caused Ellen to worry.

"Who was that?" she said.

"Nobody."

"Wrong number?"

"I guess."

"But you didn't pick up, so how can you know?"

"I just do."

Ellen could push harder, but she senses Julia has locked her out. She needs to take a different approach.

"I sometimes think how lucky I was to get cancer," Ellen says.

Julia stops reading *Vogue*. "How do you figure that?"

"Surveillance. It's like insurance. Every few months I get scans and blood tests. If anything tries to take me down again, I'll know about it."

Julia nods and goes back to reading.

"When I was sick," Ellen says, "all I wanted was someone to tell me everything would be fine. Ideally, someone who knew what they were talking about. Someone who'd been through it."

Julia sets down the magazine. "Malinowski wants a CT scan."

Ellen swallows and tries to keep her voice level. "They inject you with a dye. It's weird. I thought I maybe wet myself."

"I already had a blood test. That means he must know something is wrong."

"He's one of the best," Ellen says. "And it's not like you're sick. If there's anything going on, it's fixable."

"I'm not afraid of cancer," Julia says. "I'm afraid of the whole horrible process. The pain. The medical bills. Losing all my hair and my appetite. People coming to visit me in hospital and not knowing what to say. I don't want to be 'that woman who got cancer.'"

Ellen rolls over so she's facing her friend. "I'll be here. I promise."

"My guardian angel, huh?" Julia snorts.

"Remember when I had the first symptoms, but no one got how it was cancer? And then the pain got so bad? You told me it would get better."

"I was only trying to—"

"When I said I was finished, you promised I wasn't. That I would be back."

Julia sits straighter. "That's what friends do. They make you believe in miracles."

"But you were right. I came back."

Julia picks up her magazine once more. "And perhaps I will, too, but you need to accept not everyone deals with this the same."

Ellen decides to take a risk. Julia has so many friends. Her diary is constantly full. But how many know she could be sick?

"Who did you tell? Daniel?"

"He has enough on his plate without worrying over me."

"Anyone from our lunch club?"

Julia stays quiet.

"Denial isn't going to fix a thing," Ellen says.

"That's not what's going on here."

"I think you don't want to worry other people. You want to show the world you are okay. But I see through the shield."

"You're wrong." Julia's lips barely move. She reaches for a glass of water, and takes a sip, closing her eyes as she swallows. "Promise me you'll stay out of this. It's not you I don't trust. It's me. I'm not about to start sharing my feelings with everyone." Julia gets up and goes over to the bathroom. "We're on vacation. This isn't the real world. I would rather not think about being sick. Not yet."

The room lurches, and Julia stumbles, throwing out her hands to grab for the bathroom door jamb. A glass of water falls to the floor, soaking the carpet. A speaker set into the ceiling crackles into life. It's the captain, warning of a storm. At once, Julia's cell lights up.

"It's probably Kathy," she says. "Let her go to voicemail."

Ellen picks up the phone. "What if Patrick got sick again?"

She puts Kathy on speaker, while Julia leans on the bathroom door jamb, her face ghostly pale.

"I'm scared." Kathy sounds like a little girl. "I never learned how to swim, and I don't want to die."

Julia waves for the phone, but Ellen shakes her head. "Kathy. Listen to me. No one will die, and there is nothing to fear."

Rain lashes their tiny window, and the ship jerks. Kathy shrieks.

"Please come and sit with me. I can't be on my own."

Ellen hangs up and sighs. "Do we toss a coin for which one of us goes?"

* * *

The storm doesn't stay small for long. Far below, turbines howl. All around, lamp lights flicker, their shades rattling. Walls and floors creak and groan.

Silas watches Ken's face for any hint of worry.

"I see you staring," Ken says without looking up from his book. "Go find someone to play cards."

Silas grabs his phone and opens it. Not a single bar.

"They turn off the repeaters," Ken says. "Saves on power. You need to get above deck to make a call."

Out in the hallway, guys from other cabins sit on the floor, drinking beer, laughing, and telling stories. Silas picks his way through, taking an emergency staircase as far as the observation gallery, where giant windows offer vistas of a raging ocean. The sky is a ghostly shade of gray, and lightning forks. Far away, then closer. He opens a door and steps outside, finding the air surprisingly warm. For a moment, the universe is simple, a sliver of perfection that includes everything he cares about, and Silas holds out both arms, letting the wind lift him. A sudden clap of thunder breaks the dream.

"Sir, you need to hang back from there," a lone voice calls. "This area is closed."

A guy in a yellow jacket guides him inside, then locks the doors. The ship shudders, knocking Silas from his feet and throwing him against a wall. He grits his teeth as another violent shudder travels through the ship.

"There was an announcement." A deckhand with a bullhorn struggles to make himself heard. "Go to your room."

As Silas heads to the stairs, the guy yells after him, and he turns to see he's holding a brown envelope. The savings he didn't dare risk leaving behind.

"Dude," he says. "You dropped this."

The Atrium is deserted. Decorations that once sparkled, lie scattered and broken. Spikes of glass glint, like broken mirror shards. Silken streamers curl outward, torn from their fastening points. A tall pine tree lurches, scattering needles. Silas pulls out his cell, but still there's no signal. Though who could he call? Rose would be angry and tell him it was his own stupid fault for taking the job, and then ask if she's mentioned in his will. Ellen, on the other hand... After what happened on Nassau, she's likely terrified.

He follows a maze of corridors, lined by doors, each tightly shut. Each marked with a number in black, with a small viewing panel set into the frame. The corridors are narrow, less than three feet wide, and the walls close in. Why are there no signs? He's never been claustrophobic. Even so, Silas walks faster. Is this a good idea? Turning up unannounced. If Ellen asks why he's there, he'll make up some story about being told to check on all guests.

His throat stings with acid from an ill-advised dinner of fried chicken. A rotten sour tang causes a sticky mouth. Silas unwraps a roll of Tums, running his finger along the edge of the paper, and popping one in his mouth. The minty flavor coats his tongue, and the lingering burn of stomach-turning acid recedes. His throat still burns, and he coughs to clear his voice.

Silas pulls his jacket close and hurries, not sure why he's in such a rush.

* * *

Ellen lies back on a pile of pillows, her cheeks flushed, and her hair mussed. She stretches until every vertebrae pops, and spritzes perfume. The scent of rose, bergamot, and patchouli fills the room, and despite what sounds like the most awful storm, she relaxes. For the first time in days without one of Malinowski's pills.

Julia messaged to say Kathy had worked herself up into a state, convinced that, handsome as he might be, the captain wasn't telling anyone the full story, and they'd be lucky to survive the night. She'd agreed to stay over.

Kathy wanted to watch old movies and paint each other's toenails.

Ellen stretches with a wince and rolls onto her hip. She can't remember when she last took quality time to just lie around. Her New York life was all double shifts and pushing through stinking crowds to catch trains. Some days, she didn't see her apartment in daylight.

She's at the age where things should slow down.

Except that's not what she wants.

When she gets home, she'll make calls. Lots of people go to college late in life. It's a thing. She'll sign up for a photography course. This is a dream she never put on her bucket list, for fear it would be too much to ask. And sure, she might never get to see her work in the *New York Times*, but a true labor of love would give each day fresh purpose.

The room shudders, and her stomach rolls.

What if she never makes it home?

Determined to relax, Ellen pours herself a huge gin and reaches for the TV remote.

* * *

Silas takes one breath, then another, and another. Now he knows how a panic attack feels, he can cope. Still, his pulse jumps into his throat.

Breathe.

In and out.

In and out.

He can do this. He should go back below deck. Who turns up unannounced during a storm?

Breathe.

Take your time.

In and out.

In and out.

A cool, quiet breeze brushes past his face. Disoriented, he looks up into heavy clouds breaking apart. But how can that be? He rests his forehead against Ellen's door, and his eyes refuse to focus, as the patterned carpet swims.

He blinks rapidly.

His eyes are dry and sore.

The clouds, they open and close, they part here, and fray there, they peel, they break apart, they scatter and fly.

He breathes.

In and out.

Silas bends over, his hands on his knees, and sucks in a long breath.

Wisps of cloud dance and dart, sparkling in sudden sunlight.

The air is rich, fresh and clean. He feels light and happy.

In and out.

In and out.

"Yes," he says to no one. "I'm ready."

The door handle is cold in his palms. And then, his chest tightens. And he bangs on the door.

Take it easy, Silas. You could scare her. Knock once. Politely.

But a sharp spasm below his rib cage insists he try again.

A muffled voice calls. "I didn't order room service."

"It's Silas."

In and out.

In and out.

The click of a lock. Ellen stands before him. In a silky robe. Her expression twists, and she looks first at his feet, and then at his face.

A dull pain radiates from the middle of his chest and along one arm.

In and out.

In and out.

She says his name in a strange voice, and he presses his fingertips into the cool metal of the door frame, and when he runs a hand over his hair, finds it wet.

Like he ran here in the rain.

But how could that be?

Ellen is speaking, but the *thud-thud-thud* in his head drowns out words. The pressure spreads as his knees buckle, and the floor tilts first to one side, then to the other, and the distance between here and the sofa shrinks, and his tongue flaps like damp cardboard, and a bead of sweat trickles down his forehead, stinging his left eye.

His hands refuse to help, hanging stiff and useless, glued to his sides.

In and out.

In and out.

He's in a movie theater, and the lights dim as the main feature starts. Silas paid extra for good seats up front, and Nancy has on her new coat. An astrakhan that passes for real. Her hair is up, exposing a slender neck. Jocks stare, bewitched by her beauty.

Why is she wasting her time with that putz?

What's he got that we don't?

Silas claws for the bed, but it moves away, and the pounding in his ears blasts his brain. The room spins and roars, turning over and over, and he screws his eyes shut.

He's scared.

Where are the clouds?

In and out.

In and out.

Joey is six, and in tears because nobody came to his party. Nancy turned it into the best day. A cake baked and decorated with candles he blew out first time. At bedtime, Joey whispered how much he loved his mommy. Silas made do with a high-five.

Her face appears, filling his vision, and all he wants is to once more look into her eyes, those dark, beautiful eyes that promised a life of simple pleasures and quiet love.

Oh, my angel. Tell me what to do. How I've missed you.

Something warm and wet spreads down one leg.

In and out.

But he doesn't care.

He's no longer here.

In and out.

A world fades, going out of focus, out of tune like stations on the family radiogram. His father turns the dial, explaining how the voices come from London, Moscow, or Peking.

Home alone, Silas steals into the room and turns on the power, listening for those faraway voices. But then his folks get back early, and Father is mad, and Silas goes to bed without supper.

A woman calls his name. The voice isn't Nancy's.

Before he can pick out who it might be, the picture around fades to the most fabulous shade of yellow.

Sunshine on a rainy day.

A title card appears on the movie theater screen.

The End.

1998 - Part II

"He blames me," Silas said. "Joey thinks the rehab thing was all my doing."

Nancy clicked her tongue. "The only person blaming you goes by the name of Silas Elijah French. Give yourself a break, honey. We have our boy back."

He peered through the doorway to where Joey dozed on the sofa, his feet in thick woolen socks, sticking out from under a red fleece blanket pulled up around his face. How peaceful he appeared.

"Do we have the celebration tonight?" Nancy said. "You don't think it's been a big enough day already?"

Silas kissed the top of her head, breathing in the honey-sweet smell of her shampoo. "Let's stick to our plans."

Joey's eyes opened a slit as Nancy placed a cake on a low table.

"What's all this?" He rubbed sleep from his eyes.

"It's our way of celebrating all your hard work," Nancy said, crouching to blow out the candles and slice the cake. She handed him a blue and white china plate.

Joey sat up, pushing away the red blanket. "I did nothing."

"Exactly," she said. "You stayed clean. You did nothing. And now you're cured."

His smile became lopsided. "One day at a time, Ma, you know how it goes."

Silas came to sit next to him. "I talked to your grandfather, and there's a job for you at the warehouse."

Joey hesitated. "Oh, right, cool."

"It's not the most exciting work, but it pays the way, and you get to hang out with a fine bunch of men."

"I wanted to talk to you guys about that," Joey said. "I figured tomorrow?"

Nancy nodded, but Silas plowed on. He should have known better. Always charging at life like a bull at a gate. "Talk to us now, son. No point putting it off."

Joey sighed, and a tic fluttered in his right eye. He explained how in rehab they helped him get back on his feet and apply for jobs. Nancy glanced at Silas, and a nod of her head suggested hearing their kid out.

"I already got an interview," he said.

"That's great," she said. "Where?"

"In Denver." Neither parent spoke. "Working for United."

"United what?" Silas tried his best to sound upbeat.

"United, the airline."

A short silence took hold, and then Nancy spoke. "You'd have to move to live in Denver?"

"If I even get the job. The girl who interviewed me said I could be stationed anywhere. New York, LA, Toronto. Maybe even Europe."

"What kind of job are we talking about?" Silas said.

"Airline steward. Best way to see the world."

Silas looked first at Nancy, and then at the cake. The frosting was soft and smooth, his pretty wife's handiwork. She'd made it that morning, full of hope and joy, and now her eyes were clouded by disappointment.

"You want to serve coffee to asshole businessmen?" he said.

Joey shook his head. "I want to build a life for myself. A sober life. You get that, right?"

Fear mixed with fury rose through Silas. "It's a fag job."

Nancy placed a hand on his arm. Skin on skin. He tried to absorb her strength.

"We need to support him," she said. "It's what we agreed. Drama isn't good for nobody."

"The boy wants to travel half way across the country to interview for a job he isn't suited to do."

"Why?" Joey said. "Why am I not suited to work for United?"

"You're not a faggot, for one thing," Silas snapped. "And for another, your home is here with us, not with some prancing fairies in Denver."

The world rolled into slow motion. Nancy looked at Silas, and the way she acted made him think she was scared. Like she knew something, and wished she'd found a way to tell him sooner.

Joey dropped his gaze, staring only at the floor. "I'm gay. I like men."

Had Silas always known? Perhaps. Had he hoped he was wrong? Of course. Did he love Joey any the less? No.

"You're sure about that?" Silas said.

Joey's eyes were wet with tears, but hope brimmed as they rose to meet with his father's gaze. "I've always known."

Silas pulled him close. He needed his kid to understand how this didn't make him any different, any less loved, any less needed. Nancy sat still. Like she couldn't work out her next move. Was she surprised by how easily her husband took the news?

She clapped her hands. "We should have a second slice of this cake."

"I love you both," Joey managed, before tears took over once more.

Silas saw how Nancy couldn't reach out to touch her son. Her gay son.

"You need to be careful, Joey," he said, pulling him as close as he could. "There's so much hate out there. People who don't understand. And what if you get AIDS?"

Joey jerked away. All air was sucked from the room. A family of three fell apart. Right there. Right then.

"What if I get AIDS?" Joey sounded both shocked and pissed. "That's your answer? I tell you something I spent years building up to, and you say I'm gonna die of AIDS?"

"You are taking precautions?" From what little Silas knew, there were ways to reduce the risk of transmission.

"Are you?" Joey spat back.

"I don't need to—"

"No." Joey got to his feet. "Because you're normal."

"Because I don't sleep around," Silas called after him.

That came out wrong. He had meant to say because he had Nancy, and he loved Nancy, and wanted no one else. Joey still had to find the right guy.

A bedroom door slammed.

Chapter Eighteen

Ellen waits in a room that doubles as storage space for cleaning materials, with mops and brooms in one corner, a pile of dirty rags in the other. A small round window is half open, but fails to clear the stench of bleach and ammonia. She's still not sure she understands what happened. One minute, she was pouring herself a drink. The next, Silas collapsed into her arms, dragging himself across the floor, mumbling something about how he'd always love her, and then his eyes closed.

He isn't dead. That much she knows, but she's seen two heart attacks at the East Side Diner, and knows he had more than some sort of funny turn.

The door opens, and she tries to stand, but her knees are weak, and she rests her hand on a rickety table. It's a girl from guest relations, holding a white tray with a cup of water, a bowl of crackers, and an orange. She sets it down, sniffs, and pushes the window wider.

"Is there any news?" Ellen says.

The girl looks at her strangely. "No news, ma'am. Howard is on his way."

Ellen has no idea who Howard might be. When something bad happens, people always use first names and speak like you've lost your mind. They smile too much, and without fail, say how you're to call them if you require anything. What she needs right now is to go back to her room.

"Who is Howard?" Ellen says.

"The entertainments director."

"Why do I need to talk to him? I'm not planning a soiree."

"He wanted to see you. Before the detective…"

The girl's expression comes out pained, and she backs quietly away, grinning once more as she closes the door. In theory, Ellen is waiting to be interviewed by a police officer, flown in from Miami to check that nothing untoward happened. She fancies herself a person of interest.

She sips at the water. It's warm and tastes of plastic. She nibbles a cracker, but it's stale. She tries to peel the orange, but gets stuck on the first section. Her head aches and her throat is sore from inhaling cleaning fluids. She pulls out her phone. No messages. It's been four hours since a helicopter thundered overhead, and they wheeled Silas from her room. She was asked to leave while somebody cleared up.

The door opens again, and this time it's Julia, and Ellen is pulled into a hug, breathing in a thankfully familiar perfume.

"They've sealed our cabin off like it's a murder scene," Julia says. "What happened?"

Ellen explains about how Silas collapsed, adding her heart attack theory. "They keep saying a detective wants to talk to me."

"What do they think you can tell them?"

"It's procedure when somebody suddenly collapses."

A man appears at the door. A brown blazer with leather arm patches hangs loosely around his shoulders. Mousy fawn hair, parted in the middle, dangles limply across his brow and over the rim of his ears.

"My, it's crowded in here," he says, before holding out his hand to Ellen and introducing himself as Howard.

Julia squares up to him. "Why is Crown Atlantic keeping my friend prisoner in a cleaning closet? I have friends in high places at some of the best city law firms. One word from me and this whole cruise company can be shut down."

Howard glances at Ellen, his eyes wide with worry.

"My friend doesn't know any city lawyers," she mutters. "But I do want to know why I'm still here."

Howard manages to stay upbeat. "I spoke to the detective in charge, and she's satisfied there are no suspicious circumstances. You're free to return to your cabin."

"No suspicious circumstances?" Julia starts, and then leans in to whisper.

"Did Santa Claus die?"

Howard blinks in surprise. "Nobody told you?"

Ellen's heart leaps. Silas was awake when they wheeled him from her room. He even held up his thumb to signal things were fine.

"They say he died for three whole minutes," Howard says. "No pulse, no heartbeat. Nothing."

Ellen turns to the tiny porthole window. "But he's okay now?"

"So I'm informed. You think he saw the bright lights and a long, white tunnel? People say that's what happens."

"Was it a heart attack?"

"No, it was…let me see…" He pulls a sheet of paper from the pocket of his blazer. "Stress-induced anaphylactic shock."

Julia takes over. "I thought anaphylactic shock was an allergic reaction."

"I'm just repeating what head office told me."

There's an awkward silence.

Ellen gathers her things, and heads for the door, but Howard steps into her path.

"This is my direct line," he says and hands over a Crown Atlantic business card. "Please call. Any time. Day or night. I've also written the Miami hospital number on the back."

"Thank you," Ellen says with what little civility she can manage.

Julia cuts in. "Don't kiss up to the guy for holding you prisoner. I'm almost certain he's violated three of your basic human rights."

Howard's face turns red. "I should make amends. We invite you to dine in a premium restaurant of your choice this evening. At no additional cost."

Ellen grunts thanks, and hurries Julia from the room and back to the elevator. It's only when the doors slide shut that either woman speaks.

"He's up to no good," Julia says. "Why else be so generous?"

"I've been locked in a closet waiting to be interrogated by the cops, and the only payoff is dinner," Ellen says. "It's hardly generous."

"You saw how he blushed. That's a man with things to hide."

* * *

When they get back to their cabin, the police tape is gone, and a maid is busy making the bed. Julia shrugs off a pink cardigan and Ellen looks around. Furniture has been moved. Faint oil-stained footprints lead to the bathroom door.

"I come back to clean," the maid says. "In one hour." She holds up a finger to indicate the time, but Ellen waves her away.

"No need," she says. "Tomorrow is fine."

After she's gone, Julia reaches in to the minibar and pours two large vodkas. "That was a bucket list experience right there," she says. "Get arrested on suspicion of murder."

Ellen winces. "I wasn't arrested, and Silas isn't dead."

"Try the hospital number that idiot gave you."

Ellen turns the business card over in her hands. She wants to call, but dreads hearing bad news. And if Silas is doing fine, what then? She can hardly run to Whole Foods to buy a bunch of grapes and go visiting.

"Maybe later," she says, and drops Howard's card on the low coffee table. "First I need to show you something."

She reaches into her purse, and pulls out a brown envelope. It's folded in two, and held together with Scotch Tape. One corner is torn.

"What's that?" Julia says, and when Ellen tips the contents onto the comforter, she gasps. "Holy cow! How much is there?"

"Two grand. Exactly. I counted it twice."

Julia comes to sit. "Where did you find it?"

"Near the door. Half under your divan." She wrinkles her nose. "You think it's stolen? Maybe I should turn it in to housekeeping."

Julia huffs to herself. "How many maids carry around a couple of thousand dollars in tatty brown envelopes?" She fingers a wad of bills. "What if this is drug money?"

Ellen's mouth is dry. She licks her lips and shakes her head. "So my second theory is it belongs to Silas. I found it next to where he collapsed."

Julia nods. "Okay, so now you *have to* call the hospital."

Ellen's stomach rolls. "You think he might have been involved with what happened to Patrick?"

A note slides under their door, and both women startle.

Ellen retrieves it.

"We're invited to dine with the captain," she says. "Tonight."

* * *

Ellen must have dozed off. It was light when she shut her eyes, and now it's dark. She stretches and swallows, reaching for a drink of water and sees Julia sitting in silence on the end of the bed.

"How long have you been there?" she says.

Julia shuffles uneasily. "I'm going to turn on the lights, and I want you to be totally honest with me. Can I get away with this hairstyle?"

She flips the switch and Ellen squints at the sudden brightness. And then she yelps. "You've gone gray. How long was I asleep?"

"The imbecilic girl in the salon was supposed to add to my highlights. I said one shade lighter, not make me look like someone dug up Barbara Bush."

She heads over to the mirror and studies the results.

"It's the initial surprise." Ellen throws back the sheets. "The style is lovely."

Julia lifts a few strands. "I could purchase a color and redeem it."

Designer-name shopping bags are lined up by the door.

"I see you've also been busy," Ellen says.

"The onboard mall is uncommonly well stocked, and the girl who works there told me she's not had a patron in days. She did me a deal." Julia pulls a shimmery, dusky pink gown from one of the bags. "I'm certain this is on sale at Bergdorf for three grand." From another, she produces a pale blue off-the-shoulder cocktail dress. "She said I can return anything I don't end up wearing, but honestly, darling, they're too magnolious to take back."

"What's in the other bag?"

Julia picks it up and hands it to Ellen. Inside, she finds a pair of black stovepipe trousers and a cream jersey dress.

"These are beautiful," she says. "But I can't afford designer prices. I lost my job, remember?"

"Call it an indulgence. My gift to you."

Ellen holds up the dress. It's stunning, cut just right and made of the softest material.

"I didn't pack any nice shoes," she says.

"We'll go back to the store. They had a wondrous range of black ballet pumps. You could channel your inner Audrey Hepburn."

Size ten feet had sentenced Ellen to boy's lace-ups at school, and overhanging toes in any sandal since. Most every large shoe comes designed for wider feet, turning footwear buying into a Cinderella search. On her first date with Otto, she squeezed herself into heels a size too small, and ended up damaging the nail bed of both big toes. She'd learned to live with it. Work demanded only sensible loafers, and she spends each summer in white canvas sneakers, adding colored laces for style.

"I did spot one place that might have shoes to fit," Julia says with a wink. "Get dressed. We're going shopping."

* * *

Ellen folds her arms. She ought to refuse to speak to Julia, but then she wouldn't get to say any of the mean, spiteful things running through her head.

"Fierce Queen?" she says, spitting the store name in her friend's face.

Reflections from inside make the place look more like a disco than a boutique where Ellen could *channel her inner Audrey Hepburn*. In the window, shimmering silver sequins cover a white bodice, a silver taffeta skirt, and a red sequined tutu.

Julia nibbles on a warm hazelnut cookie. "I anticipated this sort of establishment might hold footwear in your size."

"A drag queen store?"

Julia points. "You'll look fabulous in those sparkling heels."

"No," Ellen says, and turns to leave. "No fucking way."

"You need new shoes. You said so yourself."

"I'll go barefoot."

Julia gasps. "Surely, you have standards? This is all because you hate shopping for anything original."

Julia does have a point. Ellen detests buying clothes. In impractically small changing rooms, the unforgiving overhead lights turn her cellulite into a relief map of Nevada. The most recent time she'd tried to buy something new, there was nothing to choose from, if you didn't much care for grim blobby prints—and she absolutely didn't. Ellen preferred to browse undisturbed, but that was never the way, and she found herself constantly hustled into trying on things she knew drained what little color she had from her face, or emphasized parts of her body she wanted to hide. The short dresses were too short. The long dresses too long. Shop assistants were set on forcing her into the miserable, bland, elasticized waistbands they thought a woman of her age *ought* to be grateful to wear. She dreamed of being one of those kookier older ladies, who wowed their friends with Goodwill finds. But anything she lingers over, on packed racks in musty stores, has seen better days and usually comes with a distinct whiff of the dead.

"They sell Keds," Ellen says.

Julia's eyes light up. "That might work."

* * *

"We don't need to do this," Julia whispers as the elevator doors glide open on level six. Piano music drifts from a doorway where a uniformed waiter bows in welcome. He's nothing like the snooty guy at the French place.

"The only reason I agreed is because we have to eat," Ellen says. "And this way, I don't have to put up with three hours of Kathy's inane chatter."

Julia purses her lips. "I still think we should have been allowed to bestow invitations on our two closest onboard friends."

Ellen wants to say more, but being mean can wait. The waiter nods over at a table set out with champagne cocktails, before taking Julia's bolero and nodding politely at Ellen.

"I might have a night off the booze," Julia whispers as they go inside.

183

Ellen hoots, causing nearby heads to turn. "Who are you and what did you do with Julia Hoffman?"

The Captain's Dining Room resembles an upmarket clubhouse, with rich tapestries, a deep red carpet, and ornate furniture. Shining lamps cast a warm glow, and a door opens to the kitchen, wafting through the aroma of roasted meat. Five or six couples gather in pairs, each spaced from each other. Nobody acts like they know what to do next. That's great, Ellen thinks. We're not the only ones. She sips her cocktail. It tastes of rose, apricots, and honey.

"You sure about not drinking?" she says. "This is unbelievably good."

Julia grins. "Even the toughest livers need downtime."

"Do we sit wherever we want?" Ellen scans the long, dark-wood table. "Or is there a seating chart? Like at weddings?"

Julia shrugs. "I guess we wait over by the bar?"

The staff are still busy setting up for the evening, bustling, laying out glasses and bottles, arranging napkins and straws.

"Don't worry about us," Julia tells the bartender. "We arrive early for everything."

More diners appear. A tall, elderly man, with a tall, elderly woman, who smiles hello before heading straight to the table and staking claim to their spots.

"Now what?" Julia whispers. "If we sit anywhere but next to them, it's going to look rude. And what if they grabbed places right by the captain?"

She's made no secret of the fact she considers the handsome captain to be husband material. He's a well-built man with a full head of sandy hair, graying at the temples.

"Talk of the devil." Julia digs her nails into Ellen's arm. "If I start babbling, pinch me."

Captain John does the rounds, checking in with his guests. When he reaches them, Julia's nails dig deeper, and Ellen swallows a yelp.

"Good evening, ladies," he says with a flash of perfect teeth. "I hope you're enjoying your time with us."

"Yes, thank you." Julia's voice is sharp and nasal. "We're having the best time ever."

"Thank you for inviting us," Ellen adds. "It makes a change from an all-you-can-eat buffet."

He grins, and Julia gives another high-pitched squeak that Captain John either didn't hear, or has the manners to ignore.

"Why the hell did you say that?" Julia whispers, when he moves on. "Now he thinks we hate the ship."

"I don't see how."

"Leave all the talking to me. The last thing a man of his stature wants is to converse with someone who sounds like they should be supervising Brooklyn truck drivers."

Dinner is amazing. A delicate chicken salad, followed by turbot, smothered in a fragrant sauce of citrus and herbs that melts in the mouth. Ellen allows herself three huge glasses of wine; Julia sticks to water. In a lull before dessert, Julia's cell beeps. She smirks at the screen and pushes back her chair.

"You need the bathroom?" Ellen says. "I'll come too."

Julia places a hand on her arm. "Actually, I have to make a phone call."

"At this time of night?"

"Daniel made me promise to wish the kids happy holidays."

Ellen chuckles. "Sure thing, Grandma."

Julia curls her lip. "If you ever call me that in polite company again, I'll arrange for you to go missing."

* * *

The waiters are clearing the table, and Julia isn't back. She's been gone for over an hour. Ellen finds Captain John, and drinks in one more glass of his smile, while thanking him for a lovely evening, before heading to their room, her head distinctly woozy.

It takes an age to get her card into the cabin key slot. She solicits help from two guys dressed for what she assumes to be an underwear party. As she stumbles in, Julia startles.

GHOSTED

"You could have knocked," she says, setting down a tumbler of whiskey.

"I was worried. You've been gone forever." Ellen sees how her friend's eyes are red. She's been crying. "Is everything okay? Did something happen? Is it Daniel?"

Julia shakes her head, and signals for Ellen to sit, before pouring another drink and raising her own in a toast. Ellen does as she's told and perches on the edge of the sofa, sensing dreadful news.

"I'm sorry, Ellen," Julia says. "I'm so sorry."

"For what?"

"For lying to you. I didn't speak to Daniel. I called Malinowski. After we spoke about when you were sick, I got to thinking. He already has my test results, and I made him promise not to call before I got home, but in the end, I just had to know."

Ellen frowns. "What kind of tests are we talking about?"

Julia closes her eyes and takes a breath. "It's probably nothing. Almost certainly nothing, in fact. He actually said I should fly home early, but I've decided to finish up my vacation. It's the holiday season. Nobody will be at work. Labs shut down. Hospitals run on contract staff—"

"Tell me what he said." Ellen's mind hurries to every dark place. "I want to hear exactly what he said."

"He asked after you. I told him you were doing great. I mentioned the flare-up, and how tonight was different. You were like the old Ellen Gitelman."

Ellen wants to shake her friend and scream *tell me*.

Julia's eyes meet hers. "I have breast cancer. Stage two."

* * *

It's two a.m. Julia snores gently, and the room rocks in a reassuring way that Ellen has come to love. The distant sound of engines tells her all is well.

Except it isn't.

Her best friend is dying, and she can't do a thing to change that. Despite a morbid fear of flying, Ellen suggested they both get tickets home from Miami, but Julia refused. Ellen was secretly relieved.

"This might be my last vacation," Julia reasoned. "And if I go back now, I'm going to get the kind of surgeons too crappy at their job to afford time off for the holidays. The losers you see swearing they did all they could on *Nightline*."

"Every day counts with cancer. You know that."

"I plan on making each *minute* count," Julia said. "Please don't let's talk about this again until we get home. And not a word to anybody."

"By anybody, you mean Kathy?" Ellen had said, and Julia nodded.

"This would destroy her."

From the other side of their door now, Ellen hears voices. Happy voices. Guys on their way back from the underwear party. Guys without a care in the world.

"I don't ask you for much," she whispers into darkness. "But you think it might be possible to fix it so my friend gets well?"

When they were sixteen, Julia persuaded Ellen to visit a fortune teller. An elderly woman wearing a headscarf placed yellowed fingers on a crystal ball and declared she was to meet a man with blue eyes who would be her rock and safety. Otto had brown eyes. And look how that ended. Julia was lined up to marry a millionaire and die in her bed, aged fifty. People talk such shit.

Julia rolls over, causing the comforter to rustle.

"Stop worrying," she mumbles into her pillow. "Doctors don't always have it right. I plan on getting a second opinion."

Ellen presses her lips together, fighting tears, and Julia reaches out a hand.

"When we get to Miami, I need you to promise you'll do something for me."

Some time, some place

At first, Silas doesn't recognize the room, and then he spies a thrift store table. The guy had wanted twenty bucks, but Silas bargained him to ten. He'd have been willing to pay fifteen. And then the schmuck drove all the way from Brooklyn to their building and helped carry it up three lots of stairs.

Daffodils stand in a vase, so it must be spring.

Only yesterday, he shoveled snow from the sidewalk. His back still aches from when he slipped on ice. For a while, it looked like the end of his job, but Myron Schwartz would never see his son-in-law struggle to provide, and put him to work in a delivery truck. The favor didn't sit so well with the other drivers. They whispered each time he got something from his locker.

He calls Nancy's name, but she doesn't answer.

Is she out shopping? Or picking up dry cleaning?

The TV set is on, with no picture. A faint hum and hiss, tuned in wrong. Joey told him how he read if you carried on up past W-FTY, you could pick up signals from Mars. One time, Silas might paint his face green, and hide in Joey's room and leap out, saying "Nanu Nanu" like Mork from Ork.

He calls again, and this time, someone answers. A half-familiar voice that insists on calling him *Mr. French*. How come things got so dark? A while ago, kids were playing on the stoop.

He isn't sitting on a sofa. It's a bed. A hospital bed.

And then his chest hurts. Did he have another accident? He can't afford to quit working for Schwartz. Not yet. Especially if they're ever going to

SOME TIME, SOME PLACE

make good on a promise to buy a lodge in the Catskills.

He chuckles to himself. It's great to have dreams.

"Mr. French." He can't place the voice. "Can you hear me?"

Obviously, I hear you. You don't see how I react? Are you slow? Like Ernie's boy, who got starved of oxygen at birth? He grew into a decent kid.

"Squeeze my hand."

Nancy's happy expression fills the room with light, and she asks him to dance, and he remembers the night he scored tickets for Sinatra at Madison Square Garden. He'd saved money, and kept the concert secret, telling her to wear something nice, and meet him on the corner of 31st and 7th.

Afterward, they ate at Delmonico's. He thought the lobster greasy and dry.

He squeezes the hand placed in his.

"I love you," he says. "I always will."

Chapter Nineteen

Silas watches bleary-eyed, as a bald-headed man in a brown suit drags a hospital chair to the side of his bed, takes out a notepad, and licks the end of a pencil. His breath smells of cheap coffee and peppermint.

A doctor had relayed highlights of what happened to get him here, and a nurse colored in around the lines. Silas collapsed onboard the MS Viking. A *friend* called for help, and a decision was made to transport him to the mainland. The mainland being Miami. He arrived by helicopter. That must have been a kicker. As a boy, Silas always daydreamed of flying in one. Or rather, he daydreamed of being the dude flying the helicopter, and begged his folks to let him join the air force. They finally said yes, but flat feet failed his medical.

The cheap coffee and peppermint guy explains how he's a detective, and Silas tenses.

"Did I do something wrong?" he says.

The guy writes something on his notepad. "Standard procedure."

"You interview everyone who has a heart attack?"

"We interview everyone who arrives here without paperwork."

Silas should point out that, while fighting for his life, the last thing on his mind was to scoot back to his room and collect his travel documents. And then guesses that's not going to endear him to an already-pissed cop.

"How long you worked for the cruise company?"

"Almost a week."

That scores a raised eyebrow. Like the guy thinks he hit pay dirt, and much as Silas has disguised himself as a sixty-eight-year-old native New

Yorker, in truth, he's an illegal.

"What was the nature of your employ?"

"I dressed up as Santa Claus."

The detective stops writing and finally cracks a smile. "For real?" he says. "And you fell down in the presence of kids?"

Silas suspects nothing would give the cop greater pleasure than hearing how Father Christmas clutched his chest, and hit the deck in front of a roomful of children, who screamed and wailed and begged to be let out.

"I was checking on a friend," Silas says. "There was a storm."

"And you weren't feeling well?"

"I felt fine."

The detective writes that down. "And was it the storm you refer to that led to your collapse, or something else, sir?"

Silas doesn't care for this guy, but he can't just get up and leave.

"I was fine," he says. "I took a couple of steps and I just went down."

A hard-faced woman shows up at the door, and signals to the cop that she needs to talk. They whisper together, and Silas doesn't get what he did wrong. And then he remembers the money. They'll want to know why he was carrying around two grand in cash.

The bald guy returns. "We got a copy of your documentation. Problem lies with next of kin."

Silas jerks to attention. "Rose sleeps late. Keep trying."

"Miss Schwartz already vouched for you, but she lives in New York. It's not like the hospital can put you in a cab home. Your other contact is right here in Florida."

Silas's eyes go to the clock on the wall. Early afternoon. He breathes deeply and collects himself. He always listed Joey as a contact, in case, one day, the worst happened. Not because he ever thought he might need his help.

"Did my kid pick up when you called?" he says.

The detective folds away his ring-bound notepad, signaling his questions are done. "He's on his way."

* * *

Silas wants to talk. Not because he's bored. He's nervous. On edge. Terrified. Joey is in a car and heading his way. He might be alone. Or with husband. Or with his kids. Silas's grandkids. He doesn't have their presents. How will that look? And then, there's the whole awkward meeting with Joey. A nursing assistant is busy taking readings of his pulse rate and temperature. He's kinda young, and not especially chatty.

"You mind if I ask you something?"

The young man skitters. "I can find someone."

"How long would it take someone to drive here from Boca Raton?"

The nurse had said a couple of hours at most, when Silas asked earlier.

"Traffic is bad," the guy says. "Three hours."

Silas tries to swallow, but his mouth is dry. It's been almost one, and he's not ready. For one thing, he's a mess. The plan was to dress in his one good shirt and the pants he bought the day he scored the Crown Atlantic job.

He takes long, slow breaths, his gray hair sticking to his forehead with sweat.

"You certainly have a whole lot more color than when I first laid eyes on you," the assistant says. "How you feeling?"

"Like I got kicked in the gut by a horse."

He laughs and hands Silas a cup of water. "That sounds about right."

Silas takes a sip. "What's your name again?"

"Gulliver. My mom was a huge fan of Jonathan Swift. I think she sort of hoped I might grow up taller."

He was indeed short. Five foot two at most.

The water gives Silas a stomachache, but he drinks more. Through the window, he sees the lights from a mall across the street. He should buy Joey a gift.

"Do I need to stay here?" he asks.

"As long as you don't plan on driving anywhere, I can't actually stop you from leaving."

"It's just..." Silas shakes his head. "Forget it. I'm being dumb."

Gulliver stops what he's doing. His face is kind. "I was the one who called your son," he says. "I can't say I got the warmest of receptions."

"We've grown apart."

"Boys and their fathers. That's a given."

"It's more than that."

"Let me guess." He shares a smile. "You guys had a fight, and you said something mean, and the kid's held a grudge ever since."

Silas frowns, stunned. "How did you know?"

"You get a nose for what might be going on behind what people are prepared to say."

"So what should I do?" he says.

"It's simple enough. Find out what's going on in his life. What makes him happy. What matters to him."

"And if he doesn't want to tell me?"

"I've seen the worst of people change their mind when they think their father might be sick." Gulliver rests a warm hand on his shoulder. "You got this."

His head spins. "I'm not sure I do."

"He's your family. Of course, you do. Is it rude of me to ask about your wife?"

Silas shakes his head. "I lost her. A long time ago."

"No," he says. "You lost yourself, and it's time to stop living in the past. There's a whole new world out there, and you can be a part of it."

A door opens, and a doctor comes in to explain that Joey is waiting downstairs.

Gulliver straightens up. "You need a wheelchair?"

"No," Silas says. "Thanks."

* * *

So, Silas thinks, this man who stands before me is Joey. This gentleman is my son. The resemblance is unmistakable. Tall, with a slender build and shoulder-length dark hair, and wearing a white button-down shirt and jeans. He has Nancy's almond-shaped eyes. Silas has always been able to read people—to glean emotions from facial expressions and body language. But he can't do that with his son. There's a glass door between them, like they're riding the same subway, in separate parts of the train.

Joey goes to shake hands, when they ought to hug.

Silas hesitates for a fraction of a second. "It's good to see you," he says, and the words sound wrong. Too formal.

"You, too, Silas."

Not Dad.

For several long seconds, neither man is sure what to do next, and then Gulliver appears, red-faced and out of breath. He's been running. "You forgot your jacket, Silas."

He takes it without a word.

"Your father has his tablets," he tells Joey. "It's important he takes them. They thin the blood."

Joey's eyes appear lukewarm when they meet his, and Silas can tell he's trying to think of what to say, but the right words aren't there. Not yet, anyhow.

Silas shrugs on his jacket. "I guess we should get going. Any chance I could get a ride to the bus station?"

Joey glowers past him at Gulliver, as if unsure what to say.

The nursing assistant takes over. "Like I said when we spoke on the phone, your father needs to rest up a while. He's in no fit state to go jumping on a bus."

"I see," Joey says.

Silas hates how the hospital has forced him into a corner. "I suppose you couldn't recommend a reasonably priced motel?" he says, and reaches inside his jacket pocket for his envelope of cash. There's enough to cover one or two nights at someplace better than a fleapit. Except the envelope isn't there.

"Are you okay, Silas?" Gulliver says. "You need to sit?"

"I lost something," is all he can manage to say. "An envelope."

"A letter?" he says. "Was it in your pocket?"

"Would you have put it someplace safe?" Silas asks.

Gulliver shakes his head, but offers to check with a colleague, leaving father and son alone.

"You're staying with Zach's family," Joey says finally.

Silas blinks. "Zach?"

"My husband. His folks insisted. I figured you'd rather go to a Comfort Inn. I'm right, yeah?"

Silas sees how much Joey wants him to agree not to come back home. He'll drop him off at a chain motel, maybe even hang around to make sure he checks in, and gets to his standard room, before vanishing. Back into his other world.

"I'd rather meet my grandkids," he says.

"Grandkids?" Joey makes a face. "They don't know who you are."

"So I'll explain."

"They think you died."

There's a long silence.

"Perhaps I should go to a Comfort Inn," Silas says. "I have money."

Gulliver is back. "Nobody found anything in your pockets," he says. "What exactly are you missing?"

Chapter Twenty

From the passenger seat of Joey's SUV, the passing scenery becomes a tangle of trees and buildings. An endless procession of browns, greens, and orangey grays. Clapperboard houses with pale yellow peeling paint. Palm trees throw shadows on the dusty highway. People around here don't walk. They don't come out of their homes much at all. Silas spots the occasional guy, jet-washing his oversized gas-guzzler, or watering a tiny patch of scorched turf.

The engine's roar becomes a continuous whine, restless and piercing. Joey's eyes stay on the road, his shoulders stiff, his knuckles pale. Silas has run through a thousand different ways to kick off a friendly conversation, to ask how Joey is, how the kids are getting on at school. If he has a chance of ever being forgiven.

At last, Joey speaks. "How do you feel?"

Silas hesitates. His throat is still sore, and he doesn't want to say the wrong thing. But this is a grown-up man, driving a grown-up man's car, and he deserves the truth. Though what exactly might that be? Does Joey need to listen to how Silas regrets not calling ahead, and agreeing to meet in a neutral place, and insisting they lay down their arms to hear each other out? Time is supposed to be the great healer. But why fool himself? His son is as angry now as the day he slammed the front door of their Brooklyn apartment.

Silas gets that Joey means how is he doing after the heart attack. What he ought to answer is that he's glad to be alive, and that if he'd have died, he wouldn't be here with his boy, and there might not be any chance of them making up.

Instead, he mutters one word. "Sad."

Joey's face stays expressionless. "That's it? That's all you've got to say to me after thirteen years. You're sad?"

Silas shrugs, still looking out the window. "You asked how I feel. And right now, the answer would have to be that I feel sad."

It's belligerent and childish, and Nancy would threaten to bang their stupid heads together, calling Silas a stubborn old man and Joey a schlemiel. She'd be correct on both counts and yet so wrong. Silas isn't stubborn. He wants to give ground. And Joey isn't a fool. He has every right to be hurt.

Joey clears his throat. "So...maybe if you tell me why you're sad."

He sounds less ready for a fight. This is Joey opening the door a crack, and letting Silas say his piece. This is what Silas wanted all along, and he has a speech all worked out, except his mind has gone blank.

"I can't be sure," he says, playing for time, hoping the words return. "I guess I don't have any way to fix how things have gotten between us. And that makes me...sad."

Joey stays silent.

"It's not your fault," Silas says, recalling key phrases from some *mea culpa* epic poem. "You did nothing wrong."

Joey nods, suggesting he might understand, and Silas dares steal a glance at his son. His handsome boy, with hair that would drive his mother bananas. He has the family chin, and Nancy's kind eyes.

"Are you sad too?" he says, and Joey bobs his head.

Silas doesn't want to start crying, but can find no more actual words to say. He's a man, and that means it isn't right to show frustration or emotion, but he can't help it. His son is there, sitting beside him, behind a sheet of glass, and he doesn't know what else to do.

* * *

Joey parks outside a town house on the south side of Linton Boulevard in Delray Beach, a gated development where each home resembles the next, built above carports, the lower half painted pink, with faux wooden beams on top, and windows set into plastic frames. A white picket fence guards each perfect square of manicured grass.

"This is where Zach's family lives?" Silas says, his voice husky from not talking. "Looks fancy."

"You need to take off your shoes. Tammy gets kinda weird."

It's the longest sentence Joey has strung together in over an hour. Each time Silas pointed out a sign, or a building, or happened to mention how good the weather was, and how easy it might be to forget it was December, Joey grunted to himself, and kept his eyes on the road.

"And they're really okay with me staying?" Silas says, and Joey gives him the kind of look he's used to seeing from checkout girls in Whole Foods whenever he pays for a dollar bag of nuts with a twenty dollar bill.

"It's for two or three days, Silas. You had a fucking heart attack."

He wishes more than anything that Joey would call him Dad, or Pop, or even Father. Mr. French would do...but Silas?

"You don't need to worry about me," he says. "I'll book my trip home."

"You can't fly." Joey sounds tired. Like he already thought of that and argued in favor. "Doctor's orders. You don't get to take a plane. Not after a heart attack. Something about how you could get a clot, and then they might be forced to land someplace else, and you get to piss off three hundred strangers."

It hurts to talk. It hurts even more to argue.

"Norman and Tammy said you can stay until you're well enough to leave." Joey sits for a minute, before pushing a button to unlock the passenger door. "I agreed to go along with them."

Two kids hurry from the house, a pretty young girl with long blond hair in braids, and a dark-haired boy, wearing shorts and a bright blue tee. The boy throws his arms around Joey's legs, and the girl grabs for a shirt sleeve, dragging him inside.

"This is your..." Joey starts with introductions but pulls himself up short.

"I'm a friend of your daddy's." Silas fills in for him, holding out a hand, and the girl shakes it politely. The boy high-fives, without letting go of

Joey's leg.

Silas feels his heart swell.

"Lumen and Apollo." Joey raises an eyebrow, as if daring Silas to challenge his choice of names.

"You gotta see what Daddy Zach did," Lumen says, and they pull Joey inside, letting the front door slam. Silas hesitates, unsure what to do, and then he rings the doorbell.

He's left standing a while.

"The wind," Joey says as he hauls it open. "If the veranda door is open, it causes some kind of vortex. How's about you try to keep up in the future, so I don't need to do this?"

Silas steps inside, and for one long and awkward minute, their eyes happen to meet.

"Just because you turned on the waterworks back there, we're not cool," Joey says. "Nothing between you and me changed. You get that?"

Silas swallows, his mouth too dry to speak.

A rich aroma of baking comes from the kitchen. A radio plays. The house looks like it could be held together by framed family photographs. Every space on each wall, on bookcases, on sills, and even up the stairs, is taken up with pictures of the kids, of Joey, of a handsome Black guy, who must be Zach, of a white-haired, smiling, older man, and a woman with tight copper curls. A ladder bookcase stands crammed with paperbacks against a wall of shelves, interspersed with boxes and random clutter, vases, potted plants, succulents, and a row of dictionaries. Spanish-English, Russian-English, French, German, Urdu.

"Zach's father is a polyglot," Joey says.

Silas tries for a smile. "Is it catching?"

The joke goes down like a cup of cold vomit.

"Hey there," a voice calls, and they both turn around to see the handsome Black guy who features in so many framed photos. Tall with a shaved head, and manicured beard, perhaps in his midthirties, wearing a t-shirt that proclaims: NOT SORRY.

Joey handles introductions. "Silas Zach, Zach Silas."

And then he saunters away. Outside.

* * *

Silas has been allocated one of two guest bedrooms at the end of a narrow corridor on the first floor of the house, close to the living room, where Joey and Zach watch TV with the sound down low. When the door shut, he let his face rearrange to how he truly felt. Lonely. *You'll be okay,* he told himself. *Not yet, but better times will come. You need to accept more time needs to go by. You turned up out of the blue. He wasn't ready. But how Joey feels about you right now isn't your fault.*

The lighting in his room can be on or off. With no in between. A single overhead bulb glows brightly enough to fool passing jets into thinking they've located an airport. When turned off, the darkness is all but complete.

Freshly laundered bed sheets smell of lavender, although something in whatever detergent they use in this house causes his skin to itch. The feather duvet is heavy and rustles each time he moves. It's hot in here, and the windows won't open. A nightstand clock ticks way too loud. Silas checked and there were no batteries to remove. He thought of hiding the damn thing in the closet, but found that to be stuffed to the gills with kids' toys.

The drone of Zach and Joey's conversation remains constant. One of them laughs, or raises their voice, or uses the bathroom. Now and then, their footsteps interrupt an otherwise constant chink of yellow light shining under the bedroom door.

"Come on, man." For the first time, Silas makes out words. The voice does not belong to his son. "The guy is your father."

Joey mutters something, and Silas lets his mind decide it isn't good.

"He's sick," Zach says.

Another mumble.

"It's what we do for the people who brought us into this world."

Now someone hurries past his bedroom door.

As a kid, whenever Joey lost a fight, he stormed away, either to his room

200

or to lock himself in the bathroom. Nancy and Silas always hoped for the former, as Joey was a champion sulker, and if either of them needed to pee, it called for something akin to a United Nations peacekeeping force to end hostilities.

The footsteps reverse.

"He said he wanted me to die."

That's Joey for sure. And he's talking about Silas.

"People change."

"Not Silas French."

"Why won't you call him Dad?"

"He doesn't deserve it."

The TV gets muted, and another door opens. Perhaps they guessed how Silas could hear each hurtful word, and took things outside. He could sneak out of bed, and creep through the house to listen. Not that he wants to hear whatever his kid has to say, but forewarned is forearmed. Given any choice, he'd get dressed, book a taxi, find the nearest bus heading to Miami, and board a train upstate, and then home. Rose would get to gloat about how she was right about Joey, and life will go on. It always does.

Except his clothes are in the laundry room. Tammy insisted. She's sweet like apple pie with too much whipped cream. Nothing is a trouble. She made Silas have extra portions at dinner, and gave him two pillows from her bed, fussing about how he must be in pain after everything that happened.

Joey rolled frosty eyes at each act of kindness.

Silas runs a hand across the back of his head. It's damp. Like when he went to find Ellen's room. Is he having another heart attack? He read in a hospital leaflet about how they often come in twos or threes. Building. Like ocean waves. Or earthquakes. The next one might be it.

His brow is clammy. He's sweating and short of breath. There's a glass of water by his bed, and he takes a sip of something tepid that tastes of whatever chemicals they use in Florida to maintain their huge white smiles.

Joey would have known his voice carries. The words he spat were on purpose. Deliberately cruel. Stuff he didn't have the nerve to say to his father's face.

I'm not wanted here, Silas thinks. *Not by the one man I craved to see.*

In the morning, he'll sit down to breakfast, and Tammy will once again serve up extra portions. He'll make no scene. At some point, they'll leave him alone—and if not, he'll ask if he might go for a stroll, and say he feels up to exploring the neighborhood, and when Norman suggests driving, claim the doctors at Mount Sinai wanted him to hike at least fifteen minutes each day.

For now, he lies still, straining for any sound of Joey's voice and finding nothing.

* * *

Sunlight fights its way around white wooden shutters. After a fitful night, Silas takes a full minute to work out where he might be. Not on the ship, not at home, not in some hospital bed. The sheets are soaked with sweat, but his headache has gone. Was last night another panic attack? Is this the path his life must now follow?

Tammy must have tippy-toed in while he briefly slept, for his neatly pressed clothes sit folded onto a chair. He gets dressed, wishing there was a mirror in the room.

The kitchen is bright and sunny, and the overpowering smell is of bacon frying in a square pan on the range. Tammy wears a crimson-striped apron over her pale cream velour robe, and *clip clops* around on silver mules.

"Make yourself at home," she says. "I know what they said at the hospital, but a breakfast will fix you up just fine."

"I'm not allowed fried food," he says. "Maybe a little oatmeal."

Tammy clicks her tongue. "What if I set some bacon on a plate in the fridge? That way, if you change your mind, just give it ten seconds in the microwave, and it's like new. Norman does it all the time."

Outside, Lumen and Apollo laugh and shout.

Tammy snickers to herself. "They want to get into the pool, but we're having it cleaned today. Zach is keeping them busy."

She turns on the radio and it plays "Feliz Navidad."

"Thank you for taking care of my laundry," Silas says.

"It was no problem." She stops for a minute. "Is that the only outfit you have with you?"

"I didn't exactly have time to pack."

She laughs. Loud and shrill, like he's Bob Hope telling the finest joke to a devoted audience.

"I wonder if you might be the same size as Norman?" she says, more to herself than Silas, and then turns back around to flip bacon.

Zach comes in from the yard. He beams and holds up a hand in greeting. "You sleep okay, Mr. French?"

"Not too bad," Silas lies. "I heard a car. Did Joey have to go someplace?"

Zach pours himself a mug of fresh coffee. "Into town for supplies."

A painful silence settles, and Silas breaks it by asking if he might take a shower.

"Right along the hallway," Tammy says. "I left a big old pile of towels in the guest *salle des bains*."

"My mom found out she might have French ancestors," Zach says. "She did a test where you spit in a jar and they analyze it to find out where you came from."

"I'm part French, part Norwegian, and a tiny bit Cherokee Indian," she explains, sounding proud of her upbringing. "Zach is one hundred percent African American."

Neither Norman nor Tammy are Black, and Silas wants to ask if he's adopted, but that sounds rude.

"How is Joey?" Silas hadn't planned on cutting to the chase so soon, but given he plans to be on a bus later this morning, he might as well find out.

"Okay," is all Zach offers.

Tammy rolls her eyes. "You can tell Silas. He is the boy's father."

"Tell me what?" Something rises through Silas, and it tastes of fear.

"Joey thinks he might lose his job," Zach says in a voice that makes it sound unimportant.

"At the airline?"

"They're talking redundancies, and that means getting rid of people who cost the most, on account of them being on better contracts and making decent pay."

"Are you guys good for money?" Silas says.

Zach leans back in his chair, composed. Nothing could ever bother him. "We're doing fine. I work for Chase Manhattan."

"In the city?" Silas might be about to open a can of worms. He needs to stop whoever has control of his mouth from asking anything more.

"We should meet for dinner," Zach says. "Whenever Joey is routed through JFK, we get a room at the Plaza."

Silas wants to howl. It's like someone cut off his hands, his feet, his head. Joey has been coming to Manhattan, and never once did he suggest meeting up. He knows where Silas lives. It wouldn't have hurt to get in touch, or meet for a drink. Just one beer. Did he despise his father so absolutely?

"Does Joey ever talk about me?" he says, dreading the answer.

Zach glances at Tammy, and she makes a face.

"He doesn't," Zach says.

"What about his mother?"

Zach shakes his head.

It ought to sting enough to send Silas running from the room, running from the house, and into the street to wave down a cab, and insist the driver take him to the airport, where he can fly home to New York and be safe. Fuck the doctors and their blood clots. He needs to be someplace familiar. Far away from his ungrateful son. Silas said what he said back then, and served time. But Nancy? She doesn't deserve to be forgotten.

"We have reservations for dinner," Tammy says. "It would be an honor if you would join us."

Silas forces a smile. "I truly can't wait."

2005

There's a thing with dead people. After they die, most become angels. Especially the ones who die early. Myron Schwartz was a progressive Jew, borderline secular, but still, the funeral service followed customs and beliefs based on the Torah. Everyone is equal in death. First, came the ritual washing of Nancy's body, and then she was dressed in a plain burial shroud, and lifted into a simple wooden box. Their synagogue had closed for repairs, so he found a nearby funeral home. Myron insisted Silas wear a yarmulke, even though his faith had long since lapsed. Silas joined the minyan, reciting prayers. Grief caused him to lose his place and mime the words.

At Baron Hirsch, they said more prayers, and family members tossed handfuls of dirt upon her coffin. There were no flowers, despite how Nancy often declared, if she went first, Silas should defy dumb rules and buy lilies.

He was already responsible for taking away Myron's daughter.

Why add to the man's upset?

Nancy was a great mother. Right until she wasn't. She tended to Joey through every step of his young life. His first words, when he started walking, the first day at school.

After Joey left rehab, things changed, and even though she acted like his mother, and spoke the right words, each gesture came not from kindness or love, but duty. And fear. One day, Silas came home, and found her sitting on the kitchen floor, in tears, holding one of Joey's shirts. The sleeve was covered in blood.

"He's doing it again," she said, when she could finally speak. "My baby left me."

Joey wasn't back on drugs. He'd cut his finger at work, and tossed the shirt in the laundry without a second thought, without ever considering how his mother might no longer trust him. There had been a fight. Nancy screamed, and Joey hung his head in shame.

"You'll never forgive me," he said. "Not completely."

Silas tried to intervene, but was met with such fury, that he staggered backward.

Joey hid in his room.

Two weeks later, Nancy's doctor prescribed antidepressants, promising they were mild, and suggesting they might be enough to take off the edge. For a while, Silas had his wife back. She laughed again. She danced around the kitchen with the radio on. She reconnected with friends.

But Joey spent more evenings someplace else. And Silas picked up on how Nancy still couldn't find it in her to accept that their son wasn't living a double life. Whenever he left the apartment, she'd go into his room to change his bed sheets, claiming the chore overdue. Silas once spied her rummaging through drawers.

One dazzling morning in Midtown, she walked out in front of a laundry truck.

The family sat shiva for seven days. Joey insisted on going the full nine yards, covering mirrors, burning memorial candles, ripping his clothes. He didn't shave. Twice a day, he called his father into the living room to pray for his mother's soul. Silence was where they both did their thinking, supporting each other without words.

Respecting Joey's need to not mention his mother proved tough, and Silas wanted to spell out how much his heart was hurting. Each time he tried, Joey shook his head, and said something bland.

"We require a moment of quiet."

Nancy had been so careful to make sure the apartment was filled with fun and love and joy. To experience it in darkness felt wrong. He missed the laughter and the sound of the radio.

The mourning period ended, and Joey gave permission to his father to rejoin the world.

"Go to work, Dad," he said. "It's not like we can survive on my wage."

And he promised to get the airline to reinstate his shifts.

Silas came home, bringing beer to share, along with a pizza, but found the apartment empty.

And that was how it stayed.

Chapter Twenty-One

In their room, Ellen squints at her cell. Julia's voice becomes a background hum as she focuses on the screen, and the pixels become a thousand tiny windows, each a detail of her life with Otto. There he is, dressed in full uniform, his chin held high, and a look of pride on his face, as she walks out of the room, after getting dressed for their wedding. Years later, she's in bed, shaking with grief, her cell phone laying useless on the pillow, with networks out across the city. The smell of burning in the air.

Julia is still talking. Ellen tunes her in.

"At the end of the day, it's up to you if you call her. I'm only saying. if I were in your position, I'm not sure I could stand not knowing."

Finally, she'd confessed details of her search for the woman Otto was with on the day he died. How she'd planned to visit. The hours spent in the public library, staring at photographs of the street where she lived. The searching for any sign of her having a life that might be picked apart by confrontation. Julia was all for closure.

"I've made my decision," Ellen says. "What good would it do?"

"We both know you're going to get in touch," Julia persists. "Otherwise, why keep her number in your phone?"

"Okay, so. assuming I call the woman, what exactly do I say? You think I should launch right in and accuse her of sleeping with my husband, or wait a while? Until she confesses all?"

"Be yourself. You'll figure it out."

Ellen doesn't want to figure things out. She doesn't want to be herself. What if her being herself was the reason Otto strayed? What if this Katharine woman explains how her beloved husband had been on the verge of leaving?

Ellen sits on the edge of the bed and takes a deep breath. "I can't do it."

"It's scary, I know."

"You're scared too?" Ellen looks hopeful.

"I'm scared for you," Julia says. "At some point, you're going to have to call that number. Why not now? When you're miles away from home."

The phone has gotten warm in her hand, and Ellen senses her resolve to leave well enough alone slipping away. A thought skitters across her mind. What if Katharine hangs up when she hears Ellen's voice? Perhaps she sent the cards as a way of keeping her at arm's length.

"This is pointless," she says. "I should let sleeping dogs lie."

"Okay," Julia says gently. "You don't have to call anyone. We'll watch a movie. Get dinner."

"But you think I'm making a mistake?"

Julia gets up and goes over to the minibar. "Everything is a mistake until it isn't. I want you to be happy." She crouches and glances back at Ellen. "Or at least happier."

Ellen takes a deep breath. She's not in the mood for a movie or for dinner. There's an energy coursing through her veins, and she needs to do this.

The number rings out.

"No answer," she says, but Julia shakes her head, signaling to hang on.

And then there's a click and a voice.

Ellen can't speak.

"Who's there?" the voice says. "I hear you breathing."

"My name is Ellen Gitelman."

Silence.

"You send a Hanukkah card. Each year."

Silence.

"I think you must have known my husband, Otto Gitelman."

"How did you get this number?"

"Did you know Otto?" Ellen crosses her fingers, and makes every kind of deal that the answer will be no. That Katharine Fitzgerald just so happened to pick a Jewish-sounding name at random from the phone book, and now sends cards each November. A karma credit account. One of those people who takes it upon themselves to do random acts of kindness in the hope it might make their world a better place. The more good she sends out, the more she'll get back.

"I knew Otto," she says, and Ellen's world snaps in two. She isn't sure what to say next, and wants to end the call. But Julia is watching.

"How did you know my husband?" she says, and there's a pause, like Katharine is working out the best way to explain they were lovers.

"Otto was…he was the janitor I suppose is how you call what he did. He took care of things around the place I worked. Right until…"

The voice trails away into ragged breathing.

"The janitor?" Ellen repeats. "Otto was a contractor. He fixed heating, installed bathrooms."

"Ellen," Katharine says. "I'd like to meet up."

Hearing this woman use her name is too much, and she ends the call, runs to the bathroom, and throws up in the toilet.

* * *

As Julia knocks on the Lucey's cabin door, she turns to Ellen.

"No cancer talk, deal?"

Ellen makes a face. "No Otto-had-an-affair-with-a-slut-called-Katharine-Fitzgerald talk, deal?"

Kathy hauls open the door and squeals, gathering both women into one huge hug and dragging them over the threshold into a room where Christmas has exploded, scattering holly and mistletoe, ribbon and sheets of wrapping paper.

"What's the deal?" Julia says. "Are we early?"

Kathy hugs them both again. "You caught me right in the middle of wrapping your gifts."

"That's nice," Ellen says. "But we didn't get you anything."

She waves away the protest. "You're Jewish, Helen. I get it. You probably want to go light candles. But this is all part of my plan."

210

Patrick emerges from the bedroom, stops and frowns, before shaking his head, sighing and heading for the bathroom.

"He's being a grumpy Gus," Kathy says. "Refuses to help."

Julia picks up a pack of men's woolen socks. "If this is my gift, you need to get your vision checked."

Kathy bobs her head excitedly. "I figured every guy likes socks, right?"

Ellen picks up a list of names, scribbled in Kathy's childlike hand. "You bought socks for the captain?"

"And all the senior crew members. I checked with guest relations, and there are sixteen of them."

"Well, why not?" Julia says, flashing Ellen *shut-the-fuck-up* eyes. "I'm sure there's method to the madness."

Ellen is having none of it and folds her arms. "Why are you buying everyone socks?"

"I figured they'd come thank me, and that way, I could ask if they know anything about who sold that...stuff to Patty."

"You're trading socks for information on a drugs ring. What could go wrong?"

"Yup." Kathy grabs a roll of red and gold gift wrap. "Brilliant, right?"

Julia sits on the edge of a sofa. "I, for one, think it's a brilliant idea."

Ellen isn't sure she's heard right. "Am I the only sane one here? It's madness."

She hasn't noticed Patrick standing by the bathroom door.

"I already told her it's a dumb plan," he says. "Good luck getting her to listen."

"Boo hoo. Crybaby." Kathy mocks her brother, rubbing her eyes. "Go back to whatever boring middle-aged thing you were doing in there."

He doesn't move. "What's the idea, then, Kathy? What if someone holds up their hands?"

Kathy shrugs. "I'll cross that bridge when I get there."

It's been a rough few days for everyone, and Ellen knows she ought to act positive and supportive, and that Kathy means nothing but good, and she's only trying to protect her brother. But seriously. Socks? Has the woman lost what little remains of her tiny mind?

"Patrick's right. It's a dumb idea," Ellen says, and Kathy's jaw drops.

Julia looks up from wrapping, wide-eyed with innocence. "It's a lovely thought, and it's not like anything will come of it."

Kathy looks first at Patrick and then back to Ellen. "You all think I'm dumb," she says, and before Ellen can formulate an apology, her lips tremble and spasm, her eyelids flutter. "You're right. I'm dumb. I'm so dumb."

She turns and runs into the bedroom.

Patrick rubs his forehead and sighs. "Any chance one of you ladies could deal with that? I'm so tired of it."

Dinner is awkward. Kathy is clearly brooding about the way all three of them dismissed her brilliant plan. Her fingers toy with food, as if she's a little girl and not a grown woman in her thirties. Her normally rosy cheeks are pale, and the smooth skin around her nose wrinkles when she frowns.

When she can stand it no more, Ellen fakes a headache.

"I'm sorry," she says, smiling at faces that clearly wish they'd thought of it first, "but I'm not feeling so great. Do you mind if we don't make it a late night?"

Julia jumps in fast and suggests she go with Ellen, but she isn't anywhere near quick enough.

"I'm going to lie down," Ellen says, still not sure she's completely forgiven Julia for hounding her into calling Katharine Fitzgerald. "A little time alone will sort this out."

* * *

Back in their room, Ellen fills the tub and sinks into bubbles. The soothing heat of the water is like oil on her skin. A tingling sensation forms at her ankle and crawls up her calf, spreading an intricate vine. Its prickle makes her wince, as if there's something moving under her skin. A flush of goose bumps rises along her legs and back. Her skin burns and itches, and she wants to scream out, but her throat is too dry, and her breath comes in raspy gasps.

She rolls to push herself out of the tub, and it's as if her skin is shrinking and tightening, and her legs have turned to rubber. She's out of the water, but on the floor. Somehow, Ellen pulls herself up to a sitting position, and rests against the tub, her head swimming.

She grabs for a towel, pulling it around her shoulders.

The decision, when it arrives fully formed, takes her by surprise.

In the bedroom, she pulls at the comforter, causing it to slide to the floor and, with it, her phone.

There's a crackle, a hiss, and then the sound of a line ringing out. It's still evening. Perhaps Katharine Fitzgerald is out with friends or settling in front of the TV. Maybe she goes running in the nearby park. Ellen saw online how the entrance is a few doors from Katharine's house. It looked nice.

The voice that answers sounds to be thick with sleep. "Who is this?"

"Ellen Gitelman."

Like before, there's a long, empty silence, and Ellen is no longer sure that calling so late was such a good idea.

"I hope I'm not interrupting anything?" she says and strains for telltale sounds, trying to build a picture of the life this woman would have shared with Otto, if he'd survived. There's no TV chatter, no music. Nothing. Otto always watched the news. Every show going.

"You want to ask if I was sleeping with Otto," Katharine says, and such directness takes Ellen by surprise.

She says nothing.

"The crazy thing is, I only met Otto because he was trying to keep something secret from you."

Ellen shuts her eyes. How can this be? Why didn't she leave well enough alone? Why keep poking at a sore until the scab lifted and everything sour seeped out?

"He got put on short hours," Katharine says, "and didn't want you finding out. My wife took pity and gave him work."

"Your wife?" Ellen's voice sounds weird. Like it's not been used in hours. "You're married?"

"She runs a cleaning company. Otto delivered uniforms every two weeks. They got to talking."

"You're...gay?"

Katharine's husky laughter crackles down the line. "Ellen, I liked Otto. He made me laugh. Sometimes he brought pastries."

There's one more thing to ask. "Were you working that day? When it happened?"

"I was at home." Another long silence. "There's not a day goes by when I don't thank God for giving me strep."

Ellen's chest becomes a solid block of ice. She opens and closes her mouth, struggling to form words. "I'm sorry. I'm so sorry."

"I wanted to send you a card, so you got how other people cared about Otto. Maria...my wife...she said it was wrong, and that I should write and explain who I was. I figured Otto might not want you to find out about his second job."

Ellen's head stops spinning. Otto loved her. Right until the end.

"Thank you for the cards," she says.

"I got told they're not so appropriate, but you know how it is. Once I started. I figured you might be more offended if they stopped."

"Why didn't you at least give me your number?"

A pause. "You found it for yourself."

Ellen has a million urgent questions. She's talking to someone who saw a whole different part of Otto's life.

She takes a breath. "Did he ever talk about me?"

* * *

Ellen is still sitting on the bed, holding her phone, when Julia appears.

"Hurricane Kathy blew herself out," she says, making a beeline for the sofa and kicking off her shoes. "We're donating sixteen pairs of socks to a charity. Patrick agreed to never touch drugs again. They hugged. They kissed. It was a Christmas fucking miracle."

Ellen nods.

"I'm having a huge gin and tonic. Can I fix you one? We'll order room service and turn on the TV and trash-talk the Kardashians."

She spots the phone in Ellen's hand.

"Did you call Katharine again?"

"Otto wasn't having an affair."

Julia pours herself a drink and raises an eyebrow for the full story.

"He was cleaning offices, so I didn't find out how they cut his hours."

"Why so many Hanukkah cards? Couldn't she have put all that in a letter?"

"I should be happy," Ellen says. "He was doing it to keep me happy. Don't you see? He was in that place, on that day, because of me."

Julia's eyes grow wide, and she comes to sit next to Ellen. "You can't think like that. Otto was doing what he needed to do. What he wanted to do."

Ellen stays silent, and lets her friend squeeze her hand.

"Let me regale you with a story," Julia says. "Growing up, I had a doll named Mimi. This doll was amazing. I loved Mimi to the moon and back. But one day, my parents said I was too old, and they took her away. I cried. And cried. And cried. And then, I started smashing up all my other toys. Anything I could get my hands on. I simply didn't care."

Ellen groans to herself. "Is there a point to this tale, Hans Christian Andersen?"

"One day, I woke up, and decided I didn't want Mimi anymore. I didn't love her any the less. I just somehow worked out it was time to move on." Julia's eyes well with tears. "That doll had given me years of love, and I had found a way to hate my parents for taking her away from me. But now I look back, and see how much fun we had together, and how I wouldn't trade that, but..."

Ellen sighs to herself. "It's okay. I get it. Talk about subtle."

Julia wipes her eyes with a tissue. "You're not going to cease loving Otto. But he's departed your life, and it's time to move on."

"You make it sound so easy."

"It's not. It's the most arduous of endeavors. But it's easier than holding on to a ghost. You'll go back to New York and get on with your life." Julia kisses Ellen on the cheek, stands up, and takes a breath. "I'm going to order room service, and then we'll agree what you get to wear when you visit Silas in hospital."

Chapter Twenty-Two

Silas runs his fingers over a cloth-bound menu, tracing the embossed lettering. One glance around confirms he's hopelessly under-dressed, in Norman's pants and his own threadbare sweater. This joint is fancy, ornately decorated, like the inside of a country club. Ancient books with cracked leather spines cover two of the walls, and the air is heavy and sweet with a rich perfume of sauces, exotic spices, and slow-cooked meats. The prices are outrageous. He closes the menu and sets it on the table. This is his chance. He can either sit back and enjoy the meal, cross his fingers, and offer to empty his bank account with a single transaction, or make an excuse about chest pains. It's not so far removed from the truth. This morning, soreness spread from his ribs. He sat heavily in the yard. Was *this* Malinowski's "big one"? he thought, and then he belched. The pain was gone.

"You should totally try the Kusshi Oysters," Zach says.

"Silas can't eat shellfish," Joey shoots back, before Silas can thank him for the recommendation. "He's stricter than me."

"I always struggle with kosher," Norman chips in, his tone warm and breezy. "You can't eat shellfish or pork, right?"

Silas smiles. "It goes so much deeper. There's a whole meat plus dairy embargo."

Tammy peers nervously over her menu. "Are you cool if I order a Roquefort sauce with my rib eye?"

"Pick what you want," Silas says, trying to remember if the rib eye costs more or less than fifty bucks, and what a joint like this would charge for Roquefort sauce. "We're here to celebrate. And truth be told, I veer toward the secular side of the street."

Joey makes the grumpy sound of someone ready to pick a fight, but a stern nod from Zach changes things, and his tongue stays civil. The maître d' returns with a bottle of red wine on a silver tray, and as he does the rounds, Silas holds a hand over his glass.

"Not for him," Norman says, loud enough so people at the next table turn their heads. "Our friend here recently had a heart attack."

Silas bristles. He doesn't care who knows, but he's doing his level best to fit in, and not be signaled out as different. More than anything, he planned on sitting back and watching Joey, to see what sort of man he'd become.

A server takes orders, straining to make out what Silas says, and Joey steps in. "Tuna, well done, and serve it with fries."

Silas had wanted a steak cooked medium, and he liked the sound of scalloped potatoes, but now isn't the time to cause a scene. Joey is at least trying.

Norman hands back his menu and smiles at Silas. "How long you been working on the high seas?"

"This was my first job."

Tammy perks up. "You never did this kind of thing before?"

"I played Santa, sure. For years, at a store on Fifth Avenue."

Joey groans to himself and mumbles. Silas could ask him to repeat whatever he said, but that would surely cause a fight.

"This year, I figured I might try something different," he says.

"And it was a gay cruise?" Norman sounds interested. "How did that work out for you?"

Silas isn't sure how to answer.

Joey chips in. "He means did you get freaked about catching AIDS?"

All conversation stops. Tammy glances at Norman, her eyes suggesting he should do or say something to make this right. Zach rests his fingers on Joey's arm.

"The job worked out fine," Silas says, deciding the best course out of this car crash might be to pretend Joey never spoke. "It was a nice crowd."

Their food is served, and Lumen raises her hand. "I ordered squid. This is octopus."

The tuna they serve to Silas is like leather, grilled way too long, and the fries are greasy. He eats every mouthful, declaring it delightful.

Over coffee, conversation moves to a planned beach trip.

"Silas won't be joining us," Joey says quickly.

Norman rests his chin on the palm of his hand. "And is that your decision, or did you take time to check in with your father?"

Joey's face turns red. "He's recently out of hospital. Silas needs to rest."

"Of course," Norman says. "But your father can get a ride and meet us for a late family lunch."

Silas wants to interrupt and insist that it doesn't matter, and he's not going to push to be included in any plans, but Joey isn't done.

"The man isn't family," he says. "You can't expect me to act like we're related after all this time."

"Honey," Tammy says, but he won't let her say her piece.

"This man told me he wanted me to die of AIDS," Joey says. "Screw him."

Everyone is looking, and Silas wants to be anywhere but here. Miles away. Wherever Nancy is now. She'd be shocked to hear hateful words from the boy they loved. The boy he still loves.

"Tell me I'm wrong," Joey taunts. "Tell me that isn't what you said, Silas."

"I didn't have my facts straight," he says. A line he had ready for this occasion. One he rehearsed many times in many mirrors. "I regret that I spoke in haste."

Joey sits back in his chair, and his mouth twists in a way that suggests malevolence. "It never crossed your mind to say sorry?"

Once again, Zach tries to intervene. "Not now. Some other time. Some other place."

Joey gets up and storms toward an open door.

Tammy nudges Norman in frustration.

"I'll go after him," Silas says, and Zach holds up a hand.

"Let him be. He needs to walk it off."

* * *

219

When they reach home, Tammy insists on brandy served in delicate crystal goblets. The orange flame of a gas fire dances in the marble fireplace, casting shadows on the wall. The amber liquid tastes of oak and caramel, with a hint of spices.

"You should do some sightseeing," Tammy tells Silas. "Not that there's a lot around here worth looking at. Leastways not compared with New York City. Norman can spare an afternoon and be your guide. He's always telling me I don't know the half of what goes on."

Norman guffaws. "I try to get Tammy to come fishing, but she finds every excuse. Is a tour of the sights and sounds of Boca Raton something you might be up for?"

Silas wants to say yes, but he made other plans. The MS Viking docks tomorrow morning in Miami, and he intends on meeting the ship. He needs to find Ellen and make things good. And then jump on the first bus back home.

"It's time for me to take my leave," he says. "I'm well enough to travel."

Tammy's face falls, and she places a hand on her chest. Her eyes flutter, her lips tighten, and she drops her head.

"Is this on account of how Joey acted over dinner?" she says. "You don't need to go paying him no attention. If that boy bit his tongue, he'd surely poison himself. He has too much pent-up frustration, and once he stops railing against the world, he'll find peace."

Joey has opted to shun company. He's outside, sitting on a lawn chair, smoking a cigarette. Zach is busy upstairs, reading bedtime stories to Lumen and Apollo.

Tammy goes back into the kitchen, and Norman leans in to whisper. "It's my belief your boy has anger issues."

Silas stays quiet.

"The words he uses will upset you, but it'll hurt him even more. If you let the fire burn out, then, at some point, like when you light a charcoal grill, you end up with glowing coals. Hot, but useful. Ready to work with you and produce something wonderful."

Silas grins to himself. Relationship advice served up as direction on how to grill steak has to be the most ridiculous and most manly lesson he ever got.

"You should go talk to your boy," Norman says. "I'll occupy Tammy."

* * *

Silas pulls shut the sliding doors with a soft click and steps onto the deck. The wood creaks beneath his feet. With his eyes fixed on the ground, Joey huddles on the far side of the yard. Nearby sprinklers hiss, and a sharp scent of cut grass rises into the air.

"Hey there," Silas says. There's no answer and so he moves closer. "You want to talk about what happened just now?"

Joey shakes his head.

"It's fine." Silas risks a hand on his son's shoulder. "Whatever I said and did, we'll figure it out."

Joey shrugs him away. "You can't figure this out," he says. "It's broken."

"I'm doing everything in my power to make up for my words. That's all anyone can hope to have happen. But you have to give me a way in."

"I don't want you in my life. Don't you get it? This was all Tammy's idea. And Zach's."

"Okay, so I get that, but now I *am* here, we could use this time to talk." He squats, putting his face level with Joey's. "Your mother wouldn't care to think of us like this."

"I did wonder how long before you dragged Saint Nancy into this."

So, Silas thinks, she's Saint Nancy, not Mom. He blames her too.

"Your mom used to say, there's no healing without forgiveness."

Joey's jaw tightens. "What should I tell you, Silas? I forgive you. It was years ago and you've changed. You understand better now. Hell, you even took a job on a gay cruise ship, so how can you be against my lifestyle choices?"

Silas stays silent.

"That's what they call what my kind of people do," Joey continues. "Politicians. Bigots. They say we make *lifestyle choices*. Well, I didn't choose to be or do anything. I grew up as me. I fell in love and got married. Now I have kids. You're no part of that."

"Joey, I love you."

For the first time, their eyes meet.

"The stupid thing is that I know you do," Joey says. "You cherish your notion of me. You love the thought of who I used to be."

"That's not true. I love you for the hard work and decisions you've made to get you to where you are today."

"But that's the whole point, Dad. You don't get the luxury of loving the idea of who I am now, because you're not a part of this life. The one I picked for myself. I'm who I am despite you and not because of anything you ever did."

Silas can't answer. He's stunned into silence. For the first time since forever, Joey called him Dad.

Chapter Twenty-Three

Ellen closes the door quietly, kicks off her shoes, and tiptoes to the sofa. She sits, careful not to make a sound. A light burns in the bathroom, but Julia is already asleep. She watches her a while, then leans back, and closes her eyes, trying to focus on her breathing.

"I am so exhausted," she whispers into darkness. "When do things get better?"

Her eyes catch sight of a feather, curled on the carpet by the side of the bed. She reaches down, balancing it on one palm. Julia mumbles something, turns over, and pulls the covers over her head. When Ellen was little, her mother always said feathers were signs of an angel passing by.

"Otto?" she whispers. "Is this your way of telling me to move on?"

She'd spent the evening sitting on the observation deck, staring into the night sky, and picking out constellations, tracing them to mythological creatures. A line from Draco, who towered over smaller constellations, through Ursa Minor, whirling around the great bear. In New York, you didn't get stars.

Julia rolls over and her eyes open. "What time is it?"

"Almost four."

"You can't be serious," Julia groans. "It's too early for me to be conscious."

"I decided."

Julia rubs her eyes. "This couldn't wait until the world had its first cigarette?"

"I'm going back to college."

Julia groans and pulls the covers over her head. "You woke me at the

223

ass-crack of dawn to tell me that?"

"I'm going to study photography. Pick up where I left off all those years ago."

Julia sits up and yawns, taking a moment to process the news. "That's great, Ellen. I'm so happy for you."

"You don't sound it."

"Sorry. I'm…surprised. And someone woke me right when Gary Cooper was about to ride me away on a black stallion."

"I've wasted my life waiting tables, and there's so much still to do. This is what I should have put on my bucket list all those years ago. I guess I lost sight of the dream."

She takes a deep breath.

"And I decided to hear Silas out."

Julia opens one eye. "Hall-e-fucking-lujah."

"We'll talk. He can have his say, and then I get to have mine. Whatever happens after that, I don't care. He deserves a chance to explain about the cash."

"Pass me your cell." Julia shuffles up on pillows. "I'll call the hospital before you change your mind again."

* * *

It's a bright, blue-sky morning. The birds sing to each other in the slight, sweet breeze, and Tammy has laid a table in the yard with a white cover, setting a pitcher of orange juice next to a basket of pastries.

"Hi, honey," she says, kissing Silas on the cheek. "Help yourself to breakfast."

"What's the special occasion?"

Tammy laughs. "No occasion. You're our guest."

"And you're too generous."

She rolls her eyes and raises her hand to shush him. "Joey will be out any minute."

Silas swallows. "And Norman?"

"Yeah. Perhaps." She slinks back indoors, stopping to flash one more smile.

He pours juice into a tumbler and takes a sip. Things were strained with Joey yesterday, and he has no reason to think they'll be any better this morning. Half of the night, he lay awake, worrying what happens if he can't find the right words to fix things. Do they drift back to how it was? Neither man speaking to the other?

"Hey." Joey pulls up a chair. "Sleep well?"

"Great."

He reaches for a pastry, pulling it apart and scattering flakes across Tammy's white cloth.

"You need a plate?" Silas says.

Joey stops chewing, and sits back, wiping crumbs off his shirt. "So, what's the plan? I take it you arranged all this so we get time alone to talk?"

Tammy set them both up. She meant well, of that he's certain, but a little warning might have helped. There's one thing Silas knows—he needs to pick each and every word with care.

"I'm sorry," he says at last. He ought to say more, but Rose gave him instructions. If his kid shows even the smallest sign of being ready to talk, he should sit back and listen.

"That's it?" Joey's voice is cold.

"I know that's not enough, but it's all I have right now."

Joey nods slowly, as if taking in the information, weighing it out. He smiles, more to himself than at Silas. It isn't a nice smile. It comes with an air of arrogance, of joy at deciding on some new way to twist the knife. He reaches for the jug of juice and fills his glass, taking a long, slow sip and setting it down again.

"Why don't you just stay out of my life, Silas?" he says. "Things are going great for me right now. I don't need you stirring shit up."

Silas wants to just nod and agree. Perhaps they function better alone. Instead, he speaks. "You're angry. I get it."

Joey slaps the table and leans forward in his chair. "I'm not angry because I don't care what you do. I don't give a damn what you think of me. If you take an interest in my life or not, it doesn't matter. You can go right ahead and carry on being a fucking jerk. I have better things to do with my time."

Silas recoils. "All I wanted to say was that you have to stop blaming your mother."

Joey looks like he wants to say more. Instead he pushes back his chair, gets to his feet, and heads back inside.

A door slams.

* * *

The MS Viking cuts through sun-dappled waves, gliding effortlessly to where Miami explodes up from the water, a jigsaw puzzle of manicured palm trees, ritzy hotels, and skyscrapers.

"I always dreamed of coming here," Kathy says, for once sounding humbled. "They have a Bloomingdale's Outlet."

Ellen raps her knuckles on the rail, looking out at the water and the city. "So, what's the plan? You guys spend the morning shopping and we meet up after lunch?"

Julia's hand strokes Ellen's arm. "Why don't I come with you to see Silas? Act as moral support. I can sit at another table, wear a hat, disguise myself. Whatever."

"I can give the guy his cash back."

"All the same…" Julia's voice trails away, and her eyes grow wide.

Kathy has seen something too. All along the quay, police vehicles wait.

"Do those cops have guns?" she says, pointing to the cruise terminal now clearly in view. A line of men, all heavily armed, wait in a line. As they get closer, the MS Viking slows and its engines groan, causing the deck beneath their feet to rattle.

The captain speaks from the bridge. "Ladies and gentlemen, I regret to inform you we're facing a delay this morning as we get you ashore in Miami. I can't tell you exactly why, but we'll have you on dry land as soon as I get permission." He clears his throat. "I hope you enjoy your time in Miami, and ask that you not bring ashore anything you're not willing to part with."

* * *

Norman peers into his rearview mirror. They've been stuck in heavy traffic next to the same billboard for almost ten minutes, in an orange Jeep with a palm tree decal declaring support for DeStantis.

"Things look pretty solid," Norman says. "I should have avoided the freeway."

Silas says nothing. He's been replaying breakfast. Over and over. Was that it? Are they done? He glances at his watch. It's only a few minutes after ten.

"You okay there, Silas?" Norman says. "You've been mighty quiet since we set out."

"I've a lot on my mind." He drums his fingers on the door.

Norman grins. "And all of those things involve your boy, right?"

"We had another fight. Over breakfast."

"I told Tammy that forcing you two together wasn't her best idea, but she figured giving you space to talk might work." They edge forward, two more car lengths. "Joey is kinda hot-headed. Runs off at the mouth."

Silas snorts. "He gets that from me."

"Is the stubborn nature down to you too?"

They move again. This time, rolling slowly for a full minute.

"Can I ask you something, Silas?" Norman says, his eyes staying fixed on the road. "If you didn't get sick, would you have come to see your kid?"

"I always planned on it."

"That's not what I'm asking. I always planned on one day hitting home runs for the Tampa Bay Rays, but it's never gonna happen. Did you figure, as long as you were sorry, and he was the one intent on holding a grudge, things would one day work out?"

Silas weighs his words. "I think I would have tried to make things right."

"You think? Or you know?"

The traffic crawls, and Silas sighs to himself. "I get how everyone says this, but I always knew Joey was gay. It didn't matter to me. I suppose I said that shit about AIDS because…"

227

"You were scared?" Norman says. "You didn't want to face losing him?"

Silas watches through the passenger window. "I wanted to protect him."

Norman clicks his tongue. "That's not protecting anyone. That's controlling your kid."

Neither man speaks again as they weave their way through gridlocked cars and trucks, before reaching an intersection, where Norman pulls off, claiming to know a back road shortcut.

Away from the freeway, they climb into hills, the air already fresher, and Norman turns on the radio. A string quartet plays a florid melody. When Silas thinks they're destined to travel the whole way without speaking, Norman turns off the music.

"I've told no one," he says. "So you need to keep it to yourself."

Silas nods.

"When Zachery first brought Joey home, I didn't know what to think or say. Like you, I guess I always knew he was different." He pauses a minute, as if gathering thoughts. "I do have issues with your boy, but he's basically a decent kid."

"Issues?" Silas tries not to sound defensive.

Norman inhales. "Joey can be impulsive. Nine times out of ten, he means well, but he never thinks before jumping. He takes offense pretty fast and isn't easy to win over. Is that something else he gets from you?"

"I guess."

"So keep that in mind when you next talk to him."

"I want my kid to believe I regret what I said and give me another chance."

Norman claps a hand on Silas's leg. "He already gets it. Believe me."

* * *

In the shadow of the MS Viking, three chaotic lines meander away from makeshift inspection stations. Ellen's legs ache from shuffling slowly, two steps every five or ten minutes. The sun is hot, and the back of her neck is already burning. She hates the outfit Julia picked from the onboard mall. A red and white dress with a pattern of leaves. It swallows her curves, and the sleeves are too long and too wide. She looks like a little girl playing dress-up.

Ellen has agreed to meet Silas at one o'clock, and picked out a place the city guide called "welcoming and easy to find." Still, she's nervous. When the hospital explained how he'd been discharged into the care of his family, Ellen was all for singing. It was, after all, what Silas had wanted all along. How strange that something so bad turned into something so good. When she worked up the nerve to try calling his cell, he answered right away, and sounded upbeat, agreeing at once to meet for lunch. She didn't get around to telling him about finding the cash.

A cop with a megaphone shouts at passengers like they're being processed for a spell in Rikers.

"I have Oreos in my purse," Kathy whispers. "Is that allowed? I read somewhere you can't bring food back into the country. One guy in Texas ended up in the chair."

Patrick snorts. "If all it takes is a handful of cookies, I'd have called the cops sooner."

Up ahead, Julia stands with her arms outstretched as a female cop pats her down.

"Is this normal?" Ellen whispers as an older security officer walks slowly past, eyeing them with an expression of mild disgust. "What are they looking for?"

Kathy starts bobbing on the spot. "I need to pee, real bad."

"Can't you hold it?" Patrick says, and Kathy glares.

"Maybe if you hadn't collapsed and almost died from taking drugs, the cops wouldn't need to do this."

Julia is back, a smile on her face.

"That was fun," she says. "I usually demand two courses and a decent bottle of wine before anyone gets that far."

"Did you find out why they're doing this?" Patrick says.

She glances over to where a van is parked. "I heard they arrested the priest and at least one other guy."

* * *

Silas scans the semi-circular terrace of the Monticello Café. The canopy flaps gently in a light breeze. A handful of people sit at wrought-iron tables, reading papers or chatting. Pigeons strut across the cobblestones, scavenging for crumbs. The sun beats on the white stone of the plaza, and he spots an empty table in the shade of a pink-striped umbrella.

A waiter comes right over, and Silas orders coffee, before pulling out his phone to check for messages.

Nothing.

Ellen must already be on her way.

He unfolds his newspaper and tries to read, but it's difficult to focus. He's eager for her to arrive. He's also nervous. And what the hell can they talk about? She'll want to know how it went with Joey, and he'll lie and say things are good. They're still new friends who trade nothing more than surface stories.

His stomach growls and his mouth is dry. He needs a drink and waves to the server, trading his coffee order for a beer.

All around, office workers share lunchtime gossip and tourists study guidebooks. The sun glinting off the terrace stones makes him scowl and shade his eyes. Ellen agreed to meet at twelve, and it's already ten after. She'd struck him as the kind of woman who was always on time. What if she isn't coming after all? His stomach clenches, and he pulls out his phone. After a few rings, her number goes to voicemail. He doesn't leave a message.

* * *

Julia leads the way, with Kathy and Ellen keeping up. It's hot and humid, and the harbor is a stew of scents: gasoline, asphalt, rotting fish. Seagulls and cormorants scavenge along the water's edge.

The three women take a sharp right onto a broad boulevard past hole-in-the-wall restaurants and massage parlors. Everyone seems to be speaking Spanish.

"Miami is a mini-state," Julia reads from an information guide handed out onboard. "It's a city like no other and totally different from the rest of America. Not only a city, a whole country."

"I love it," Kathy says. "This reminds me of Disney World."

Ellen isn't so sure. Take away the palm trees, and Main Street Miami is like any other US city with the same old store signs—McDonald's, Starbucks, 7-Eleven, Dunkin' Donuts. They pass a hotel with a pink flamingo fountain, and an almost-empty bar.

"I need a drink," Julia says. "Something tropical and strong enough to knock me off my feet."

It's almost midday, meaning Ellen has an hour to find the café where Silas suggested they meet.

Three cute servers descend in full-on flirt mode.

"My brother is single," Kathy tells them, pointing out Patrick, whose face is already red. "And ready to mingle."

"We're in Straightsville USA," he mutters. "Not every guy we meet is potential husband material."

Julia insists on a jug of mimosas, and even after two sips, Ellen's head spins. They skipped breakfast, and now she's starving. She needs a clear head to meet Silas and suggests snacks to soak up the booze.

Julia laughs. "Won't that spoil your romantic lunch?"

The last thing Ellen has on her mind is romance, but now she sees things through the eyes of other people. She's meeting a man alone in a strange city for lunch. More than anything, she wants to cancel. She should send a text message and say the ship arrived late or claim she's feeling sick.

"You're certainly thirsty," Kathy says. "You finished that cocktail super-fast."

Ellen looks around. Every other glass is half full. Hers is empty. Kathy laughs and goes to the bar, and when she returns, slides a fresh drink in front of Ellen.

"This will help with nerves," she whispers. "Don't ask what I told them to put in, just drink it."

Ice cubes clink gently against the sides of the glass. Ellen takes a sip, and the liquor burns her throat. Her eyes water.

"You got them to make up one of your specials," Patrick says and he sounds annoyed.

Kathy waves away his irritation. "One of Kathy's Ku-ku-ba-ras won't hurt anyone."

Ellen dares another sip, then another. It's mostly whiskey, with something else she can't identify. Soon, it feels like her cheeks and ears are blushing red.

"You guys should come with me," she says suddenly, and the others stop drinking. "I mean it. Come with me to meet Silas. Sit at another table and keep watch. Make sure nothing terrible happens."

Julia shakes her head. "What do you think the guy is going to do? You're about to hand back his life's savings. He's gonna want to kiss you."

"That's the problem."

Julia looks first at Patrick and then at Kathy.

"Do you guys understand what's going on here?" she says, "because I sure as hell don't."

Kathy starts to say something, and then appears to think better of it, instead placing a hand on Ellen's arm.

"Julia told us about how you never have much luck with men," she says.

Ellen glances up and Julia looks quickly away.

"The thing is," Kathy continues, "they always say the best way to get over one man is to get under another. And while, technically, this is you getting under the same man—"

"I don't want to get under anyone," Ellen splutters.

Her phone beeps with a call that goes to voicemail. It's Silas. And she's already late.

Ellen waves for a server and asks if he can flag a cab.

Chapter Twenty-Four

As romantic lunch dates go, Ellen meeting with Silas barely counted as a date at all. It was about as romantic as an Excel spreadsheet. Whatever had been in Kathy's specialty cocktail interacted with the pill she popped to settle frayed nerves. Ellen has no recollection of entering the Monticello Café, or of ordering food, or of eating it. Silas became a jumble of sounds, as the surrounding space twisted into weird shapes. On the way to the bathroom, she tripped, and a pitcher of water upended itself, and two waiters descended. Silas was on his feet, thanking them, and reaching out a hand to help her up. The ground pitched again. And staring around at the mess, Ellen had never been so mortified. She pulled a wad of cash from her purse and thrust it at Silas, who protested how she wasn't to blame.

"Tip the staff," she said. "And delete my number."

A small crowd had gathered for the show, and the café manager rushed to apologize as Ellen fled. She has no idea how she got from there to the ship.

"Silas will have seen the funny side," Julia says, clicking her tongue. "One day, it'll make a great story."

Ellen's eyes narrow. "There is no funny side."

"I guess you'll see him next when we get to New York."

"Were you even listening to what I said?" Ellen wrings her hands in frustration. "I told him to be sure he forgets we ever met."

Julia reaches to squeeze Ellen's hand. "He's not going to do that."

"Fine. He can keep my number, for all I care. I'll not answer. Better yet, I'll get a new cell."

"You want to know what I think?" Julia's tight expression suggests Ellen will hear what she thinks, regardless. "I reckon, if Silas French is worth anything, he won't give up that easily."

"I just want to forget today ever happened."

"You look kinda pink," Julia switches subject, and places her palm on Ellen's forehead. "And you're burning up."

"There's no way I'm spending another minute in the medical center."

Julia goes to the bathroom and returns with a small pot of green cream and a face cloth.

"I know you probably agreed to meet Kathy, but could we please just order room service?" Ellen says as she leans back as she accepts the cream. "I can't deal with any more crap today."

*   *   *

The taxi driver's eyes flick to Silas in the rearview mirror. The guy is young, in his twenties, with the look of a brawler—strong arms, flat nose.

"You okay, buddy?" he says. "You talking to me or yourself?"

Silas exhales. "Thinking out loud."

Through the greasy cab window, the buildings, the cars, the people blur together. Silas is numb, disconnected. She told him to lose her number and ran away.

"Drop me off here," Silas says, figuring he needs to clear his head.

He gets out and pays the fare.

A huge truck thunders past, throwing up dust. The afternoon light is fading, and the air has a chill. He spies an abandoned lot and climbs through a break in the wall, pushing through long grass until he finds a stump and sits. How could he misread every sign and signal? First with Joey. Then with Ellen.

The sun sinks behind nearby buildings, and Silas shivers and pulls his jacket tighter.

A hand is on his shoulder. "Don't be so hard on yourself."

Silas looks up and gasps. Nancy's face is inches away.

"How long were you watching me?"

234

"Only a few minutes."

He pulls back. "You're not really here. I get that."

She smiles weakly. Like she used to do when he lied about stopping at Ziggy's Bar on the way home for a beer, or told her he didn't bet money on a race.

"Something needs to change, Silas," Nancy says. "You can't float through life like you are now. I got all of eternity to discover, and right now, you're taking up most of my free time."

Silas gazes out across the lot, over the tops of the trees. Somewhere, he hears kids playing.

"He blames you too," he says.

"Joey blames the world, Silas," Nancy comes to sit on the ground at his feet. "He always did. That's how he ended up taking drugs. Some people just can't cope with the world. They need something else."

"I want him to know I love him, no matter what."

She gazes into his eyes. How he's missed that face, those lips, that smile. A new idea forms. One that will end all the torment of the last few days.

He pulls out his cell and finds the number for a local cab firm.

"Can I book someone for tomorrow?" he asks the dispatcher. "To pick me up. Around seven a.m.?"

* * *

Ellen leans against a railing and surveys the ocean. The sun sits low on the farthest horizon, setting the sky on fire. Waves crash against the side of the ship, and the air smells of salt. She thinks about her parents and how much she misses having someone around who'll excuse most everything. She thinks about Otto. And Silas. She did the right thing by running away, she gets that now. Why drag another person into a life that holds little promise? She's sick and likely to get sicker. She lost her job. All she has to offer are silly dreams of going back to school—dreams that will never come true. She's an old dog who can't learn new tricks. It's all she can do to use Google on the public library computers. She almost always ends up calling someone over for help, and they speak to her slowly, like she's gaga. Cameras these days are digital. How could she ever hope to keep up with kids who live their lives online? And who would want a sixty-seven-year-old woman taking their photos?

The sky turns deep purple and red.

Life is so fragile. Everything can happen in an instant, yet we live these long lives, hoping for a better future.

"Ellen?"

She turns and sees Patrick, dressed in a black tuxedo, tailored to fit his tall frame.

"Did Julia send you to find me?" she says.

"She told me what happened with Silas."

Ellen turns away. She feels stupid enough without everyone knowing. "I'm glad I've given you all something to laugh about."

"I'm not laughing." He moves beside her and looks out at the water.

"People my age don't fall in love," Ellen says. "We've been through too much."

"Whatever happened to never being too old?"

Ellen shakes her head. "That's what Julia always says. She's fooling precisely nobody."

Patrick puts an arm around her, and at first, she stiffens, and then relaxes, resting her head on his shoulder, thankful for the comfort. The lights from the ship dance across the water.

"How come you're dressed up?" she says.

"Kathy wants me to go to the Christmas Eve Ball. She figures I might find Mr. Right."

"Perhaps you will."

He pecks her cheek. "It's like a wise old woman once said. I've been through too much."

* * *

There's a soft knock at the bedroom door. A chill climbs the length of Silas's spine, and he hides his half-packed bag in the closet.

"It's only me," Tammy calls. "Just wanted to make sure you know, Norman is firing up the grill any minute."

Zach's parents have invited neighbors and friends to celebrate Christmas Eve. There will be food and drink. Silas is their guest of honor.

"I'm about to step into the shower," he says.

"I'll leave your clean laundry by the door."

Silas knows he has no choice but to put in an appearance. If he doesn't, it gives Joey one more reason to hate him.

"I'll be out in a couple of minutes," he adds, and her mules *click clack* along the polished wooden hallway floor. Tammy and Norman are good people and Silas doesn't want to make them think him ungrateful. They've been generous, but he's not sure he can stand one more evening of pretending everything's fine, when it so obviously isn't. A doorbell chimes, and the front door opens and Norman greets early guests.

Silas flips open his cell phone and punches in a number.

Rose picks up on the first ring.

"Merry Christmas Eve," he says.

She snorts. "They converted you?"

"No, but I'm about to go downstairs and act like one big family."

"I take it you're not having a good time?"

"Joey hates me, and I made a total ass of myself with a woman I care about."

There's a silence, and she draws an audible breath.

"I miss you," he says. "I wish you were here to find this shit funny."

Rose's voice becomes gentle. "I'm sorry you didn't find your happy ending."

Silas doesn't want to cry, but tears in his eyes blur the pattern on the bedspread.

"I'm probably not the best person to give you advice," Rose says. "I've had zero luck with men. The only guy I ever talk to is a loser who spends the holidays on a gay cruise ship."

His laugh is a little hiccup. "I sound like a whiner."

"No, you sound like a man who needs to be loved."

"Yeah, well. That's me." Silas hesitates, and then says what he needs to. "I'm lonely, Rose."

Silas hears her swallow and knows she understands.

"Go downstairs and be with your new family," she says. "Show that kid he can't always get what he fucking wants."

* * *

The MS Viking Christmas Eve Ball is in full flow. The room is alive with music and laughter. A mirror ball cascades colors, as hundreds of hands clap and hundreds of feet move in time. Silhouetted by the warm glow of chandeliers, handsome men laugh and raise glasses.

Ellen is on the balcony, watching, wearing a long black dress, with her hair piled on the top of her head, a few stray strands falling around her face. She's never been good at dancing. Her movements look awkward and uncoordinated. A clumsy giraffe flailing between graceful deer. Otto called it endearing. That only made it worse.

"It is a lovely party, is it not? I love the elegance." The man next to her speaks with a heavy Spanish accent. His olive complexion, black hair, and striking eyes set him apart.

Ellen sighs to herself. "Yes, it's lovely."

She has no interest in small talk and wants to be alone.

"I have seen you before," he says. "With your handsome friend." He nods over to where Patrick stands, talking with Kathy and Julia. Ellen gets it at once.

"Can I introduce you?" she says, and he holds out his hand. His cologne is a mixture of sandalwood and spice. "I didn't catch your name."

He grins. "Miguel."

* * *

Norman and Tammy know many people. Their backyard is filled with neighbors, some sitting, and some standing, and the air is heavy with the rich aroma of barbecue and spices. Music plays over the steady hum of laughter and conversation. The party is in full swing.

Dressed in a yellow floral shirt, Tammy greets Silas with a boozy kiss.

"Come and join in," she says. "Make sure you eat."

Silas looks around the yard. "Where's your husband?"

"He's around here someplace. I'll find him later when I'm done flirting." She takes a plate and fills it with chicken and ribs before handing it to him. "It all has to be eaten, so help yourself to a refill."

Silas has never been a socializer, and everyone looks to be comfortable talking with folks they already know. He spots Joey and Zach over by the grill. Zach has on a striped apron. Lumen and Apollo are there, too, wearing chef hats. Joey glances over and catches him looking before turning away.

Asshole.

One of Tammy's neighbors corners Silas in the kitchen.

"Norman tells me you're Joey's father," she says.

He nods, hoping that's enough, and that he can grab a beer and head back outside, but she turns out to be a talker.

"Joey told me all about you. You live in the Big Apple, that's right?"

"Don't believe everything he says."

"Your wife died?" The neighbor sighs sympathetically. "Took her own life."

Silas splutters. "Where did you hear that?"

"Joey. But don't be too hard on the kid. I asked, and I guess he needed to say something."

Silas breathes slowly, forcing himself to stay calm and not rush right outside and rip his son's head off. "My wife was hit by a truck."

"Oh." She grins awkwardly and pats Silas on the shoulder. "I hope you're doing okay."

Silas watches her drift away and join some other group.

Right now, he wants to find his son and ask why the hell he told those lies. What kind of kid does that? How can Joey even call himself a man?

There's no sign of him as Silas moves around the yard, so he takes another beer and finds a spot to wait. The crowd kicks into gear, people hooting, clapping, and whistling, and he spots a figure stepping off the porch and dragging a chair into shadows. Silas knows at once who it is.

He walks across the yard, fine gravel crunching.

"Hey, Joey," he says, his voice cracking on the last note of his name.

"Hey, Silas." Joey looks up, his eyes dead.

He swallows an angry lump in his throat. "I was talking to some woman. Told me she was sorry to learn how your mom took her life."

Joey shrugs. "You trying to say that isn't what happened?"

"No," Silas bites out. "She didn't kill herself. She was involved in an accident."

Joey pulls something from his pocket. "You go on telling yourself that, Silas. Nancy went out to get something, nobody knows what, in the middle of the day, left the apartment door unlocked, and she was totally sane."

"Sane? Your mother wasn't the one who was taking drugs."

Joey laughs to himself, refusing eye contact. "Saint fucking Nancy. You don't get it, do you, Silas? The reason she killed herself?"

Silas says nothing. His hands shake, and he wants to punch his kid. Hard.

"Thing is, Silas. Saint Nancy was sick. Not just sick in the head. She was sick of you."

A sob rises through Silas, threatening to break him apart. He tries to speak, but words refuse to form.

"What's wrong, Daddy?" Joey's voice is mocking as he pulls a bag of something from a pocket. "Truth hurting too much?"

"What do you have there?" Silas says, his voice thick with a new dread.

"Just a little weed. You care to smoke with me?"

Silas stumbles back, his insides burning. "Drugs?"

Joey laughs. "What's wrong? Did you think little Joey was a good boy now? You think he turned straight?"

Silas stares, struck dumb.

"Straight is exactly what you want though, isn't it? No chance of this dirty little fag dying of AIDS then."

Silas's eyes flicker over this man. He has Joey's hair, Joey's eyes, Joey's

240

mouth. He's as much his son as he ever was.

"We gave up everything for you," he says, forcing his voice to stay even. "Everything. And what good did it do? You're still the same selfish piece of shit you always were."

Joey's smile falters, before he ratchets it back, bigger and brighter. "I'll take that as a no, shall I, Silas?"

* * *

Miguel leads Ellen onto the dance floor. It's been years since she last dared make a fool of herself in public, but knowing that, tonight, nobody is watching makes it into fun. And she's on a mission. Ellen's body tries to remember how to move, how to bend, how to sway. Dancing makes her whole body relax, leaving her cheeks warm with a blush. Kathy and Julia watch open-mouthed as Miguel's arm slips around her waist.

And then she realizes who's missing. Where did Patrick go?

The song ends, and Ellen looks around, sure everyone thought her ridiculous. Miguel links arms and leads her from the floor.

"You dance well," he says.

"Come meet my friends," she says, willing herself not to blush.

This handsome guy is gay. He likes Patrick. She has a chance to make someone's day. Or night. She just needs to know where the hell he vanished to. She can't just ask Kathy, because that would make this into a big deal. She's not beyond getting the DJ to stop playing music, have the lights turned up high, and putting out an all-points bulletin to locate her brother.

"Who is this?" Julia says, all but dropping to the floor in a curtsy.

"Just some guy I met."

Kathy jiggles on the spot. "Jeez Louise," she says. "And there I was thinking every other man on this trip was a homosexual. Trust you to find the one straight guy."

Miguel looks confused. Ellen needs to find a cover story.

"Where did Patrick go?" she says.

She motions toward the bar. "Patty went to join a line for drinks. Tell me more about your new friend."

Ellen glances around and spots Patrick, a drink in each hand, and a third in the crook of his elbow, talking to a cute redhead. Her heart sinks. Miguel hasn't seen; he's too busy answering quick-fire questions from Kathy and Julia.

She can't let the moment pass.

"Come with me," she says, grabbing his hand.

She pushes in between Patrick and the redhead.

"This is Miguel," she says. "I think you two should talk."

She takes the drinks, shrugs an apology at the third-wheel guy, and ducks away.

* * *

Silas shuts the door of his bedroom and sinks onto the bed, pulling out his cell and paging through to find Ellen's number. She told him to delete it, but he can't. Silas had wanted to suggest meeting up in New York. Rose keeps saying he should make new friends.

If he calls, Ellen might hang up. But then at least he would know for sure.

"You sound too much like a man who needs to be loved," Nancy's voice echoes, and from outside, there's a cheer and more laughter.

The party is in full swing. Joey is somewhere in the middle of it, smoking pot, not caring about him. Not caring about his mother.

Loneliness pangs, and Silas types a message.

Hi Ellen. It's Silas. Just checking in.

He backspaces. Checking in or checking up?

Which sounds better?

Is checking up creepy?

How are you?

Delete.

How are things?

Delete.

He doesn't know what to say. Isn't technology supposed to make everything easier? In the old days, he'd show up at a girl's front door, ask her father if he could ask her out, and that was that.

A cool breeze blows through an open window. Silas takes off his borrowed jacket and drapes it over the back of a chair. Fireworks light up the sky.

He can do this.

Maybe we could have dinner sometime.

Delete.

What the hell is he doing, anyway? She made it clear, there was no way she wanted to stay in touch.

Silas puts away his phone.

There's a sudden burst, as another firework pops and fizzes into the darkness. He lowers the shade and lies back.

How could Joey do that? After everything.

* * *

"That was a nice thing you did for Patrick," Julia says, as Ellen unzips her dress and steps from her shoes.

"Everyone deserves a little happiness."

Julia stops taking off her face. "Says the woman who told an eligible single man to delete her fucking number."

Ellen looks at her cell phone, but the screen is blank. She folds her hands in her lap.

"I know it might have sounded callous, but it wasn't like we were going to become love's young dream. I didn't want to lead him on."

The screen lights up.

Silas is online and typing a message.

Her heart leaps into her throat.

Three dots pulse, first gray, and then white, fading in, fading out.

"What I can't get is why you pushed him away," Julia says, oblivious to what's going on. "Silas seems like such a nice guy."

The dots stop pulsing.

"There isn't room in my life for a nice guy." Ellen tosses the cell aside.

"Truth be told, I don't know why I bothered meeting him at all."

"I do." Julia goes over to the minibar. "You wanted to have fun for a change and forget about the big bad world."

"Perhaps."

A miniature bottle of champagne opens with a pop.

"You're a brick wall," Julia says. "And I get why you're like that."

Ellen frowns. "I don't know what you mean."

"You're impossible to get through to. The Energizer Bunny of loneliness."

"I am not lonely!" She snatches a glass and swallows the contents in one gulp. It burns her stomach.

Julia shrugs. "Whatever helps you sleep at night."

Ellen clears her throat and exhales deeply. "I don't think Silas needs another complication in his life. And right now, what with me being sick, and you being sick, that's all I have to offer."

Julia laughs. "You're so full of shit, Ellen Gitelman." She holds out her hand. "Give me your phone."

* * *

It's after midnight, and Silas sits on the edge of the bed. Ellen sent a message.

Sorry about before. Let's meet up for drinks when I get home. We can talk. x.

The kiss might mean anything. Don't all women end their messages that way? Rose does, and she's hardly known for affection. He ought to reply, but what does he say?

Sure. Name the time and place.

Or does that sound too eager?

I'll call you.

Delete. Too dismissive.

He's been listening to Joey and Zach argue for the last hour. The strident rise and fall of fury travels through tightly shut doors. How could they be so angry with each other? And is this all because of him?

He opens his bedroom door a crack.

"It's not fair," Joey says. "It's not fair at all."

Silas's stomach lurches. He sniffs and wipes his eyes with the palm of his hand, and then creeps along the hall to the bathroom, reaching for the faucet to splash water on his face. He's had a headache since the party ended, and his insides hurt like they've been scooped out with a spoon. Footsteps in the hall have him holding his breath, afraid if he goes out and runs into Joey, the fight will drag him in. He waits for the muted sound of a television set and slips out of the bathroom. The door opposite is half open, and Zach sits on the bed, his back to the room, head in his hands.

"Are you okay?" Silas asks.

Zach turns, and fixes on a tired smile. "Did we wake you?"

"I needed the bathroom."

"We didn't mean to be so loud."

Zach's happy expression is supposed to be convincing, but he acts so defeated, as he rubs his neck and fixes his eyes on the floor.

"Joey couldn't sleep," he says. "Neither could I."

Back in his own room, Silas pulls a hospital shopping bag from the closet. The one they gave him in Miami. Sadness forms a vast black hole where his weak and failing heart should be. He got Joey wrong. The guy is a jerk. He has a right to be pissed at Silas, but not to keep being so mean. Lashing out at everyone. Silas reaches for the envelope of cash. It isn't his money. Not really. He'll take enough to cover a bus ticket home and a gift for Rose, and leave the rest for Joey. He can buy something for the kids. He can do whatever he likes. Silas knows when he's beaten.

None of what happened this evening makes him love Joey any the less. They can't be together. Not yet, anyhow. Maybe never.

In six hours, Silas will be in a cab and heading for a bus, taking him home. Where the heart is.

Chapter Twenty-Five

Silas brews a coffee in Tammy and Norman's kitchen. Morning breaks. The table is already set for breakfast, with dishes, mugs, and a wire basket for bread. The silence is bliss, nothing but the creak of a house and the hiss of hot water pipes. He'd crept around, taking a shower in the downstairs bathroom so as not to wake anyone. It's half past six. His taxi will be here soon enough.

Is he giving up too soon?

Grass isn't even illegal in many states. And who's to say it's any worse a drug than coffee or beer or regular cigarettes? And, for most people, it isn't. But Joey is an addict. He didn't go into rehab and emerge fixed or cured or made better, made whole. He will always be an addict, and Silas was told by the doctors how it was his job to make sure Joey steered clear of temptation. He'd taken his eye off the ball. But was there really any ball to watch? It's better they go back to the way they were. He knows he has a son. Joey knows he had a father. And never the two shall meet.

Tammy appears, yawning and dressed in an old sweatshirt, with her hair tied up in a yellow scrunchie. Her cat-face slippers shuffle to the refrigerator.

"Happy Christmas, Silas. You're up bright and early. Couldn't sleep?"

"I need to go home. You know what they say. A guest and a fish both smell after three days."

She cups his cheek in one hand. "We'll miss you."

Tammy and Norman are good people. Zach is a great kid. And so is Joey. But together they form a family that isn't his. Silas gives her a quick peck and pulls on his jacket. He needs to do this now.

At the door, she drags him into a hug, clinging tight. He gently pries her arms from around his waist and steps back.

"Norman can give you a ride to the bus station," she says. "It's no trouble."

"I'll be fine."

"You need money for that taxi?"

He hurries away the beginnings of a tear with his hand. "It's taken care of."

For one last moment, Silas stands still, wrapped in the comfort of a happy house sleeping.

"Give Joey my best."

* * *

Ellen sits down to breakfast. Alone. Everyone else on board seems to nurse a Christmas morning sore head. Julia didn't stir as she rattled around their room, taking a shower, drying her hair, trying on shoes. She pours herself a coffee and picks at a croissant. It's another stunningly beautiful day, with bright sunshine pouring through huge windows, glinting off a pale blue sea. And then she spots Kathy, holding a tray and searching for someplace to sit. It's too late to hide; she's been spotted. Kathy squeals and heads over.

"I'm so glad you're here," she says, as she sits. "I really need to talk to someone. Patty didn't come back last night. He just sent a message to say he's having breakfast in bed with Miguel."

Ellen summons a lukewarm smile. "How lovely."

Kathy takes a sip of her coffee, then sets down the cup. "Helen. I have to talk to you."

"Shoot."

"Tomorrow is a sort of anniversary for me. Not a good anniversary. One I would rather forget. It's just that Patty might try to do something." She looks quickly away, chewing her lip. "I don't know for sure. Otherwise, why insist on me coming on this trip? He could have sold the tickets. Instead, he wanted me to be here. With him."

Ellen stays quiet, sensing Kathy will share as much as she wants to share.

"I lost a baby," she says with a heavy sigh, and Ellen's hand moves to offer comfort. "A little girl. She was due in late spring, and I'd already picked out her name. Rachel. I started feeling sick, so Patty insisted I see somebody, but no. I knew better. I figured it could wait. Nobody disturbs their doctor in the middle of Christmas, right?"

A fat tear falls, and Ellen's heart aches.

Kathy wipes at her face. "This is stupid. I haven't cried about this in so long. Rachel is a part of my past, but I still miss her. I guess the pain is always there."

"You don't have to talk about her if it hurts," Ellen says.

Kathy leans her elbows on the table. "They made me go to the hospital and told me to get on a table. The nurse turned the ultrasound screen around, so I could see the picture. She was still there. I could see her. It was like she was waving."

"I'm so sorry." Ellen squeezes her hand.

Kathy clears her throat and sits up straight, as if to signal she's done with confession. "Is Patty planning something? A party? A memorial? Anything?"

Ellen shakes her head. "Nothing I know about."

The answer seems to comfort Kathy. "Thing is, Helen, I want tomorrow to be…I don't know…normal."

"You need me to double-check?"

Kathy sniffs. "I want to be prepared."

* * *

A blue cantilever bridge links two gray towers, their facades curving and smooth with large, square windows. The Boca Raton bus terminal, like any bus terminal, sits in the worst part of town. Silas crosses the road and heads inside, finding the ticket office deserted. The clerk at the only open window glances up from reading his newspaper, his brow furrowed at being disturbed during a shift he likely only agreed to cover on the promise of being away from either an empty home or one overstuffed with family and friends.

"You looking to travel this morning?" he says. "We're on a limited service on account of how this is Christmas Day."

He confirms an interstate bus leaves Boca just before seven, giving Silas an hour to kill in the desolate departure hall, where someone has turned out the lights, adding to a sense of him scoring front row seats for the end of the world.

"The basic price don't come with a reserved seat," the clerk says. "And you board last."

Silas glances around. Does this dude not see what he sees? There are no other passengers.

"I figure that's not a problem today," he says. "I mean, it's hardly rush hour."

"Not down here, for sure, but I can't promise the same when you reach Jacksonville. If the place you choose to sit in is already booked, you'll likely have to wait around for the later service."

"When might that be?"

"Next Greyhound departing here is five before nine tonight. It's not a gamble I would advise."

"Should I change my ticket?" Silas says.

He's never been one for leaving anything to chance. Nancy often laughed at the way he wrote to-do lists each time they took a weekend away, and the methodical manner he worked his way through their apartment: turn out the lights, check all power outlets, make certain the fridge door is closed, double-check windows, close all internal doors. Check the outlets once more. Locate the iron. Confirm Nancy didn't leave it plugged in. And then do the same with her hair dryer. Finally, he'd go around making sure every faucet was shut off and, if Nancy didn't jump around and scream and shout too loud, he'd head to the basement and shut off the water completely.

For someone so obsessed with leaving nothing to chance, the thought of not being able to reach New York tomorrow morning is too much.

"I'll book a seat," he says, but the clerk has already put his feet up on the counter, and is reading the sports pages.

"All sales are final, sir," he says without looking up. "There are no refunds."

* * *

"Kathy isn't a bad person," Patrick says after a five-minute diatribe, where he outlined each of his sister's many, many faults. She gossips, she thinks herself better than others, she cheats supermarket scales to pay less. "More than anything else. Kathy never stops to think before she speaks."

Ellen stays silent. She tracked Patrick down to the side of the pool, desperate to offload about Kathy's worries. He jumped to every kind of wrong conclusion, guessing his sister had been making a nuisance of herself.

"I mean," he continues, "why is she still getting your name wrong? And why don't you ever correct her?"

"Honestly? I find it endearing. I suppose I always quite liked the name Helen, and when I started working at the diner, it's what everyone called me."

Patrick glances up, his face a picture of surprise. "When she calls you Helen, it doesn't drive you wild?"

"Should it?"

"I'm being unreasonable, right?"

She decides to come straight out with it. "Kathy told about losing the baby."

He deflates. "I kinda hoped this trip would take her mind off things. It was a year ago tomorrow."

"That's what she told me, and I have to know…are you planning some kind of memorial?"

He sighs and closes his eyes. "It crossed my mind, but then I couldn't decide. I wanted to call our folks for advice, but they don't want anything to do with her."

"Kathy told me she wants tomorrow to be like any other day," Ellen says. "She was adamant. She said she's fine and nobody needs to feel guilty."

Patrick lets out a humorless laugh. "Is she fine, though? Really?"

"No…but that's what she told me would make her happy."

He glances up. "You get what the worst part of this is? Mom and Dad still choose to blame her. She hasn't spoken to Mom since it happened, and Dad tells everyone he only has a son. Even if I am a disappointing faggot who never made the soccer team."

Ellen nods, unsure what else to say or do.

"It's tough," he says. "To see Kathy like that, and think how much hurt she's carrying around, and to not be able to take even one bit of it away." Patrick studies her, his eyes wide. "I have to say or do something. No matter what."

Ellen glances up and spots Miguel heading their way. He's dressed in white canvas shorts and a flowing blue shirt.

"Leave it with me," she says. "I have an idea."

Chapter Twenty-Six

The ticket clerk in Boca was right. The Jacksonville Greyhound terminal is loud, crowded, and chaotic. Holiday season passengers push and jockey for places to sit and stare into space. By the time the bus parks, a pale amber sun is setting, and Silas wonders if a three-hour comfort break is overly generous. By now, Joey will know he's gone. What story will he spin for the kids?

"Daddy, where did Grandpa Silas go?" Lumen will ask.

"Don't call him that."

"But Daddy Zach said—"

"That man was just a guest. You'll never see the guy again."

Asshole.

Silas aches with fatigue, after eight hours on a bus where the driver played religious music. Not your regular "Hark the Herald Angels Sing" shit—this was full-on southern gospel. Two hours in, one brave passenger asked him to lower the volume and scored a mouthful of pious abuse, including the threat of being offloaded by the side of a deserted road. Silas fashioned earplugs from a torn paper napkin and tried to sleep.

Like any other municipality, Jacksonville has a homeless problem. And like in any other place, it centers on the bus station. Zombies shuffle, eyes vacant, hauling possessions in hefty bags, piled on makeshift carts. Armed security guards patrol, yelling at anyone who stops to catch their breath. A mangy dog weaves between legs, sniffing for food. The few working streetlights cast a dirty yellowed glow.

Silas sits on an uncomfortable metal bench, with cracked padding, and squints at a fuzzy TV screen above a sign that thanks him for *Going Greyhound*. On the other side of a grubby plastic divider, one overworked woman cooks and serves fried food to hungry travelers. He'd waited in line awhile, before opting, instead, for a vending machine sandwich. Now, he eats the last mouthful, wiping a sheen of grease from his fingers. Not long and he'll be home.

"Dude, you got money?" The kid asking can't be older than sixteen, and is wearing a dirty orange sweatsuit. "You gotta give me something. I'm hungry."

Silas digs into a pocket. "I got five bucks."

Loudspeakers announce the New York bus is ready to board.

"Don't buy food in here," Silas says. "Find a 7-Eleven."

The boy turns away and vomits. Thick, yellow chunks pool, causing other passengers to cry out. Within seconds, a heavy guy in uniform descends, barking orders, pointing a gun, and screaming at everyone to stand clear.

"Stop!" Silas says. "Give the kid a fucking break!"

The guard lowers his weapon. "Is he with you, old man? Get your boyfriend out of here."

* * *

When Ellen asked after the woman who taught gingerbread house building, the nebbish at guest relations shrugged and suggested the poolside bar.

"That's where she hangs out," he said, flashing a fake smile. "Mary drinks."

He was right. Mary isn't hard to spot. Hers is the only white bob on a line of high poolside stools.

"Excuse me," Ellen says, tapping a shoulder.

Mary turns around, putting a hand to her chest. "Jesus, girlie. You scared the living shit out of me. Give me some kinda warning."

"I'm so sorry," Ellen says and climbs onto the next stool. "I was at the gingerbread house workshop…"

"Oh sure." She looks Ellen up and down, her thin upper lip curling. "The broad who found the whole fucking thing to be some sort of joke."

Removed from a festive lair, Mary isn't anything like the apple-cheeked old lady with a whimsical love for Christmas. She's pale, with ghostly eyes, and a face that's seen a lifetime of cigarettes and alcohol.

"So what can I do for you?" she says, snapping her fingers for another drink.

"Do you do special one-off classes?"

"Who wants to know? You're not from the IRS?"

Ellen shakes her head. "A friend of mine lost a baby, and it's been a year."

Mary cuts her off. "Other women lose babies. Tell her to get on with life."

"She's having trouble letting go. She's…stuck."

"Then you're looking at the wrong person. I don't know how to get some ditz unstuck any more than you do."

Ellen's eyes water. "I just need someone to help."

Mary groans and her shoulders slump. "These are tears of pity?"

"I suppose I thought you could do something. Make figures. Angels. Anything, really."

"What the hell would that achieve?"

"Perhaps nothing," Ellen says, "but it might help my friend open up and talk a little more."

"You think it might help if this friend of yours gets in touch with her emotions?" Mary says. "Is that your plan?"

"I'll take that as a no," Ellen says, and gets up to go. "And I'll be sure to let the IRS know it's only the gingerbread houses they need to investigate."

Mary reaches out a hand and claws for Ellen's arm. "I said you were an idiot. I didn't say I was one too."

* * *

Silas sets a plastic tray on a grubby Formica table. They're in an almost-empty McDonald's looking out onto a divided highway. A tattered tinsel tree flickers in one corner, and a sign on the window wishes everyone *Happy Holidays*.

The kid doesn't look up. The hood of his sweatshirt covers his features.

"It is manners to show your face at the dinner table," Silas says.

It earns him a sucking sound. A full minute later, the kid pulls off his hood, and Silas can't help but see his skin is sallow, like cheap soap, his eyes red and rheumy, weighed down with the worries of someone many years older.

"How long since you ate?" he says.

The man-child opposite picks up his burger and gnaws silently. Silas drinks a strong black coffee.

"You want I should get you more?" he says, when the food is all gone.

The kid glances up. "I'll let you fuck me. Fifty bucks."

Silas gawps. What exactly do you say to that? Does he break off into how he isn't offended, and isn't gay—not that he's anti-gay, because his son so happens to be that way inclined, and Joey has a husband and kids.

"Forty," the kid says. "Final offer. No kissing."

"I only wanted to do something nice for you," Silas says. "It's Christmastime, for fuck's sake."

"Your loss." He wipes a dirty hand across his greasy mouth. "You look as if you could really hurt me. I'm into that."

Without invitation, the kid lifts his shirt, and Silas sees how the skin around his ribs has a green and yellow tinge from what can only be a recent beating.

"Who did that to you?" he says.

The kid shrugs. "Another guy. Looked a lot like you. Paid me well."

"What's your name?"

"Victor."

"Do you live here...in Jacksonville, I mean?"

Victor shrugs. "For now. Thought I might head for someplace else soon. Perhaps New York City. That where you're heading?"

"Do you have friends there?"

He stuffs french fries into his mouth and chews listlessly. "I don't got friends nowhere. My old man kicked me out on account of how I'm a cock-sucking fag and all."

"What about your mother?"

"She died. Meth."

Silas peers out at the street, then back at the kid. "When did you last speak to your father?"

"A while ago. He used to smack me in the mouth. And I let him. At least that meant he was listening to what I had to say. He knew I was alive. That was all before Mom got sick. Now we don't talk at all." He rests his head on the stained table. "Final, final offer. I'll suck your dick for ten bucks. You strike me as a pretty cool guy."

Silas pulls out his wallet. "Take this. Find a place where you can sleep tonight. Call your father."

Victor's eyes widen. "No fucking way!"

"Why not?"

"Because he wants me dead. Dude hates my guts."

"That isn't going to be true," Silas says. "A father can't hate their kid. He—"

The boy pushes away from the table and stands. "You don't know shit. Nobody does. Nobody gets what it's like to be me and to go home and tell your old man you're a faggot and let him beat the life out of you for daring to breathe. Nobody knows shit!"

He grabs the money anyway, and Silas watches him scoot across the busy road. Cars sound their horns.

The next bus leaves in two hours. In his pocket, his cell phone vibrates.

"What the hell, Silas." It's Rose. "You took off from Joey's place without saying goodbye?"

* * *

Mary is back in full apple-pie mode, wrapped in a shawl, and wearing a floral dress and a straw hat. Her cheeks are rosy with blush, and the corners of her mouth are turned up in a smile. She hums a soft tune as the others file into the room.

"This is a special class," she says, clapping her hands. "A chance for us to remember someone lost before their time."

Kathy makes a raspy sound, like she's strangled herself. Her nose is red and dripping, her lips pursed and puffy. Ellen sees how Patrick squeezes her hand.

"I'm talking about your baby, honey," Mary says. "Your sweet little baby."

Patrick looks like he's turned to stone, and Kathy's eyes swim with even more tears.

"It's a good time for this, because you've been feeling the loss for too long. And now it's time to let it go." Mary's voice is as smooth and sweet as caramel.

"I can't," Kathy mumbles. "I can't simply forget."

Mary chuckles. "I know you can. You want to."

And then, in a rush of words, Kathy is telling her story.

She was on the pill, and it shouldn't have happened. She was having her period. She was at the gym and left her pills in the pocket of her jacket. She didn't even want a baby. She's dreamed about Rachel every night since.

"It's not fair," she says. "I couldn't really love her. I told myself how I didn't even want her." She looks up with red-rimmed eyes. "Now I miss her. All the time."

Ellen straightens in her chair. It's all so sad. She turns to Patrick and tries to catch his eye. But he's staring at Kathy. His face filled with fear.

"Okay, now it's time for your baby girl to rest," Mary says. "We're going to make her a gift to show her how much we all care."

She leads the four of them to the center of the room. On a table are several bowls of brightly colored yarn.

"It's very simple," Mary says. "We work in unison to create a chain, wrapping the yarn around our fingers. Then we wrap the chain around a special cloth. And we keep wrapping, making a cocoon for your baby."

Mary demonstrates, first wrapping pink yarn around her left index finger, and then she wraps the next thread around her right index finger. Ellen looks at Kathy. Her eyes are shut. Patrick's too.

Around and around and around the yarn goes.

"When we're finished, we put our cocoon in a special place," Mary says. "And we let it rest there until the baby's spirit leaves you and finds its peace."

"Will any of this hurt?" Kathy asks.

"You'll perhaps sense a little tug, but it'll be okay," Mary says. "Everyone. Let's weave this motherfucker."

∗ ∗ ∗

Silas is one of the first to board the next funky-smelling bus bound for New York. The recycled air weighs heavy on his skin as he heads for the back, fingers brushing against the grime of other people. Slowly, the empty seats fill, and the engine rumbles into life. He'd been scouring the street, hoping to spot Victor, needing to know he's safe. A stoplight turns green, and the bus lurches forward. Silas leans his head against the window, the glass cool against his cheek. His mouth is dry, and he reaches into his bag, pulling out a bottle of water and flipping off the lid, taking a long slug. He checks his phone. One full day and no call from Joey. And still nothing more from Ellen.

Empty stretches of road blur. The sky is clear and peppered with stars. All around him, strangers sleep, some wrapped in blankets, others with the hoods of jackets pulled over their faces.

And there she is. Nancy. Sat right across the aisle, smiling. Like always. He goes to call out her name, but she signals for quiet. Other people need to sleep. There's no reason to be rude.

"I still love our boy," he whispers, after checking nobody is listening. "That won't ever change."

Nancy nods. She's young again, or maybe that's how he's chosen to remember her. How might she look now if the world had turned in a different way and they'd grown old together?

"I don't think I *like* our boy," he says, trying the words out for size. "Is that okay too?"

She cocks her head to one side and winks—like she always did when she had the upper hand.

"Them's the breaks. You do what you can. You can't live his life."

Chapter Twenty-Seven

Ellen vows she'll never drink again. And this isn't one of those proclamations everyone makes when they wake hungover like hell. This one is serious. Even her hair hurts. After Kathy's ceremony, they decamped to a place on level three, and took up residence on high stools, talking long past when they should have broken for dinner. The only food she recalls eating was a sandwich from the midnight buffet. At least she thinks she ate it. There's the vaguest memory of being too drunk to get the wrapper off. She's hungry now. But hunger is nothing compared to a raging thirst.

"Orange juice," she says with a hopeful nod to the guy serving drinks on the otherwise-deserted pool deck. "The biggest glass you can find."

She closes eyes that sting, despite wearing shades. With New York just days away, the Eastern Seaboard winds blow colder, and a shiver climbs her spine. Last night, Ellen told literally everyone about how she was going back to school. At age sixty-seven. People clapped and cheered.

"I'm planning on being a photographer," she'd said, hoping it might be true.

Nobody looked at her with pity. They told her what a great idea it was.

Mary's ceremony woke something deep in Ellen. It was more than the will to live out her college dreams. She saw how you could let go of love and still cherish the good things about it. Kathy hadn't been the only one weaving wool and saying her goodbyes.

"Hey there." Patrick pulls out a chair. "You okay? You were miles away."

"Enjoying the last of the sunshine," she says. "Before New York takes hold and hell literally freezes over."

He laughs. "I had a pen pal at school, who lived in Australia, and he wrote me about how they went to the beach on Christmas Day."

Ellen takes a lungful of ocean air, willing it to settle her rolling stomach. "This is going to sound weird, but I miss the city in the winter. I know everyone bitches about the snow and the sleet and the sludge and how they can never get warm, but did you ever go through Central Park early in the morning, right after sunrise, when there's frost on every tree?"

Patrick shakes his head. "Maybe that goes on *my* bucket list."

"Look me up next time you come to town. I'll take you tree spotting."

For a while, neither of them says anything, and then Patrick clears his throat. "Kathy had a great time last night. It was super kind of you."

Ellen manages a smile. "We all had a blast. I'm paying for it now."

He gazes out across the surface of the pool. "I'm not quite ready to go back to normal life."

She sighs to herself. "It's too soon, right?"

"Miguel wants us to have some kind of long-distance love affair, and I told him okay, but we both know that isn't going to work."

Ellen nods. "Reality can be a bitch."

"Couldn't have put it better myself." Patrick sounds thoughtful, as though he's had a strange and wonderful idea. "What if we make *this* a thing? You and me, and Kathy and Julia. How about, every year, we meet up and hang out? Even if only for a day or two. Even for the one night."

She grins. "I mean, there's no reason we couldn't."

"It could be our way of closing the year. The four of us, in New York. Or wherever we want to be. Perhaps on some other cruise ship."

Ellen's stomach flutters. "I love that idea."

More than anything, she needs someone to report back to. Someone who won't let her get away with excuses why she never mailed back her college application papers, or what made her take another waitress job, rather than live her dream. Or why she never called Silas for that drink.

"And the rest of the year," Patrick says. "We live our lives, making sure we do stuff worth talking about when we meet up."

Warmth spreads through her, remembering Otto, and the way he used to insist she was worth so much more than waiting tables at some shitty back-street diner. The day he died, so did every one of her dreams. It's only now she dares hope there might be another way.

"They serve mulled wine," she says. "What say we drink to the future?"

* * *

As the Greyhound bus rumbles over the Manhattan Bridge, midmorning sun peeks between glass towers, turning their tips coral and gold. Silas shifts in his seat, lifting his chin and shading his eyes. The buildings pulse with power and elegance. Speeding along Flatbush toward the beating heart of the city, he fumbles with his phone, and tries Rose's number. Silas isn't sure what she'll want from him. The full story or his side of what happened.

She sounds sleepy but insists he come over.

His life is normal once more. He's home. He still has Rose's friendship. He still has Ellen's message. Unanswered.

We can talk, she wrote.

He can't think what to say back. *It's not you, it's me* is a classic cop-out. Even if it happens to be true.

The sun slithers around buildings and creeps along the sidewalks as the bus lurches into the Albany Terminal, where Silas tugs at his bag, before stepping out into frigid Manhattan air. He pulls up his collar and tightens a scarf around his neck.

Halfway along the next block, he ducks into a doorway and pulls out his cell.

Ellen deserves better.

* * *

When Ellen was a kid, Christmas in her household was much like any other. She envied kids in nearby homes with their decorated trees, paper streamers, and visits from Santa. Throughout December, billboards advertised Christmas movies, and the radio played Bing Crosby. The magic of the holiday season beckoned with all its sweetness, cinnamon, and spice. She asked a teacher why she was missing out, and why there was no history lesson on the birth of Jesus and rededication of the Temple in Jerusalem.

"People celebrate different holidays," the teacher said. "Some celebrate Christmas, but your family gets to celebrate Hanukkah."

Naturally enough, her folks did all they could to stop her feeling different. They lit the Hanukkiah, hung lights, cooked latkes, ate jelly doughnuts, and gave gifts each night. She still got to marvel at department store window displays. Each year, they took the D Train to Brooklyn and joined the crowds of people heading to the decorated houses of Dyker Heights to witness life-sized Santas, sleighs, and snowmen. Some homes pumped carols from loudspeakers. But as soon as they boarded the train home, that was it. They left this version of Christmas behind.

On the MS Viking, Ellen can't jump on a train and be someplace else. Instead, she finds herself in the shower, humming songs that would send her grandmother into flitters.

"You gotta see this," Julia calls from the other room. "We finally got a card. Crown Atlantic respects religious diversity. They wished us Merry Winterval."

Ellen emerges wrapped in a towel and sits on the edge of the bed.

"I had a message from Silas," she says, trying to keep the excitement from her voice.

Julia brightens. "Did he tell you he can't live without you? Each minute alone is painful?"

"He told me to call when I'm free for a coffee."

"It's a start. The guy was always going to need time to get down on bended knee."

"So, you think I *should* call him?"

Julia throws up her hands in despair. "Have you learned nothing on this trip? Life is very short, and we get so few chances to be happy. Why would you not?"

Julia is dressed in a white running suit, her hair tied back, her face left bare.

"Are you drying out?" Ellen says. "Is this some New Year thing?"

"Kathy made me promise to go bowling. I blame the champagne cocktails."

"You can't bowl."

"Neither can Kathy. She caught me at a weak moment right after the whole baby funeral."

"It's for two more days," Ellen says. "And after that, we only need to see her once a year."

Julia spins around, her mouth hangs open. "Say that last bit again."

* * *

Silas stops and pays for two coffees, one with extra sugar and cream, just the way Rose likes it.

"Who the fuck is it?" her voice spits when he rings the buzzer.

"Do you want to make friends with Jesus?"

There's a short pause. "Silas?"

"In the flesh."

The door clicks, and he's inside. She isn't waiting by her apartment door. Instead, it's left half open, and Silas picks up on the smell of incense. A burned stick lies cold in a saucer in the hall where he hangs his coat.

"You playing hide and seek?" he calls, and Rose appears in the bedroom doorway, wrapped in a sheet, wearing no makeup with her hair loose.

"What the actual fuck?" she says. "It's Boxing Day. Shouldn't you be out someplace else...boxing...or whatever."

The apartment is messy, with cups and plates still in the sink, and he feels her eyes burning into him.

"You look rough," he says.

The backs of her legs disappear into a pair of black jeans, and her feet into grubby gray mules. "What exactly are you doing here, Silas?"

"Spending quality time with an old friend."

She shrugs on a cardigan and moves past him to the kitchen to light a cigarette, hacking at the first puff. "Want one?"

He shakes his head. "Filthy habit."

"So sue me." She inhales and holds the smoke, letting it out slowly, and picking up a crumpled packet of Luckies. "You want to talk about what happened with Joey?"

"I've got something to show you." He hands her his phone.

She reads and then sniffs. "I assume Ellen is a she, and you need wardrobe advice. This isn't just you being a prince and dropping by with a cup of joe?"

"She reminds me of Nancy."

Ash tumbles on the carpet. "In what way?"

"She's smart. She knows how to handle herself."

"Did you fuck her yet?"

He laughs. "Seriously? No, I didn't."

"What do you want from me, Silas? What do you want from us?"

The sudden change in her tone makes him frown. He moves toward her and puts his hands on her waist, pulling her close. She doesn't resist, and he kisses her forehead. It's warm and tastes just a little salty.

"I missed you, Rose."

"You're an asshole," she says, and drops her cigarette in a not-quite-empty wine glass. "What the fuck are you even doing here?"

He watches as she goes into the bedroom. Does she want him to follow?

Chapter Twenty-Eight

Rose runs a hand through her hair. Even without makeup, and woken from sleep, she's pretty. Her skin is flawless and colorless, like polished best porcelain. She lights a cigarette and waves him over to a lounge chair. After taking a long drag, she sighs with lustful satisfaction.

"A good fuck was what I needed."

Silas grins. "Happy holidays, I guess."

She pulls a chair from under the cluttered kitchen table and sits. "Tell me everything. I need to know what really happened in Florida."

"Didn't Joey already call and tell you how I was Satan in borrowed clothes?"

She grins. "Spill already."

Silas aches with tiredness. He had hoped to sleep on the bus journey, but each time he closed his eyes, faces came to visit. First Joey, his expression twisted and resentful. Then Ellen. She acted disappointed. Tammy stopped by to remind him he's a decent man. One thing struck him. Nancy stayed away.

"The smart money says I don't get to win Father of the Year," he says, with a heavy sigh, part of him hoping Rose has talked with Joey and will contradict this. Instead, she half-smiles.

"Is this your way of admitting I was right all along?" she says. "Now you agree on how you should have let sleeping dogs lie?"

"I got to meet my grandkids."

"Big fucking deal. That leaves you with two extra lives to hanker after."

Silas wants to tell her to shut up. He aches with the newness of another day. Rose is so much like Nancy, and yet she couldn't be more different.

"You asked me why I came to see you," he says.

She winks and reaches for a jug of coffee. "I think we both know why you came calling, Silas."

He takes a breath. This is it. He needs to say out loud what he rehearsed already a dozen times.

"We have to end whatever…this is, Rose. We have to end us."

She raises an eyebrow. "Suddenly, there's an *us*?"

"Can we go back to how things were? Back to how we acted around each other when Nancy was still alive? We can't carry on…being together."

Her head jerks. "We're friends with benefits, right? Nothing heavy."

"Be honest with me," he says. "That's just the two of us finding a way to explain why we're being disloyal to Nancy. And for all the big talk, I know you think that."

She takes another drag of her cigarette. "And then there's Ellen."

Silas feels a stab in his gut. "She's not like you. She doesn't have your…"

She raises an eyebrow. "Be very careful what you say next."

"Your…freedom."

"I'm not so free." Her eyes grow wide. Serious. "I keep things in check. Like with you, now. I have to make sure I'm saying and doing what's right. I'm not sure that's really me. I was always the good sister. Nancy got away with shit."

Silas grins. "You're telling me you've never done anything wrong in your life?"

"That's not what I mean," she says and places a hand on his. "I don't know if I want to be the person that life made me."

"Fine," Silas says. "Give me both barrels. What did my kid say?"

"He called to see if I knew where you might have got to, and we got to talking. I figured he should know what's been going on between you and me, and so I told him. Laid it on the line."

For ten whole seconds, Silas says nothing. Did he imagine what she just said? Is his mind playing tricks? He kinda thinks Rose just told him she spilled everything to Joey. She told him they were sleeping together. Surely not. She wouldn't just blurt that out. Not without discussion.

"How did you figure out that might help?" he says, eventually, trying to keep his voice even, while a scream takes hold between his ears.

"The kid wasn't fazed. If anything, his take on it is that life's too short to keep questioning what comes your way."

"This still has to stop," he says. "We're done."

Rose strokes his arm. "I know that, Silas. I've known it for a while. I guess I didn't want to be the one to say it."

Outside, cars and trucks rumble over the bridge. A world goes about its day, not caring that, behind one of the many windows, in one of the many buildings, a man is breaking ties with the one woman who connects him to a life he once loved.

"My kid grew up and became an asshole," he says without thinking.

Rose throws back her head and laughs. "At fucking last. You got there in the end. My nephew is an A1 asshole. Graduated cum laude."

"He's still my son."

"And you're an asshole too. Just a nicer kind of asshole. Joey needs to learn a few more lessons about life. And you can teach him the most important one."

Silas isn't sure what she means.

"It's simple enough," she says. "You start by giving up. You stop sending him cards, stop leaving messages. You write him one last letter and wish him well, and say you hope he gets to enjoy a full and rewarding life."

"And then what?"

Rose shrugs and sighs. "You wait until the klutz works out that he can't have every damn thing he wants each time he fucking whistles. You stop dancing to his tune and trying to win him over. That's how Joey gets his kicks, seeing you turn yourself inside out."

She stubs out her cigarette, like that's her final word on the situation, and she knows she's right. For Rose, the road ahead appears straightforward and simple.

Silas can't help but shake his head. "You reckon that's going to work?"

"After my sister died, you spoiled that kid. You wouldn't let nobody help.

I had to tiptoe around and never mention Nancy, in case it upset poor little Joey. All he wanted was a world where the people around him let him share in the grief. You assumed you were protecting him, when, in fact, you changed him into a thoughtless punk. He created his own version of the world. His own reasons for being. And, somewhere along the way, he turned you into the enemy."

Silas balls a fist into his mouth. "I never meant for that to happen."

Rose leans back in her chair. "Nobody ever does. The thing you need to do now, is to be ready to let him back in, but to make that happen, first you need to slam doors."

"How does that work?"

"Joey wants what Joey can't have. He's an addict. It's in his blood."

"So what? I sit and wait?"

"It might take a while, but he'll work out for himself that he lost something even bigger than his mom, and the only way he can get *you* back is to reach out."

Silas gets to his feet and goes to the kitchen window. New York City. The place where you get to reinvent yourself, and nobody gives a shit about the version of you left behind for rats to pick apart.

"What do I do about Ellen?" he says.

"Are you asking your former fuck buddy for dating advice?"

"Who else do I got?"

Rose thinks for a minute, then grins. "You're already screwed up enough to fill a big-ass stadium. You don't need somebody else to add to the confusion. But Silas French doesn't work well on his own. He needs a body with the same amount of grit, who might put up with his crap and give it back."

Silas is quiet for a moment. "So you're telling me to go for it?"

"I'm telling you to get back out there. Nancy is gone, and you're still a hot commodity. The world wants you, so why are you wasting time with a woman who can't let herself love you back?"

* * *

Ellen slept well, but feels no better for it. This morning, her feet hurt for the first time. Malinowski warned it might happen. Pain she can deal with, the fatigue is something else. He said her to pace herself and keep things on an even keel. That if she pushed too hard, there would be down days. Ellen has never been a layabout, and being told to change the speed at which she lives is like trying to leap over the moon. In the shower, she found a new rash on her thigh, like psoriasis, and no matter how much body cream she slathers on now, it refuses to fade.

She moves around their room, trying to work out a kink in her back.

"You okay, hon?" Julia says, as she folds clothes into neat stacks ready for packing. "You're still kinda pale."

"Just a little tired." Ellen's voice is flat, and she grunts as she sits and lifts her left leg onto the coffee table to massage the sole of her painful foot.

"Why don't you call Silas?" Julia says. "You're not sixteen. Why all the text messages?"

"I'm scared that, if I do, he won't pick up."

"Then he's not the man you thought he was." Julia sniffs. "People get hurt, hearts get broken. But you need to know that at least you tried. Maybe he didn't see your message. We already know he's careless. The guy left two grand lying under our bed. Maybe he lost his phone."

Ellen picks at the skin around her fingernails. There's a tick right next to the message she sent Silas that signals he read it. Ten seconds after she hit send. Her stomach is tight, and her hands shake.

"He's ignoring me," she says.

Julia rolls her eyes. "Did it ever cross your mind the guy might be nervous?"

Ellen's fingernails leave red half-moons in her palms. "I get what you're trying to do, but I put myself out there and got knocked back. I've sent a message, and he didn't answer. Unless the guy got kidnapped by aliens, what excuse is there?"

"Try one more time. Normal people meet up all the time. It doesn't mean they're committing to spending the rest of their lives together."

Ellen glances up from her phone. "What exactly do I say?"

"Tell him to meet you at that ghastly tourist trap on Columbus Circle, where you insisted on taking me? That's as far from a romantic gesture as New York gets."

In a little over forty-eight hours, the MS Viking will dock, and Ellen will be home. Even though she's thought of nothing but the comfort and privacy of her tiny apartment, part of her dreads a return to normal.

She tosses the phone aside. "I can't do it."

Julia stops what she's doing. "Give me one good reason."

"I just…it's stupid." Ellen brushes her hands over her face. "Everything is different now. I lost my job. I'm going back to school."

"It's not like we live in a war zone. Friends do still drink coffee. I have it on good authority."

Very few good things had happened in Ellen's life, and Silas might well become one of them. The last thing she wants to do is get it wrong. Build up hope, where hope isn't welcome.

"I'm not ready for a relationship," she says.

"That's fine. You're ready for a friend." Julia gestures toward the phone. "And he's right there."

* * *

Ziggy's Bar never changes. The same dark wood and the same dim lights. And Silas finds his stool empty, right where he left it, waiting for his inevitable return. He's missed the stench of stale beer, the always-sticky floor, and Larry acting pissed at having to get off his lazy ass and tend bar.

"They fire you from the cruise ship?" Larry says, as he reaches for a beer. "You good for this?"

Silas shoots him side eye. "I had a heart attack. Next question."

Larry's eyebrows arch. "You sure beer is the right thing to be drinking? Don't they got you on some kinda health kick?"

"Does this shithole serve fancy mineral water?" Silas pulls his first swig.

Larry leans back against a shelf and crosses both arms over his gut. "How come you're back and not in Florida with Joey?"

"I'm giving the kid space."

"Space to do what?" He glances over to where Rose shrugs off her jacket before climbing onto the next stool. She surveys the joint before nodding approval.

"So this is the famous guy you pay to listen to your crap?" she says and holds out a hand in greeting. "I'm Rose. Silas told me you were one ugly motherfucker, and shit, but he was spot on."

Larry shakes his head and fixes another beer. "One day, when you're ready, you can fill me in on what happened."

Silas grins as he and Rose clink bottles together in a toast.

"You finally good to be seen with me in public?" he says.

"I'm your sister-in-law, what's the harm in the two of us sinking a friendly beer?"

"We should make this a regular thing."

Rose shares a smile. "You think you might run that past your new girlfriend?"

Silas flinches. He promised to call Ellen. And he really did mean it when he said he would. It's just, he couldn't work out what to say. How to avoid sounding like a fool. Right now, things between them were on hold. Either could pick up where they left off.

"Let me guess," Rose says. "You still didn't call?"

He sighs and rubs his face with his palm. "It's complicated."

The stool squeaks as she turns to face him. "Let me give you some advice on relationships, Silas. They're as complicated as you fucking care to make them. Most women want a ballsy guy who's gonna make them feel good. He has to screw them hard one minute, and the next tell them they look pretty, especially when they feel ugly. If a guy can fix a broken shelf, that's all to the good. I truly believe you can hit that low bar."

"Thanks." He takes another swig of beer. "What makes you think I need your dumb dating advice?"

Rose shrugs. "You've made a habit of dating the same type. I know you better than anyone. If a lady comes even close to my sister, you go looking for a problem. This Ellen sounds like she just might make the grade."

Silas raises his bottle in another toast. "She does."

* * *

Ellen sets down her book and holds her breath. She hears the soft splash of water and then a sigh. Julia is in the tub. She stares at the phone. His message is still there, still showing it was read. Still lacking an answer.

She taps on the bathroom door.

"Come in," Julia says. "The plan is to soak until my whole body looks like a California raisin."

The door creaks open, and she steps into steam. Julia's hair is piled on her head in a sloppy bun, her face free of makeup, her skin flushed.

"Is everything okay?" she says, without opening her eyes.

"What exactly do I do about Silas?"

Julia's lips purse. "What do you want to do?"

"I...I truly have no clue."

"Perhaps now might be as good a time as any to decide."

Ellen tries a deep breath, hoping it might go some way to calming her nerves. It doesn't. "Am I too old to be acting like this?" she says. "People our age—"

Julia raises a hand for silence. "People our age have every right to act like schmucks. We've earned it. Call it a badge of honor."

"Okay, so let's put it another way. What would Julia Hoffman do?"

"I'd call his physician and check for lasting heart problems. If Silas gets the all-clear, I'd invite him for dinner. The obvious advantage here is you share a doctor, and that makes it easy."

"What happens after dinner?"

"I'd ask if he wanted to pay for a room at the Ritz-Carlton. Better yet, a suite."

Ellen laughs. "Seriously?"

"I'm kidding. I'd probably say thanks, but let's take it slow."

Ellen smiles to herself. Julia's right. She's doing what she always does and letting one tiny seed of doubt grow into runaway creepers of despair.

"I'm going to message him," she says.

"Good."

"Except…I have no idea what to say."

Julia blinks. "Say hello and see where that goes." She reaches for a loofah. "Now get the fuck out. The deal is, you act on my advice, and I get a whole bunch of quality *me time*."

* * *

Ellen sits on the edge of a bed and studies the screen of her phone. She could call him, but is it easier to send a message? What if she gets tongue-tied and says the wrong thing? Or she hears something in his voice that suggests she got it all wrong? He was just being friendly. Not that friendly is a problem. She doesn't have nearly enough friends. One more would be welcome.

Her thumbs tap against the screen.

Hi Silas,

I wanted to say that I hope you're well.

Ellen x

Too formal. She might as well be asking if he ever considered paying up front for a funeral plot. And given the guy had a heart attack, he most likely won't be well.

Think on, Ellen, Think on.

Hi Silas,

I have been very busy, but I hope you are okay.

Ellen x

Now she's making excuses, and he knows she's on the MS Viking. How can she be busy? Busy doing what? Busy putting off getting in touch. She can do better.

Hi Silas,

I wanted to say that I have been thinking about you, and I hope you are okay.

Ellen x

There's a sound from the bathroom. Ellen drops her phone like it's on fire and holds her breath. Soon enough, Julia starts to whistle, and water runs.

Silas,

I cannot say this in person, but you were right. I was wrong. I understand now.

Ellen x

She frowns at the screen, unwilling to press send. What if this backfires? What was she wrong about, anyway? She needs to sound more sincere.

Hi Silas,

I think about you all the time. I would like to meet up. I hope you are okay.

Ellen x

She takes a deep breath. It's not perfect, but there's a chance it will get him to reply.

Chapter Twenty-Nine

Through the tiny porthole, Ellen sees the weather has changed. Gunmetal gray clouds hang pleasingly low and threaten rain. The ocean has become a wild, rolling plain of darkening water. All is well with the world.

It's almost three o'clock, and Julia isn't back. She left late morning to buy gifts for the ladies who lunch, promising to return within the hour. Ellen tries calling, but as always, it goes straight to voicemail. Why does Julia bother with a cell phone? She never picks up.

Today is not a good day. Her bones ache, her toes and fingers tingle, and even dimmed lighting is proving too much. Some unseen force drained her energy.

When she makes it to the bathroom, she needs to sit on the edge of the tub, catching her breath, as a sharp stabbing pain in her midriff renders her almost breathless. She places a hand on the cold tiles to steady herself and takes slow, even breaths. In the dim light, her reflection is drawn and tired, with dark gray circles under both eyes. Her hair is limp and lifeless.

She turns on the faucet, brushes her teeth, and stumbles her way back to bed.

It's dark outside when next she wakes, and still there's no sign of Julia. Her phone says five o'clock, so she's slept two hours. And yet, she feels no better. If anything, her body is more exhausted. The pain in her abdomen has subsided, but a dull ache remains.

This is what Malinowski talked about. This is lupus in all its glory. And there might not be a cure. She could be feeling like this every day. Until she feels nothing at all. She tugs the covers up around her chin, wishing she could simply disappear.

How can she possibly go back to school when it hurts to blink? When she can't hold a pen? How will she deal with the stares, the whispers, and the inevitable pity?

That old girl. What was she thinking?

There's one blue pill left. She'd been saving it, just in case, planning on breaking it in two. Without a second thought, she swallows it whole, choking on water, but keeping it down, even when her stomach protests.

It's ten after six when next she wakes.

The wave of exhaustion has passed, and she reaches for her phone and tries Julia again. When there's no answer, she calls Malinowski. At home.

"I'm so incredibly sorry," she says. "This is out of order."

"Ellen?" He sounds concerned. "Where are you? What's wrong?"

"Nothing. Not really. I was wondering if you could arrange a refill of my medication."

"Are you okay? Are you having a flare?"

"I need to not be in pain. I can't think straight, and I can't do anything. I'm so tired all the time."

"Are you at home?"

She swallows what tastes a lot like vomit. "I'm a day away. Still at sea."

He sighs to himself. "I guess I can try. But the ship pharmacy might not carry what I prescribe."

"I'll take whatever you got to get me back home in one piece. Valium. Whatever."

"Okay. Let me see what I can do."

There's a click as he hangs up.

* * *

Silas gets his hair cut once a year by a guy called Ali, in a tiny shop where one worn and well-used chair sits in the window next to a neon sign. A single blue bulb shines on a small mirror. The only source of heat is a paraffin stove, which doubles to warm-up water.

"So, Silas," Ali says. "What we gonna do today?"

"Trim it."

He sprays the back of Silas's head with water, and the sound of the electric clippers becomes hypnotic. Silas gazes at the far wall, covered in posters of sportsmen and celebrities, trying to clear his mind.

Ali sets aside the clippers and picks up scissors to *snip, snip, snip* with amazing speed.

"You need a shave," he says. "Want me to take care of that?"

"I had one last month."

"A proper shave. No more of this designer stubble."

Silas lies back in the chair and closes his eyes as Ali works his magic, and when done, he wraps Silas's face in a hot towel scented with rose oil. They're still chatting when Ali's wife, Fatima, comes in to cluck about and insist both men share homemade soup and warm bread.

"Hasn't your boy been to see you?" she asks. Like she did last year and the one before.

Silas shakes his head. "I visited with him in Florida."

Fatima's eyes open wide. "Why did you ever come back here to the cold?"

"You know me," he says. "My heart is in the city."

They talk about the New Year, and Ali explains how his whole brood plans on standing in Times Square and watching the ball drop. Silas has no family. Apart from Rose, and she already said she's staying in to watch Anderson Cooper.

"Please join us," Fatima says. "We would be so honored."

He mumbles something he hopes sounds like a vague yes, then tries to make his excuses, but Ali insists on making a fresh pot of coffee. Silas catches sight of his face again in the dimly lit mirror. Sixty-eight years old, and he might as well be a hundred. Of course, Rose agreed to end things with him. She must have danced a jig.

He takes his time walking home, past the same buildings, doughnut shops, dry cleaners, florists, pet stores, and in front of his door, he glances up at the apartment where he's lived for the last forty years.

He stands on the threshold.

He could go to the bodega and buy wine, but he's had enough of being on his own. Life didn't end when he boarded that Greyhound.

* * *

A pretty young nurse holds a penlight inches from Ellen's eye and tells her to look this way and that. She asks if Ellen wears glasses.

"Only to read. Even then, I squish up my eyes. I never know where I leave the damn things."

"What about the light in here?" She nods toward a circular ceiling lamp. "Does that bother you?"

"Someone could take a cloth and wipe away the dust, but no. It's okay."

"Any loss of consciousness? Any family history of seizures or strokes?"

Ellen gets that the girl is simply doing her job, but all she came here for was to collect medicine. Malinowski made no mention of needing to undergo any sort of examination. From the other side of a plastic curtain, tinny music plays, and a man's voice speaks in heavily accented English.

"I'm sorry about that," the nurse says. "We're having a small party."

Ellen can't help but ask if she's being a pain by getting in the way of what sounds like a celebration. She's about to excuse herself, when a thought occurs. "If you don't mind me asking, how old are you?"

"Twenty-eight, why?"

"Obviously, you studied at college."

"I have a Bachelor's in Biology and a Master's in Nursing."

Ellen sighs to herself. "I'm going back to school. In spring. To study photography."

"That's a great idea. Nobody is too old to try something new."

This is Ellen's big chance to quiz someone who's been there, done that, and she has a million questions. Will there be anyone else her age? How heavy is the workload? Does she need to brush up on miserable computer skills? Do young people even know how to use pen and paper? What about lunch breaks? Do they serve food in the cafeterias or does she take a packed lunch? Will she find some way to fit in?

She settles for one question. "What's college like?"

The nurse laughs. "A lot of work. A lot of drinking. And a bunch of guys fresh out of diapers who think they're some kind of gift to mankind."

Ellen tries to picture herself in a lecture hall, carrying a pile of books, wearing a backpack, surrounded by people a quarter her age.

"Were there many women like me at your college?"

"You mean Jewish?" The girl shares a winning smile. "One of my best friends was around your age, and he landed a job at the New Amsterdam. I fucking hate him now with a passion. Lucky bastard owns a brownstone in the Village. I get by sofa surfing."

"I'll bet he's smart." Ellen presses her lips together when she realizes how silly this sounds. "By which I mean, I bet he's smart for someone so old."

The nurse rolls her eyes. "Some of the dumbest fucks were my age. All they cared about was getting drunk and having a good time." She hands Ellen a plastic bottle. "If your breathing gets worse, I'll need to speak with your doctor. The last thing Silas needs is you making yourself sick."

The mention of his name causes her to startle. Ellen's eyes narrow. "What's he got to do with the price of fish?"

She stops writing something in Ellen's notes. "Seriously? You don't remember? He was across the hallway that time you almost drowned. He saved your life."

"We're friends."

The nurse blushes. "Jesus, I'm so sorry. I guess I assumed...I talk a lot of crap. Forget I said anything."

From along the hall, someone cheers. Party poppers explode, and the music gets louder.

"I'll go check on that," the nurse says. "You stay here a while. I'll let them know you need quiet."

Ellen shakes her head. "It's good to hear people having fun."

* * *

Ziggy's Bar enjoys a bump in the lull between Christmas and New Year, as people still pretend to love strangers enough to talk, instead of rushing by caught up in their thoughts or glued to cell phone screens. It's early evening when Silas leans against the counter, nursing a beer and watching the crowd, scanning faces for someone he knows. Next to him, a couple laughs and jokes. The girl, in her twenties, is red-cheeked and drunk. The man is older, in his thirties, with that air of a guy with a great job, a beautiful wife, and a nice house, yet desperate to act young and single.

Silas checks the time. 7:45 p.m. He drains the last of his beer, pulling on his jacket. If he hurries, he'll make Whole Foods in time for when they mark down prepared food at the deli counter.

The older guy with the younger girl cries out. "Look what the fuck you're doing!"

Silas turns around, summoning up his best apology face. "Did I catch you, dude?"

The guy stinks of booze. His face is hard and angry as he pushes a hand into Silas's chest. "You made me spill my fucking beer...dude."

"Easy man," Silas replies. "Didn't see you there."

"You need to say sorry. And that means buying me a drink."

Silas chuckles to himself. The guy's going to fall over any minute anyhow, and it's Christmas. What the heck? He'll cut him some slack.

"Alright. Sure," he says. "I'm sorry. Now, what are you drinking?"

The guy isn't done. "Don't talk to my dick. Talk to my face. Cock sucker."

Silas feels each muscle tense, and his hands tighten into fists. He could take this jerk. He knows he could.

"I said I was sorry," he says.

Bartender Larry appears at his shoulder. "You guys want to take this outside?"

"This queer touched me up. Dirty fucking fag."

"Hey now." Larry tries to settle things. "You both need to leave."

The guy lunges at Silas, grabbing for his shirt, but misses and goes sprawling to the floor.

"Hey!" a woman's voice yells. An older woman. "You want to try that macho bullshit with me?"

Silas blinks. He can hardly believe it. "Rose?"

* * *

Ellen gasps as she steps back into their room. Tornado Julia has swept through, scattering clothes into piles on the bed, the floor, and the sofa.

"Is that you, Ellen?" Julia calls from the bathroom. "I'm almost done. Can you hand me a towel?"

She picks her way through the mess and opens the door. Julia is in the shower with the curtain pulled.

"What happened out here?" Ellen says. "I thought we were meant to be packing."

"I can't lay my hands on my strapless bra. Have you seen it? White with a thin gold bow on the back." The curtain slides open. Water drips from Julia's body as she grabs the towel and hurries past. "I want to wear my blue dress, so I need to find it."

"Are you in the middle of a psychotic episode?" Ellen says. "Should I call someone to come sedate you?"

"Captain John finally invited me for dinner."

Ellen does her best to smile. "I don't think I have an appetite."

"Good, because you didn't get an invitation. Just me. Hence the call for something strapless." She goes over to the bed and searches some more. "Are you sure you haven't accidentally got my bra mixed up with your stuff?"

Ellen shifts aside a stack of sweaters and sits on the sofa. "Did you not wonder where I might have gotten to?"

Julia doesn't look up. "I figured you went for a walk. That's something you do, right?"

"I was at the medical center."

Her face changes. "Again? Are you okay? What happened?"

"I had a weird turn. I needed tablets."

"And now?"

"I guess I'm better." She holds up the small brown bottle.

"Great, so pop one of those, and help me find my fucking lucky bra." Julia squats to peer under the bed. "I know I packed it."

Julia was like this one time before. The day when Ellen dropped by unannounced to break the news she had cancer and was having surgery. Julia became distraught, a cornered, wounded animal, lashing out, and insisting Malinowski must have got everything wrong, that her best friend couldn't be sick. She looked fine. It was all Ellen could do to stop her calling her own doctor and demanding a second opinion.

"Where did you check?" Ellen says, but Julia isn't listening. She's locked in some world of her own.

"The mall," she says, and grabs a pair of shoes. "Let's go see if they have a bra in my size."

Ellen bars the door. "Something is wrong. Tell me what happened today."

Julia sits heavily on the edge of the bed. Her face goes blank, and her shoulders sag. "Malinowski scheduled my surgery for three days' time."

Ellen sits beside her. "That's good, though, right? The sooner they get you in, the better."

Julia closes her eyes and shakes her head. "I told him to cancel. I can't go through with it. I'm not as indestructible as you. It's New Year's. We have to sit on my sofa and see the ball drop. And anyway, I can't lose my breasts. I won't."

Ellen puts a hand on her arm. She doesn't know what to say.

"I thought I could deal with all of this shit," Julia says. "I've looked online and seen all those women who had surgery and how they claim to be proud. That isn't me. I was willing to try, but...I'm not strong enough." She gets to her feet and goes over to peer through the tiny round window. "My mother was the strong one. She never gave up. She had this fucking cruel disease twice, and the second time she kept it to herself until it was too late. She decided to keep on living and working and laughing, right until she passed. Mom was the bravest and strongest person I ever knew. I want to be like her."

Ellen wants to suggest that maybe Julia's mother was dumb as all hell, but holds her tongue.

"You can't change my mind. I've made peace with the decision," Julia says.

"Cancer no longer scares me."

What can Ellen say? Julia has always been the most positive person she knows. The idea of her giving up like this is unthinkable. Julia is also stubborn as a mule.

"What if I *want* cancer to scare you?" Ellen says.

Julia comes to sit. She takes a hold of Ellen's hands. "Don't think of what I'm doing as giving up," she says. "I'm just letting nature run its course. Every one of us has to perish. I guess you could say that I'm the lucky one. I get to know roughly how long is left. I get to tick stuff off my bucket list. How's about if you ask the doc for pills, and we take an airplane to Europe? I really do want to see Paris before I die."

Ellen swallows. Everything Julia says makes sense. And yet it doesn't.

"A few hours back you were full of life and energy and now you're ready to…give up?"

"I'm going to live each moment to the fullest." Julia takes a deep breath and lets it out slowly. "There's no point you trying to talk me out of this. I'm at peace with what comes next."

In every version of what comes next, Ellen has carved out a space for her best friend. Even if the lupus gets worse. Even if Julia gets sick. Together, they would fight, and be there for each other.

"This isn't how it ends," Ellen says. "We're going shopping."

Chapter Thirty

The last night at sea finds five friends sharing a table, each acting like they're happy, each lost in thought. While all around, guys party, drink, and cheer, Julia sits across from Ellen, a smile pasted in place, and her arms folded. Patrick and Miguel play the role of happy new lovers, but now and then, Ellen sees how Patrick looks away and chews his lip. Kathy isn't herself. It's all down to Julia, who acts like a needle stuck in the groove on a song about the sun coming out tomorrow.

After dinner, the guys call it a night, leaving Ellen, Julia, and Kathy to finish what's left of their wine. Ellen pours a glass for herself, and no sooner does she put down the bottle, than Julia picks it up.

"We should order champagne," she says. "This is meant to be a party."

Kathy glances at Ellen. "Sure, but…"

"Sure, but nothing. This might be our last night together."

She signals to the server, who nods to say he'll be right over.

"So," Julia says, sitting back in her chair. "I already told Ellen, now I need to share my news with you."

Kathy nods.

"I have cancer, and I'm going to die."

"Oh my God." Kathy's hand flies to her mouth. "Can't they do anything?"

"My doc suggested chemo, but it's too late." Julia sips her wine and gives a sigh of satisfaction. "It's my time."

Ellen stares down at the table. More than anything she wants to argue with her best friend, but this isn't the time or place.

"What are your treatment options?" Kathy asks again.

"None."

Ellen, still staring at the table, shakes her head ever so slightly.

"I never thought I'd have a death wish," Julia says, "but I do. I'm ready to die."

The server places a bottle of vintage champagne on the table. "Shall I open it, ladies?"

"Yes," Julia says. "Please do."

Ellen isn't sure exactly when Julia's mood flipped. In the mall, she tried on outfits and acted like tonight would be fun. She even let Ellen do her hair. When the captain's office called to apologize for him being unable to make dinner, she shrugged and said it was easy come easy go. Ellen had treated herself to a long soak in the tub. The warm water was a blessing, soothing muscles, and taking the edge off her fatigue. When she emerged, red-faced and relaxed, Julia was perched on the sofa, staring at the carpet, wearing a pair of Ellen's blue jeans and a pink top. She refused to wear the low-cut blue dress, insisting the sweater would do.

The server fills three glasses, and Julia gets to her feet to propose a toast.

"To the future," she says. "However short a time there might be."

Kathy's lower lip wobbles and tears run down her cheek. "Do you need anything?" she says. "Are you in pain?"

"Nothing." Julia takes a sip of champagne. "And there's no pain."

Kathy and Ellen exchange glances, searching for a sign, anything to indicate Julia doesn't mean what she says.

"I don't want a big farewell. I don't want anyone wasting their time on me."

Kathy's tears flow faster. "This is all too much," she says. "How can you find out like this and there be nothing anyone can do?"

Ellen can hold her tongue no longer. "There's plenty the doctors can try, but Julia decided to refuse treatment."

Kathy's eyes widen.

"She's a fucking fool," Ellen adds. "And she knows it."

She's never spoken so sharply to her best friend. Not even when they've had fights. This time, though, she has no choice.

Julia slams an angry hand on the table. "It's up to me. Not you. This is my turn to say what happens next."

Nobody speaks.

"And as for you." Julia pokes a finger at Kathy. "Who the hell are you, anyway? We don't know each other. Why the waterworks?"

Kathy opens her mouth, but then closes it without speaking. Ellen tries to calm the flare-up.

"It's been a long day," she says. "I guess we're all tired."

"Speak for yourself." Julia sits back in her chair, holding up her glass. "I only just got started."

Conversations at nearby tables go on hold, and heads turn to listen in.

"I've known Ellen most of my life," she says. "We've seen each other at our best and our worst. When she was around, even the bad days were better. I never thought she'd hurt me."

Kathy looks first at Ellen, then at Julia. "Did I miss something here? What happened?"

"A doctor told me I'm dying. And Ellen fears being left on her own. She wants me to put up with treatment that can only make me sicker, so she gets to act the hero and rock up at my bedside holding flowers and candy."

"That's not fair," Ellen says.

"Then quit." Julia clicks her fingers. "Stop acting like you know what's best for me. Stop telling me what to do."

It's too much, and even though she knows this must be fear and frustration speaking, Ellen teeters on the edge of tears.

"We're all tired," Kathy says, pouring her quart of oil onto troubled waters. "We should call it a night."

Julia swallows her champagne and pushes back her chair. "Fine by me."

When she's gone, Kathy turns to Ellen. "Is this my fault?"

* * *

For Silas, letting Rose see inside his apartment is unsettling. He sees the place he calls home through her unforgiving eyes. The depressing gray walls, the orange drapes, stained and worn. The place is shabby. Unloved. Uncared for. The overall stench is of loneliness. He pushes shut the front door and turns five locks, and Rose doesn't move. She stands in the middle of the room, surveying his domain.

"Sit, please," he says.

She does, perching on the edge of an ugly tan Goodwill sofa, like someone waiting for a chance to bolt.

"This is a dump, Silas," she says, eventually. "How come you live this way?"

"It was *your* idea to not go back to your place."

"I didn't know you had a cave for a home."

Silas isn't sure how to respond. He knows Rose is right. He has done little with the apartment. The reality of his living conditions sinks in. He surveys piles of newspapers, dishes stacked on the sticky low living room table, dust balls that lurk in every corner.

"Nancy would have a fit," she says. "This joint is crying out for a woman's touch."

He wants to lighten the mood, and grins. "Is that you offering?"

Rose glares. "I wouldn't touch it with a ten-foot pole."

"Maybe I could paint. Buy new furniture." He gestures around the room.

"Let me ask you one thing, Silas," she says. "Do you care that this apartment got in such a state?"

"I've been busy. The maid quit. It's tough to find good help."

"Quit with the bullshit, Silas. That's not an answer."

She gets up and goes through to the kitchen and returns, shaking her head. "You might have warned me. Is that an active crime scene? Did someone die in there?"

Silas laughs and then quickly stops himself. It's not funny.

"What went wrong with you?" she says. "You live like a pig."

He blinks away tears. "I guess I should try to do better."

"Am I the first woman who scored an invitation back here?"

He says nothing.

"So what gives? Are you too lazy? Did you give up on life?"

"I took a break, that's all. Things got out of hand. I always meant..."

Rose gives him a skeptical look. "Nancy said the road to hell was full of people who meant to do shit."

Mention of his wife sends the sharpest of pains through his chest. Silas sits heavily on the couch. "I was trying to figure out where I was going."

She comes to join him, this time sitting, too, no longer perching on the edge.

"You need to get out there and date someone more suitable than me," she says. "Did you ever try online?"

"You mean like cybersex?"

Rose groans. "I can't work out if you're being deliberately dumb."

Silas shrugs. "What if I don't want to meet anyone new? What if I'd rather date *you*."

She leans forward. Her eyes are alive, her face flushed. "I am not the woman for you. I thought we'd agreed on that. It's why I'm here."

He isn't sure what to say.

She gets to her feet, brushes down her skirt, and looks around. "Let's make a deal. I won't lecture you about this pigsty of an apartment, if you promise to get back out there, date around, and live your life."

"Deal," Silas says, and then after a pause adds, "I have beer."

"Cold beer?"

"I keep it in a bag on the window ledge."

Rose smiles. "Hit me up."

* * *

Julia and Ellen's room ought to look bigger with their clothes packed neatly into trunks. Somehow, though, everything is smaller. Like walking through a place where a party happened, right after the cool crowd moved on.

"We're going to miss this," Ellen said.

Julia picks at a thread on her sweater. "'If all the year were playing holidays, To sport would be as tedious as to work.'"

Ellen isn't sure what to say. The words will be from some or other show. Julia quotes theater when she wants to make Ellen feel small. Like she's the dumb kid who never went to college.

"The funniest thing is," Ellen says, "I wasn't that excited about coming on this trip, and now I don't want to leave."

Julia clicks her tongue. "I suppose not."

"Do you?"

A direct question is often the only way in when Julia gets this way. She can sulk and choose not to answer, or mumble one-word replies, but until Ellen knows what she's supposed to have done wrong, what chance is there of making things right?

"No," Julia says. "I don't want to leave. Not yet."

They stay silent for a minute. Ellen shifts, and tries to put her hand on Julia's arm, but Julia pulls away.

"About what happened after dinner," Julia says. "I'm sorry. I had no right to lash out."

Ellen already gets how her friend didn't mean to hurt her. "It's okay. We all have our moments."

Julia goes over to the minibar and peers inside. "There's a tiny gin, one tonic, and three lemon slices."

"My liver put in an official request for time off," Ellen says. "It's all yours."

Julia makes herself a gin and tonic, and comes to sit. "You won't tell anyone, will you? About what I said back there?"

"Such as who?"

"The fucking ladies who lunch. The last thing I need is a bunch of supportive shoulders to cry on. People always mean well, but seriously, it gets to a point where I'm sick of explaining my decision."

Ellen smiles for the first time. "Your secret is safe with me. And Kathy. And about 300 gossipy gay men."

Julia shakes her head. "I always envied you, Ellen."

"Why would anyone in their right mind be jealous of me?"

"You have everything figured out."

"I lost my job, and until a few days back, I was sure my late husband had an affair. Yeah, I've got a really fucking great life, thank you very much."

Julia chuckles gently. "At least you have a life."

"And you don't?"

"Daniel makes excuses for why he can't come to New York, and whenever I suggest a trip to San Francisco, he's away at some conference. I was supposed to go to Hawaii for the holidays, but the hotel mysteriously overbooked."

It's the first time Ellen has ever heard Julia lavish anything but unconditional love on her son.

"Does Daniel know about the cancer?" she says, and Julia flinches.

"Nobody knows. Except you…and Kathy…nd 300 gossipy queens."

Ellen grabs her hand. "Why haven't you told him? He's your son. He should know."

"He'll just act guilty about not being here."

"Is that why you said you didn't want treatment?"

"I saw how sick it made you, honey. And I'm not half the woman you are. I scream blue murder if I so much as get a paper cut."

"That's no reason to give up."

"It's like my fate's already been determined, and there's nothing left to do but wait for the final curtain to fall."

Ellen gets to her feet. "Do you want me to argue and insist you talk to Malinowski about chemo?"

"I want you to help me get out of my head," she says. "Tonight, while we still can. Before we go back to the real world."

"Sharing one gin and tonic?"

Julia gets up and picks up the phone. "That's why the Almighty and Crown Atlantic invented room service."

* * *

Silas has slept on his sofa almost as often as in his bed. When the neighbors opposite play music late, the windows rattle and he can't sleep. Tonight there's no music, but Rose is here. She refused to get a cab home after dark, since she doesn't trust the drivers. He suggested an Uber.

"Are you fucking insane? They're just regular drivers with no criminal checks. I might as well hand over a meat cleaver and sit back while they hack me in two."

He makes out the sound of Mrs. Blatter's television from the downstairs apartment. Upstairs a door slams, footsteps follow. It's probably the heavy guy he sees on the stairs, getting home from work. He's a welder or something. Silas barely recalls. There's only so much useless trivia your brain will process before it gives up. He looks at the clock. It's a quarter to three in the morning, and he's hungry, but can't bear the thought of going to the kitchen. Not now that he's seen the filth through Rose's eyes.

She coughs in the other room. Wet and throaty. Silas has tried a million times to talk her into quitting the cigarettes, but she shakes her head, and says, "It'll be the death of me, but it's a good death."

He rolls over. Padding footsteps wrench him to consciousness.

"That sofa isn't good for your posture," Rose says. "You want to come to bed? We'll cuddle."

He says nothing, but tosses aside the scratchy blanket and follows her into the other room.

"We'll spoon," she says, and Silas climbs in after her. She wriggles until they're touching from shoulder to toe.

"Just a cuddle," she mumbles into the one pillow. "Tomorrow we shop and buy you better clothes. Then we'll go to a bar I know. In Brooklyn. There are people who'll accept cash to torch this place."

Her breathing slows to a steady rate.

Rose is asleep.

* * *

Ellen lies on rumpled sheets and scowls at the ceiling. Mixing room service champagne with Malinowski's pain meds has her brain spinning, but it's a nice kind of spinning—a carnival ride with all the sharp edges made blunt.

"You reckon this is how rock stars get right before they drown in hotel tubs?" she says.

Julia lifts her head from the far end of the bed. "I think it's more like how rock stars get after doing lines off the tits of a groupie."

Ellen groans and rolls around, untangling herself, and sitting against the headboard, rubbing her eyes and laughing. More than she remembers laughing in years. It hurts her stomach. She sits up and rests her back against the headboard.

"I want to stay this way forever," she says.

Julia snorts. "I'll get right on that."

All at once, Ellen is sober. Reality crashes in. Her mind races, and she swallows down a sick sensation in her gut.

"Why don't you come stay with me?" she says. "You could rent out your place, and we'll become the new Golden Girls."

Julia holds up a *good idea* thumb. "We'll hire a limo and drive around construction sites whistling at men."

The knot in Ellen's stomach loosens. "You do like to whistle."

"And I'll open a petting zoo," Julia mumbles.

"A what?"

Julia snores. Her perfect rosebud mouth opens, and her pale pink tongue slips out to wet her lips. Ellen clumsily unfolds a blanket, covering her friend's legs, and lifts her head onto a pillow.

"What about Silas?" she whispers to herself. "Is there any place for him in this?"

She lies back and pulls sheets up around her face. She has his number. He still has hers. If he calls, what will she say? Her thoughts are a mess. Ellen doesn't have the strength to fight sleep. Moonlight streams through the porthole, bathing the swirling carpet with soft silver. Julia mumbles something and rolls over.

"What?" Ellen whispers.

"I said, if you speak to Silas, what will you tell him?"

"Ask me again tomorrow."

Julia sniggers to herself. "You know the old saying? If you don't want everyone to think you're a shiksa, leave a decent period of mourning between men. Seventeen years feels about right."

Chapter Thirty-One

When Kathy nudges Ellen, it hurts, and she's about to pass comment on just how much, when she spots Miguel, down on one knee, and pulling a blue velvet box from his jacket pocket. Kathy signals crossed fingers. Ellen looks around frantically. Julia is busy laughing with two stocky guys about the *Cats* movie.

"Quick," she says, grabbing her friend's arm. "I think Miguel is about to propose."

Patrick gazes down with a wistful look, frozen to the spot, and Miguel shifts to his other knee, the box now open. Kathy jumps up and down, and Ellen swallows a lump in her throat.

"Say yes," Julia calls. "The putz is hot."

Guys all around laugh approval.

"She's right, Patty," Kathy joins in. "And it's not like you're likely to get asked again. Grab him with both hands."

He purses his lips, glares over, and then back at Miguel. "Get up, you fool," he says. "We can talk about this later."

But Miguel is having none of it. "Patrick Garfield Lucey. Will you marry me?"

Julia pulls a surprised face at Ellen. "Did you know his middle name was Garfield?"

Kathy winces. "Mine is Pooky."

Patrick grunts in frustration. "Fine. Yes, Miguel. I do...I mean, I will... whatever it is you want. I'm in."

"We're engaged!" Miguel cries, pulling Patrick into a bear hug.

Julia, Ellen and Kathy clap happily, and when Miguel looks around at the faces, he puts back his shoulders and holds his head high.

"I should have asked your permission," he says to Kathy. "Do you give your consent?"

She hoots. "Are you kidding me? I've been waiting for this day all my life. I honestly thought it would never come, on account of how Patty isn't such a catch and all. Do you have any opinions on a wedding venue? I have a whole list. Some of them do themed weddings. I always wanted to recreate the Civil War."

Patrick pulls Ellen in close. "Am I crazy? Does long-distance love ever really work?"

Julia cuts in. "Does it have to be long distance? There are so many jobs for teachers in New York, right now, and if it helps, I happen to know a gentleman on the board at Felician."

He frowns, dumbfounded. "You're kidding, right?"

She shakes her head. "All it would take is one little telephone call. I also happen to have photographic materials he wouldn't want made public, so, you know…everyone wins."

"Thank you!" Patrick all but bursts into tears. "That would be so lovely." And then he stops. "But wait. Isn't it like a million bucks to rent a shoe box in New York?"

"Housing is, indeed, outrageously expensive, but I might suggest a bridging solution." Julia pulls Ellen closer. "I'm taking a short break, and I'll need someone to apartment sit. I plan on staying with a friend. If she agrees."

Ellen's heart sings. "You have to stop with the fucking whistling."

"This is all so sudden," Patrick says. "I'd have to leave Kathy behind. And she…"

Now it's Kathy's turn. "I'm old enough, and ugly enough, to look after myself, Patty. If anything, having you around kinda cramps my style. Nobody with a stable income wants to date a woman who drags around her nerdy gay brother."

They hug. "You're one of the most wonderful women I know."

Kathy reddens. "I'm going to miss you, all the same."

"You can come for Thanksgiving," Ellen says. "We'll make that our once-a-year celebration."

* * *

"I see a clown." Silas tells the full-length mirror. "A clown who should take off these dumb clothes and leave this stupid store."

"You look like a Disney prince," Rose says.

The jacket she picked out is so stiff he can barely move his arms. The pants hang awkwardly over his boots. The last time Silas stood in front of a full-length mirror in a Fifth Avenue store, he had Nancy by his side, fussing around, pulling out his shirt so it hung right, brushing lint from the shoulders of a well-cut jacket. Today is different. This is Rose in full *get Silas laid* mode. Like she's doing her best to make sure she hands him on to Ellen in showroom condition. Two careful lady owners. Good for another ten thousand miles.

"Remind me again why I'm letting you do this," he says.

"Because I know what women want," she says and steps back to look him up and down, a slow smile finding her lips. "And women don't want a man who walks around in stinky Goodwill clothing."

The store assistant descends, holding even more shirts. One white, one black with green stripes, the other polka-dotted and red. Silas groans.

"Can't I wear my regular clothes?"

"I already had them bagged up and sent to an incinerator. It's this or you walk home naked."

"At least then I wouldn't look like a fucking circus performer."

The assistant steps discretely away, and Rose pulls out the shirt with the polka dots. He slips it on; the fabric feels soft against his skin. She rests her head on his shoulder, and he breathes in her perfume. Sweet and floral. A bouquet of wild roses, a heady mix of woods and wildflowers.

There have been dark days where he missed Nancy so much, he'd have given up life to be with her wherever she went. He didn't believe in any kind of heaven—though was rather taken with the concept of hell for his bongo-playing neighbor—but Silas couldn't believe that our time on Earth just ended and that was it. The idea they had had their time together and there would be no more is too painful. Nancy lives on inside his head. In memories. What hurts the most is there can be no new memories. Nothing more to share. No new life to build.

"What do you think Nancy would say if she saw me trussed up like a turkey?" he says.

Rose squeezes his arm. "She would be fucking furious. You off to greet some up-herself broad with flowers. Nancy would scratch her fucking eyes out with her perfect red nails."

Silas stares for one minute. Shocked to hear Rose talk this way. Nancy was a perfect human being. Someone without a bad word for anyone. Loving. Beautiful. Caring. Except Nancy could also hold her own. She swore like a trooper. She wasn't some perfect angel spirited to Earth. One time, she blacked a man's eye at the bodega for trying to shortchange her.

"Ellen looks like she could fight back," he says. "She's pretty tall, and her hands are huge."

Rose laughs and stares into the mirror. "Admit it, Silas. I got you worked out."

* * *

In the cocktail lounge, Ellen raises her drink in a toast. Julia does the same.

"I put you on the spot back there," she says. "If you want to tell me to find a hotel to recuperate after surgery, that's fine by me. I have savings. I might even jump on an airplane and make Daniel step up."

"I would *love* to have you stay," Ellen says. "What you did for Patrick was kind."

"He's a sweet kid. And if I can't play matchmaker for you and Silas, this has to do."

Ellen leans back in a battered leather armchair. The observation lounge walls are painted black and lined with mirrors and framed photographs of tropical islands. The setting sun lends everything a mysterious, melancholy quality. Within two hours, the ship will dock in New York.

"I'm so glad we did this," Julia says.

"Even though we didn't get to swim with dolphins together?"

"I reckon it's time we wrote new bucket lists." Julia waves for a server and asks for pen and paper.

"You go first," she says. "What would you like to do the most?"

Ellen scribbles on the pad and hands it to Julia, who squints to read.

"See Paris in the rain? But you hate flying."

"True, but business class on United with a load of pills, and I might just about make it." She pushes the paper back across the table. "Your turn."

Julia writes something and slides it back. Ellen reads and looks up, laughing. "Ellen should go on a date with Silas?"

"Well, why not? You saw Patrick and Miguel. Despite the odds, they found a way."

"Miguel is less than half my age."

"Excuses." Julia bats away the argument. "Just one rendezvous. But I'm not talking coffee or a friendly walk through Midtown. This has to be dinner at a top restaurant, three courses, and a horse-drawn carriage ride through Central Park."

"In January?" Ellen makes a face. "Why not just toss me out into the snow and leave me to die from exposure?"

"Okay, so a *taxi* ride through Manhattan. Whatever. Point is, go on a serious date with the guy."

"I'm not even sure he thinks of me that way."

"If he doesn't, then the man's a fool," Julia says. "It's almost twenty years since Otto died. You deserve to be happy."

Ellen studies the list one more time and grabs the pen.

Julia reads what she's written and cries out. "I already told you, there's no fucking way I'm going to Vegas for Celine Dion. If the woman gains thirty pounds, ask me again."

* * *

Silas steps out of the beauty parlor Rose insisted he visit. She has a friend, who agreed to fix up his bitten-to-the-knuckle fingernails as a favor. It was nice to have someone take care of him for a change. The girl worked quickly and expertly with a tiny drill, grinding away ragged edges, until he studied clean, sharp nails. His hand looks alien now.

"My work here is done." Rose adjusts the collar of a new woolen jacket, and he can't deny that, for the first time in forever, he doesn't feel like himself. And that's a good thing. If he so wishes, he now has it in him to march into Goering Brothers, fill out an application form, and nobody will dare call his Santa Claus smile fake. Except he's done with all that. Last night, he spoke to the boys, and officially quit the band. The others agreed they should meet up soon and celebrate the end of an era.

Rose pulls him close and brushes her lips against his cheek. "This isn't goodbye forever, Silas," she says. "It's goodbye for now. Don't be a stranger. A card on my birthday would be nice. And if you happen to slip twenty bucks in the envelope, even better. March 7th. I'll call ahead and remind you."

He grins and holds her at arms' length. "Why did you do all this for me?"

"Because Nancy made me promise to take care of you if she went first. And I figured what we were doing wasn't quite what she had in mind."

She hands him a bunch of white roses bought from some fancy store on Broadway, paper-thin petals, wrapped in tissue, to keep them fresh for their rightful owner.

Rose sticks her fists in her pocket. "You give Ellen these, and tell her you want to start over. Nothing more. Don't go saying you're sorry for not calling ahead or any of your usual crap."

Silas takes a deep breath and steps back. She checks his collar one last time, as he stands straight, his chest puffed out.

"Thank you," he says, swallowing tears. "I'll never forget this."

When their eyes allow themselves to meet again, it's too much.

"Don't forget me either." Her voice wobbles. "And don't forget the twenty bucks."

He grins. "March 7th, right?"

* * *

The icy air hangs pungent with the scent of salt. Tiny silver pinpricks twinkle in an inky sky. The stark, electric lights of office buildings blur as the MS Viking sails slowly home. She's missed New York. The streets, the car horns, the smell, the rats, the people always rushing other places. Roadblocks. Sirens. The noises that prove there's life out there.

The metallic clang of an anchor being dropped into place drags her back to the here and now. A guy runs past and bumps her shoulder, yelling sorry. She thinks about her father, taken too soon. About her mother, who worked so hard to make sure Ellen had everything. About Otto. And she can't help but shed a tear for what might have been. But now a new chapter begins.

She'll go to school. She'll meet new people. This is Ellen reborn.

She will call Silas.

They will have that drink.

And one day, she might even suggest booking a room at the Ritz-Carlton.

This sickness. The one that bites her bones and threatens to overwhelm. It isn't going to win. Julia will survive, and so will she.

Snow flurries swirl and dance in the wind, like a million tiny feathers filling the air and blanketing the deck in white.

She sees him now, in the distance. Tall and elegant, just like he always was.

Her Otto.

"It's all going to be fine," he says. "Just you wait and see."

Rebuilding Alexandra Small

MO FANNING

This is the first chapter from my previous novel, set in Brighton, England, it tells the story of a woman who everyone thinks has it all, until she very publicly doesn't. A romantic fanciful novel of love, loss and unexpected newfound love.

Married to a successful and wealthy man, Alexandra Small feels diminished professionally as well as personally, since she is unable to give her husband a child. What transpires during the story provides a backdrop of greed, dishonesty and betrayal-with a surprise ending that warms the heart. Truly touching and oftentimes sad, but the delicious ending makes it all worthwhile.

Megan Macmillan is the reigning queen of daytime television. She's everyone's best friend. And this morning–between *lunch on a shoestring* and a man with twelve toes–she's mine. A ray of light on the darkest of mornings. Today, however, finds the three-time TV Guide award winner simmering with anger, and in the foulest of moods.

'Did some cretin leave a door open?' she says, aiming filthy looks at every member of the studio crew.

Sprawled on a beige leather sofa, her permatanned husband Clive chuckles and smirks, much like he does on screen whenever Megan goes off on *one of her rants*. Under bright lights and thanks to the combined efforts of three makeup artists, Clive looks half his age, in clothes hand-picked by their gay stylist - who Megan thinks might have a crush on Clive, since he insists on putting her in yellow; her most hated colour.

'Well?' she says, tapping her foot. 'Does the star of this show have to die of pneumonia before someone takes her seriously? It's cold enough in here to freeze a witch's tit.'

Clive pulls his *oil on troubled waters* face and leans in closer to whisper in my ear. 'You must excuse my wife,' he says. 'I've no idea where she picks up such colourful expressions.'

His liver-spotted, podgy hand pats my knee.

'Where the hell is Simon?' Megan looks around for their producer. 'Is *nobody* in charge?'

'Take cover,' Clive whispers. 'Any minute now poor Simon will inform her she did that last segment with a piece of spinach lodged between her front teeth. It won't be pretty.'

I shuffle along the sofa before he makes another beeline for my knee.

It's already been a long day. A car arrived at 5am, and the driver spent the entire journey from Brighton to London quizzing me about my footballer husband. He turned out to be a Brighton and Hove Albion fan. They almost always are.

Saturday with Megan and Clive is far from a happy workplace. As a long-married couple, they've ruled the hangover telly roost for years with a chintzy mix of recipes, makeover tips, weight loss routines and human-interest stories. The second I left the makeup chair, I sensed an atmosphere.

During an earlier break for the news, a row broke out, with Clive berating his wife for flirting with a reformed boy band. She'd stroked honed biceps and fanned herself with programme notes as the drummer lifted his shirt to reveal a six-pack.

Their screaming fight ended with Megan calling Clive *pencil dick*. He shot back that she was a sad, desperate tart. And then they spotted me, and professional smiles slotted back into place as Megan swished blonde extensions and Clive leaned in for a 'welcome' kiss.

'Such a treat,' he said, acting like I was a long-lost friend. 'We've wanted you back since forever.'

This, I doubted. Producer Simon had called late yesterday afternoon on the off-chance I *might* be free. The Hollywood A-lister he'd booked had collapsed in an airport toilet, and an ambulance crew rushed her to rehab. Simon had once wangled me tickets for Hamilton, so I couldn't refuse. He said that seeing as how everyone was tipping Jed for a place in the England squad, would I mind coming on?

The floor manager calls us back to the set as the signature tune plays.

'My tummy hurts from eating all that cake.' Megan flashes the best dentistry money can buy. 'I just can't resist chocolate. It's my bête noir.'

This is a lie. She refused leftovers from the baking slot. A runner waved a slice of Sachertorte under her nose and she glared as if he'd been sick on the plate.

'Our next guest has it all,' she says. 'And is about to rocket to the top of the WAG league... if her gorgeous husband lands the job we're all talking about.'

The camera pans my face, and I do my best to smile.

'Alexandra Small,' Megan says. 'It's been *way* too long since we had you on our sofa.'

Before I get to speak, Clive takes over. 'How's the old man? Still telling the referee he needs glasses.'

'He's at a training camp,' I say. 'Preparing for the weekend.'

'So, you're young, free and single. Hot in the city? Perhaps I can tempt you out for lunch.'

Is he chatting me up? On live TV. In front of his wife?

Megan interrupts. 'Tell us, Allie, are the rumours true about Jed? Our viewers are dying to know.'

First, I hate it when people I don't know well call me Allie. It's a name reserved for my closest friends. Second, I doubt the people who watch Megan and Clive's show give two hoots about Jed's try-out for the national squad.

'It's all hush-hush,' I say, and mime zipped lips.

Megan guffaws like I've told the best joke ever. 'But you're not denying it?'

Clive's sweaty hand finds its way back onto my knee. 'Come on, Allie. It can be our little secret.'

He winks at the camera, and I brush him away.

'How does it work with the WAGs?' Megan pulls a serious face. 'Is there a league table with Coleen Rooney at the top?'

'I don't really know her,' I say. 'We've met, but...'

Megan's having none of it. 'It must worry Coleen that you'll grab her crown.'

'Her crown?'

She directs a vapid smile into the camera rather than at me.

'I know there's not an actual crown, Allie,' she says and exchanges a smug smile with Clive, 'but this news *must* put you in line to become the new WAG Queen.'

I die inside. The one thing I refuse to let define my life is the fact I married a footballer.

Megan wants an answer. 'I can see she's thinking about it,' she says and nudges her husband.

'It's not like that.' My voice sounds nothing like mine. 'Or at least I don't think it is. I tend not to mix with the other wives.'

The way she shakes her head suggests she doesn't believe me.

'I bet you all meet up and compare notes,' she says.

'Notes about what?'

Her eyes narrow and ice forms.

Clive must sense the cold front, because he takes control. 'If Jed gets into the squad, how are you going to reward him?'

His hand makes yet another bid for my knee. If I shuffle any further along the sofa, I'll be on Megan's lap.

'We'll go for a lovely meal somewhere,' I say.

'With champers?'

'I don't drink.'

Megan pounces. 'You had rather a problem, didn't you, Allie? You're a reformed alcoholic.'

'I still call myself an alcoholic,' I say. 'Reformed or not. It's an illness. Nobody says reformed about people in wheelchairs.'

Megan's upper lip curls. 'Are you comparing yourself to a disabled person?'

'I would never...'

'Because *you* can drink or not drink. They can't walk or not walk.'

'That's not what I said.'

The floor manager gestures to wind things up, and Clive grins into a camera. 'After the break, decorate or decimate. We'll hear from a woman who claims her hapless hubby is the world's worst handyman.'

The theme music plays, and Megan is on her feet and across the studio, vanishing into makeup.

'Thanks for coming on last minute,' Clive says.

Off-air, he's more composed and less of a creep. With the lights down to natural levels, his face is creosote brown, his jeans are way too tight, and his French-tucked white shirt struggles to stay buttoned.

Someone comes to unhook my microphone.

'I think Megan's having a rough day.' Clive shuffles closer. 'Take nothing to heart.'

I scoot along the sofa and hold up surrender hands. 'It's fine. I get it.'

'We should have that lunch sometime. Just the two of us.'

I freeze.

'Clive, love,' says Producer Simon. 'We need you in the kitchenette for the next segment.'

My phone beeps. It's Jed to remind me we're meeting for coffee at 1pm.

Today is an anniversary.

We've been seeing the same fertility specialist at a swanky London clinic for exactly one year.

About the Author

Mo Fanning grew up near Birmingham in the UK but left for pastures new as soon as he could legally drive, spending much of his grown-up life in the Netherlands, before returning home just before lockdown took hold.

He has contributed to *100 Stories for Haiti and written for the Observer travel section. His first novel 'The Armchair Bride' was nominated for Arts Council Book of the Year,* and his work was turned into a short play for BBC America. After having lived in Manchester, Amsterdam, Lyon and Brighton, he's back in the West Midlands determined to get on top of his geraniums.

You can connect with me on:
- https://mofanning.co.uk
- https://twitter.com/mofanning
- https://www.facebook.com/mofanningbooks

Subscribe to my newsletter:
- https://mofanning.co.uk/mailing-list

Also by Mo Fanning

Mo Fanning writes contemporary fiction with an (often dark) romantic edge. 'The Armchair Bride' was a UK bestseller and nominated for Arts Council England's 'Book of the Year'.

Rebuilding Alexandra Small
When push comes to shove, how far will you go?

Alexandra Small is almost seven years sober and married to one of *Britain's Ten Hottest Footballing Hunks*. They live in gorgeous Brighton, where she has a fabulous job.

Allie has it all. Until one dreadful day, when she very publicly doesn't.

When her perfect world crumbles, a face appears from Allie's drunken past, hell bent on revenge.

Can she rebuild her life before a stranger destroys it forever?

BUY THE BOOK

The Armchair Bride
That grass you thought was greener. It all too often isn't!

Lisa Doyle is nearly 40. And single. Very single.

Fed up with being the girl most likely to die alone, eaten by feral cats, she invents a husband, bragging online about their perfect life.

When a lifelong friend puts her in charge of her dream wedding, Lisa needs to think fast. Does she come clean or change her name and move to Argentina?

Or dig an even bigger hole by getting her best friend to play along?

BUY THE BOOK

This is (not) America
When the world falls apart, do you do the same?

A collection of short stories set against a world in flux. Lives lived on both sides of the Atlantic.

Fanning takes a break from romance and comedy to chew over the things that make life less fun. The body count is high.

BUY THE BOOK

Lightning Source UK Ltd.
Milton Keynes UK
UKHW010634011122
411449UK00001B/21